The Magic Thread

Astrological Chart Interpretation using Depth Psychology

by
Richard Idemon

Edited by Gina Ceaglio

The Wessex Astrologer

Published in 2010 by
The Wessex Astrologer Ltd
4A Woodside Road
Bournemouth
BH5 2AZ
England

www.wessexastrologer.com

First published in 1996 by Samuel Weiser 087728864X
© The Richard Idemon Trust

ISBN 9781902405469
A catalogue record of this book is available at The British Library

Cover design by Dave at Creative Byte, Poole, Dorset

Printed and bound in the UK by MPG Biddles,
Kings Lynn, Norfolk

For more than 20 years, Richard Idemon counseled, taught and lectured on astrological techniques, speaking on the synthesis of psychology and astrology at numerous conferences throughout Canada, Europe, South America, Africa and the U. S. A. He spoke at universities, medical schools, and clinics around the country, taught astrology at Sonoma State College in California in the Humanistac Psychology program, and counseled prisoners in the California State Prison System. he established the School of Astrological Studies and Pegasus Tapes, which ditributes audio cassetttes of his and other world-class astrologers' work, and served as a consultant to therapists in both private practice and clinical settings. Richard was a founding member of AFAN, and was affiliated with both NCGR and the Jungian Society. He died in 1987.

TABLE OF CONTENTS

Foreword

Richard Idemon's untimely death in 1987 was a tremendous loss and deprived the astrological community of his dynamic "in-person" style. However, many of his innovative presentations synthesizing depth psychology, myth, Jungian archetypal imagery, dreams, and drama, with the rich symbolic language of astrology, have been preserved on tape. Outstanding among these are three never-to-be-repeated six-day seminars in which Richard's and Liz Green's talents were alchemically combined. First was "The Hero's Journey" in 1983; next came "Through the Looking Glass" in 1985, and finally, "The Magic Thread" in 1986.

Richard Idemon's first book, *Through the Looking Glass*, was edited by Howard Sasportas and published by Samuel Weiser in 1992. It is a transcription of Richard's portion of the seminar of the same name and is a search for the self in the mirror of relationships. This second book by Richard Idemon, *The Magic Thread*, bears the same title as the seminar from which his lectures were transcribed. It is an exhaustive study and depth investigation into natal chart interpretation replete with new techniques, case studies, and lively audience participation. I had the great good fortune to work very closely with Richard for many years—to coordinate, oversee, and be present at all three seminars—and I am honored to serve as editor of this book. Without reservation I promise you that although you may not have been there to hear and see it "live," as Richard leads you through the labyrinth to the heart of the astrological chart, it will excite personal insights and facilitate a transformational experience.

— Gina Ceaglio
1996

Preface

Our title comes from the wonderful tale of how Ariadne, out of her love for the Greek hero Theseus, betrays her father King Minos of Crete and gives her lover the marvelous magic thread to guide him through the inextricable maze known as the Labyrinth. The magic thread, twisting and turning and ever unraveling, always avoiding the cunningly devised false passages, unerringly finds the true road and leads swiftly downward to its secret heart.

For ages philosophers, alchemists, and psychologists have been fascinated with the intricacies of the Labyrinth, viewing it as a many-faceted metaphor of the human condition and as a model for the complex but ordered universe. The journey to the center of the labyrinth was referred to as an initiation into sanctity and a commitment to absolute reality through facing the innermost core of one's being. The astrological chart, as a symbolic model of inherent universal order, is like the Labyrinth—a logical but complicated and elusive structure. The interwoven symbols in the horoscope are made up of a single thread that, when unraveled like the magic thread of Ariadne, will lead us through the maze to the heart of the chart and our own nature

— Richard Idemon
1986

MYTH, PSYCHOLOGY, ASTROLOGY, AND METHOD

I promise you a very intense week of good experience—a "meat and potatoes" conference full of solid stuff. I'm going to take you on a journey and our theme is *The Magic Thread*. I chose that title because it's a story that has deep mythological meaning for me, and for all of us in our journey through life.

You may remember the myth about King Minos of Crete who had a daughter named Ariadne. Because of an insult to the god Neptune, a very special white bull was sent from the sea, and King Minos was to sacrifice this bull. Well, he was so enamored of the bull that he could not bring himself to sacrifice this beautiful creature, so he played a trick on the gods. He substituted another bull that he wasn't quite so fond of and thought, "Well, that will do." This is a theme we'll be talking about during the week—*the proper sacrifice to the proper god.*

Anyway, Neptune, or Poseidon, is not a god to play tricks with because he plays tricks back, and Neptune was not well pleased with this substitute bull. He sent another bull, and in this case, he enchanted King Minos' wife, Pasiphae, to become so enamored of the bull that she hid herself inside a heifer's outfit and was actually impregnated by the bull. When she gave birth to the Minotaur, a monster that was half-human and half-bull, it was seen with such great horror that it was placed into the heart of a maze or labyrinth. Now,

this Minotaur, like many misbegotten monsters, had a great appetite for the innocents, and sacrifices from Athens and other cities
were demanded regularly. Some say it was once a year, others say it
was once every two or seven years, that seven maidens and seven
youths were sacrificed to the appetite of this Minotaur.

The labyrinth was so deep and entangled that, although many
tried, nobody could find the way inside to slay the monster. Finally
Theseus, a Greek hero, was sent to put a stop to all this. He began by
seducing King Minos' daughter Ariadne, who lent him a golden
thread. And the magic of this thread was that if he would stand at
the opening of the labyrinth and unroll this golden, magic thread,
the thread would guide him all the way to the heart of the labyrinth
where the Minotaur lived. And so he did. It's beautiful to hear how
the myth is related, that golden Theseus, the Greek, the hero destined to save his homeland from these terrible sacrifices, followed
the magic thread as it twined and rolled its way unerringly through
the labyrinth to the very heart where dwelt this profound figure
who, maybe in some way, we can call a *shadow*. A collective something that lies at the heart, not only the heart of the potential for the
Minotaur because he met his destiny at the end, but the heart that
made Theseus a hero by confronting this.

I see that story as the approach to an astrological chart. If you
look at it, it's labyrinthine, for there are so many things to see; there
are so many twists and turns. Once you see all the network of aspects in a chart, you look at it and say, "Where do I turn next here?"
Often we're like a kitten with a ball of yarn. Have you seen what
happens when you take one kitten and add one ball of yarn? You get
a mess. The yarn is all over and the kitten is twisted up in there,
hollering dreadfully. This is often what happens to us astrologers.
What do we look at first? What do we discount? Another theme that
speaks to an unwinding is taking the thread of a sweater. If you gently pull the thread it will gradually unravel the entire thing, so there
is a gentle, definite, focused way of pulling out the thread. In the
same manner, trust that there is a way of unwinding the astrological thread and letting it guide you through the labyrinth to the heart
of the chart.

I want to begin by saying we are not going to offer cookbook
astrology here. Cookbook astrology, although it's fine in its own

way, is something you can get out of a book. What I hope to do during this week is not only to present techniques, but also to give suggestions and ideas that you can run with and make part of your system. So please remember that what I'm sharing with you are things from my experience as a working astrologer, and I may not always agree with you, nor you with me, and that's okay. Take from this what is useful for you. There is no "right" or "wrong" per se.

We're going to begin with some of the basic ideas I have about the psychological and mythological approach to chart interpretation. Look at the chart—not as a round array of bits and pieces—but as a living organism that belongs to a person. I call myself a "born-again" astrologer. The reason for this is that I've been practicing astrology for twenty-one years and for the first seven or eight years I was what I would call a traditional astrologer. Then I began to discover psychology and mythology, and I tell you, it was very lonely out there in the beginning. I remember speaking at conferences where, literally, half the audience would get up and walk out. They'd say, "We didn't come to hear about psychology and mythology, we want astrology." And that meant Saturn in the 5th house is, and Saturn in the 6th house is, and so on. Well, that's not what will be happening this week.

I rejoice to see the movement now, the integration, the divine marriage between astrology and psychology. They properly belong together. Just as psychotherapists are moving more and more toward astrology as the most perfect, beautiful, qualitative language of the human condition, astrologers themselves are moving in the direction of psychology. Not that there is anything wrong with any of the other psychological models, but astrology to me is the most perfect, all-encompassing, universal model of the human condition. But what astrology does not have inherent within it is a practice, a therapeutic technique. How do you actually take this morass of information in the chart, what I would call the archetypal patterns, and hone them into an individual with unique pains, struggles, and differences? These are the kinds of things that we are going to be focusing on during this week. We change slowly and open gradually. It's not easy for astrologers who have been practicing for many years—often very good at what they do—to suddenly begin to open up to seeing things from a vastly different point of view.

For me a good analogy for astrology is music. I see the symbols in the astrological chart as akin to musical notes. Musical notes, in and of themselves, don't mean anything except perhaps to a musician. A musician can scan a sheet of music and get very excited over a mass of notes that trill and run through one octave and another. Ever watch one of those musicians? He or she is quite involved in the music and you're not hearing anything. It's like astrologers do when they see a chart, "Oh, Moon opposed Pluto, T-crossed to Mars with the focal point in the 6th house, out-letting into the 12th and transiting Uranus going over the outlet point." Anybody who is listening is thinking, "What in the world is the astrologer getting excited about?"

So, astrological symbolism is our music. Our musical notations are the symbols in the chart; the symbols of the basic building blocks—the signs, the planets, the houses and the aspects. We do not want to do musical theory, we want to put this all together and *play music*. I don't want to create disciples—the best I can do is add to your collection of useful information and help you see from a point of view that may contrast with yours. It may trine you, it may square you; I hope it won't quincunx you, and throw you into paradox. It will stimulate you to find out that you learn as much by knowing what you *disagree* with as what you agree with.

Astrology really comes alive, as far as I'm concerned, when you are dealing with a live human being, with an entity. Music does not come to life when Beethoven writes his notes; it only lives when the music is played and there's an audience there to hear it. Astrology comes alive when the chart belongs to somebody, and the somebody is there beginning to give you feedback. For me, the astrological chart is not an analysis, not just something to take apart to examine its component parts and pieces. And it's not even a synthesis. It's not "putting it together," because in astrology 1+1 are not always 2; 1+1 sometimes = 11. What it gives us is *synergy*. That means that the component parts act upon each other in such a way that the whole is greater than the sum of its parts. And the one thing I think we're going to be stressing is that there is an inherent mystery in the human condition. We have a tendency to get trapped into the hubris. Astrology tells us so much, widens our perspective so greatly, enables us to see so clearly, that the danger is—the *trap* is—we think we can see everything. And we can't.

I think one of the main differences between the so-called traditional astrology that I originally learned and the kind of astrology I see being practiced more and more now, is the fact that *people are in process*. People are not static. They are dynamic, they are in motion, always changing. The gods are constantly coming into our lives, knocking on the doors, tapping at the window, showing themselves in various disguises. Sometimes kicking down the door, sometimes running us over. And with each exposure, with each major point in our life, comes the opportunity for transformation. So, as far as I'm concerned, there is no way of looking at the chart of a human being without that human *being* there to give you feedback.

One of the things I'm going to be talking about is how to determine "level." How do you determine the level that a person is living the chart on? If you use traditional astrology and look at Saturn in the 5th house, how many interpretations can you come up with? I imagine we could go on until tomorrow morning and find valid interpretations for what that is. Do you say that Saturn in the 5th house is "old children," or "strict pleasures," or "tight creative activities," or "constricted heart valves," or "thin lovers?" Well, we could go on and on having fun with that, but you see, the whole is greater than the sum of its parts. We want to spend very little time talking about the *ingredients* of the cake. What we're going to be doing is a lot of *cake-making*. Most of you know what vanilla is, what sugar is, the proper use of flour, and what 1 tablespoon means. We're going to start making some cakes. This will not be a course in basic astrology; we assume that people here are knowledgeable about planets, signs, and houses, although I'll be doing some contrasting material. I'm going to talk about some of those issues and contrast the traditional with the psychological interpretation.

I think Einstein's theory of relativity—that what we observe depends on the position of the observer—is adaptable to astrology, most definitely. Give 100 astrologers the same chart and you will get 100 different interpretations. Is astrology a science? Well in that sense it isn't. The *construction* of the astrological chart is a science, but the *interpretation* of it is an art. And you cannot teach an art, you can only invoke it. So I cannot make you artists in astrology, but what I can do is help to invoke the artist within you and that's what I plan to do.

So what does it mean "...depends on the position of the observer?" A person who sees astrology as a given thing, as a destiny, as something static, is going to interpret the chart very differently than the person who is in process. The depth of work that you have done on yourself (I call it homework), the amount of homework that you have done, the level, or I should say, the depth, of your consciousness, will equal the depth of your ability to read an astrological chart. Jung[1] said it perfectly and clearly, and he said it over and over again, that you cannot take a person any deeper than you yourself have gone. You cannot see anything more clearly in another chart than you can see in your own mind, or in your imagination. The breadth of your experience, your education, and your insight into yourself, is what will enrich you as an astrologer, not further techniques and cookbooks. The deeper you become—the more broad you become—the better astrologer you will be. And we're going to study some very exciting concepts in connection with that.

One of the things I want to do is share the chart and story of a person I met on a recent trip to New York. There's about seven pages of reading material and a chart to go with it, so a little later in the week I'll ask you to give about twenty-four hours to think about that chart. Think about it in the way you are used to looking at an astrological chart. Then in session we'll share a discussion to compare and contrast our ways of looking at her story. This woman is uncommonly open in describing some very painful, traumatic things in her life and in my mind, she's a heroine. She has triumphed any number of times and I think the chart shows that very clearly. Can you look at an astrological chart and tell how an individual will actually live out the experiences in the chart? No, you can't. How can you find that out? Listen! Listen! Listen! That's one of the things I will be talking about this week.

One of my favorite sayings is that we were given two ears and one mouth, which means we should listen twice as much as we talk. And a very important lesson for astrologers is that the chart comes alive with *dialogue*. I will be talking a lot about dialogues this week.

1. Carl Gustav Jung (July 26, 1875–June 6, 1961): Swiss psychologist who founded analytical psychology using myths, dreams, and the psychology of religion. C. G. Jung, *Memories, Dreams, Reflections* (New York: Vintage/Random, 1961), p. 132.

Every relationship between two planets is a kind of dialogue; every planet in a sign is a dialogue. The gods are speaking to each other constantly. There is this cosmic, or Olympian *dramatis personae*— these actors who constantly come on and off the stage. They have their own natural relationships with each other. Zeus and Hera relate in a certain way, no matter what kind of drama you put them in. Venus and Pluto, astrologically, relate to each other in a particular way, and it doesn't matter what kind of aspect you put them in. So there are *archetypal themes.* How do you know how the person is going to live out the archetypal theme? You learn to listen and the person then tells you the chart. This is one of the most important differences, at least for me, between a traditional and a psychological approach to the chart. In the traditional approach one tells the person what is in the chart. In a more psychological approach we discover together through dialogue what is in the chart and how it effects the life.

I want to talk a lot about myths, too. Personal, social, collective myths, and how these come to affect us in our lives, how we can determine what mythological components may be within the astrological chart. I'm going to teach you what I call my shortcut method to chart interpretation, which are the psychodynamic highlights of the chart, and where you can do a quick scan of an astrological chart. I tend to feel that astrologers over-prepare for a consultation. We not only over-prepare, but we also overload the chart. The danger seems to be, "When in doubt—add." Put in some asteroids, some midpoints, and a few unknown planets and other cosmic debris, and then add all the minor aspects and the Arabic parts, and pretty soon what you really have is a mandala instead of an *astro-logos.* Logos meaning reason, rational, logical science. What we have instead is *astro-mancy,* an art of divination. There's so much in the chart you cannot comprehend it, so you switch into alpha, into your basic Neptunian intuitive thing, and then you might as well be reading tea leaves.

I want to warn you about what happens at our seminars. Transformation is afoot. This seems to be the case from the people I've talked to who have been at our seminars. Something happens here. There's a synergy that goes on. I don't quite know what the magic is, but it does happen and that's why more than half the people who were at our last seminar in Vermont are back again this year. Something special seems to happen. Not only does it happen for you, it happens for me and there is a renewal cycle that is important for us all.

I want to begin with a few things I find very basic to chart synergy with the idea that the chart is more than an analysis, it is more than a synthesis, it is greater than the sum of its parts. So one of the first things I want to look at in the chart is the mythology that the person is living out—what is his or her *mythos*, if you like. I will be spending the next couple of sessions on discussing what I mean by the mythos and how you can go about piecing this out of the chart to get the bare-bones structures of the personality.

The chart does not come alive, does not become real, until the living person is there dialoguing with you, or until you at least have the biography. One of the great advantages of dead people is that they have biographies (there may be other advantages, but I can't think of them just now), and one of the ways to learn astrology is to work with the chart of somebody in history who fascinates you. There are ample recorded times of people, now dead, to use and trace their biographies. Do an astro-biography and check the chart with the biographical study. That, as far as I am concerned, is the best possible way to learn astrology. If you like Mozart, look at his chart, read his biography, listen to his music, see the play or the film *Amadeus*, take a couple of music appreciation courses, and I tell you, you will refine your astrological skills no end. That is the way to learn astrology and the advantage of working with somebody dead is that you can't do any damage. It's why, when I am teaching beginning and intermediate astrology classes, I do not work with case studies, although I will be doing that here. I always work with famous people because there is no chance of damaging them.

So let's get back to this idea of *mythos*. What in the world do we mean by that? Well, first of all, what is a myth? A myth is a metaphorical story, a metaphor to describe something that we perceive in our reality. It is a tale told as a metaphor describing a perception of reality, and these myths can be personal, social, collective, or transpersonal. Every society has myths. Some of these myths are universal and we call them archetypal. Some of them are social, within a particular society. Obviously certain myths that exist here in the South are different from those that exist in the North. So they are comparative and they differentiate, depending upon the time and place in which an individual is born.

What if you're doing the chart of Machiavelli?[2] We have four basic variables here. We have you, coming from your orientation in time and space, looking at the chart of him, plus his orientation in time and space. So you see the number of variables that have to be matched there. You've got you, and remember what we said about Einstein—that which we perceive is in the eye of the beholder. So we have your eye that is beholding or perceiving this chart from the position of your social conditioning and the myths that you carry around, trying to interpret the chart of Machiavelli, who lived in the Renaissance in Italy, and trying to interpret how he would have lived his life through his own personal mythos.

Now that all seems very complicated, but it really isn't so complicated, and astrology is the bridge that gaps that. But will astrology bridge the gap alone? No. That's why we as astrologers have to have some background in sociology, social psychology, history, and literature. Jung said a wonderful thing, well, Jung said many wonderful things, but here is one of them. He said that unindividuated people of any age tend to think that people either are like they are, or they ought to be.[3] We might say, then, that the unconscious people— people living in shadow—tend to assume that everybody else is like them and if they're not, they should be. And, of course, this is what happens from the point of view of astrologers looking at a chart.

Not only do we do myths on a collective and a social level, we have our own personal mythology. The point is that people do not *know* that it is their mythology. What they say is, "Well, this is what my life is about and these are the facts. This is how it is with me." But they don't see it in terms of being a myth. To show the vast contrast, people can have the exact same experience, but how do they interpret the experience? Every time I get together with my

2. Nicolo Machiavelli (May 3, 1469—June 22, 1527): political and military theorist who argued the pursuit of stable government; condoned force and amoral actions; whose name became synonymous with cynical brutality and atheism.
3. C. G. Jung, *The Development of Personality, The collected Works, No. 17,* trans. by R. F. Hull, Bollingen Series XX (Princeton: Princton University Press, 1954), p. 179.

brother, it's amazing. He talks about his mother and I talk about my mother. He says, "My mother didn't do that," and I'll say, "Well, *my* mother did." And then we say, "But isn't this the same person?" The answer is no, of course it's not the same person. Not only does she relate differently to me and my brother, being born seven years apart, but obviously her progressions and the transits influencing her have changed. Also, people do not relate the same way to the same person, and my brother and I have mythologized her differently. Do you see what I'm saying? We each have created an entirely different person, so reality is in the eye of the beholder.

We're going to look at the chart to find out what assumptions we can make about reality in the eye of that person. So the first and most important thing for astrologers to do, as best we can, is to get ourselves out of the way. This means that we must, as far as is absolutely possible, look at a chart avoiding value judgments or results, and go for an understanding of the process. I'll go into that a little later to explain thoroughly what I mean, but let me talk for a second about what I mean by reality being in the eye of the beholder. Imagine yourself walking down a street. You see a very good friend, your best friend, scurrying down the opposite side of the street, with her hand up shielding her face. Now, you have observed a phenomenon, but how do you *interpret* that phenomenon? Well, it depends on what your perception is, your first impulse, and it is based upon your mythos about who you are, your relationships to other people and your relationship to the universe. So what happens depends on you. You may say, "Ah, she's running off from a meeting with her lover," or "Oh, the poor woman, she has a toothache and is rushing off to the dentist," or "She saw me in my new dress and that's the one she wanted, so she's furious at me," or "She phoned me and I never returned her call, so she's never going to speak to me again." Now, how do you find out whether your perceptions have any basis in fact or reality? You check it out, don't you? I mean, hopefully, if you have a good relationship with this friend, you'll phone her and say, "I just saw you running down the street, what was going on? Was something wrong?" and you get clarity on it. The astrologer who is looking at a chart does the same thing. You come up with your own individual perception of what it is you're seeing in the chart and the way you find out if there is any basis in reality for that is by checking it out with the client. And that is why the astrological chart consultation is a dynamic procedure.

There is a phenomenon that I call a *psychological basic ground*. What I mean by that is this. As you probably know, all animals are territorial. They mark the perimeter of their borders by scent, if they are animals that move in herds like buffalo. The herd somehow knows the boundaries of its territory. Territory is essential for the survival of all life. We human beings can become a little unaware of our own physical boundaries and territory, but nevertheless, it is just as important for us as it is for all other living organisms. A jack-rabbit being chased by a coyote knows the limits of its own territory and will double back on itself, even into the jaws of the coyote, rather than to leave its basic territory. The same thing happens to human beings on a psychological level. We have our own basic psychological territory that gives us security. This is reality for us. Usually this is based on a mythos, the mythos that says, "This is who I am, this is what relationships with other people are like in the world for me and this is what the collective has for me." In other words, "This is my fate." Or, "This is what the gods have to say to me."

Very often these myths (the fundamental matter that goes on in this psychic basic ground) are established very early in life. The process in psychotherapy is to identify the nature of this basic ground, and, once it is identified, to help facilitate the person to extend the boundaries, or even to break out across them. That is why some people can be in analysis for years, or study their own astrological chart for years, or go to every psychic in the world, and not really change. And the reason they do not change is that insight is not enough to get through the boundaries. There is psychic barbed-wire. It's like the land of Eden, where Cherubim and Seraphim, angels of the highest order, guard the way with flaming swords, isn't it? As long as we're innocent, we may never have to go out, but once we've bitten into the apple (which all of us psychically do at some point by severing the umbilical cord to our parents), we must break through that ground. Then Cherubim and Seraphim, with flaming swords, guard the way and we can't go back. So, in a sense what's happening is a psychic death. Change equals a kind of psychic dying and that's one of the reasons why people resist change so desperately. Consequently, insight does not necessarily equal change, but it's a great beginning and what we can get from astrology is insight.

Now, what is the material in this basic ground? Well, the material is mythos. It is mythic material made up of a combination of personal, social, and collective or transpersonal myths. Let's go backward and talk about *collective* or *transpersonal myths.* C. G. Jung referred to these as *archetypes* —archetypal myths—and he even gave them archetypal names like the desire for the archetype of the Great Mother. The mother is an archetypal force. She exists everywhere, in every culture and every time. Her function is nurturing, protecting, giving birth, being fecund. That is so for everybody, so there are certain archetypal myths, universal and collective, about what the function of mother should be. We have digested those and, as Jung puts it, it comes right in with the mother's milk. We breathe it in with the air, simply by being a collective part of the universe we're living in. Jung addresses an enormous number of these collectives and that's his particular specialty.

Then we have what I call *social myths.* We all live within a particular time and place where the social mythology is different. How does a woman behave in the Antebellum South as opposed to how a woman behaves in 1980? How does an unmarried woman behave in Greece as opposed to one who is married or a widow? It's vastly different from the way a widow behaves in California, isn't it? So social myths come from a particular cultural milieu, a particular time and place from which a person comes. We also take those in, we digest them and we learn them very early. What is the role? What is it to be a man? What is it to be a woman? And there are also myths about professions.

Close to that are *family myths.* Every family has their own mythology. Now we're getting closer to the realm that Freud[4] spoke about. Who is powerful in the family? Who gets the nurturing? What does it mean to be a woman in your particular family? What does it mean to be a man in your particular family? Who gets the strokes? How is power divided? How is anger dealt with in your particular family? Maybe the myth is that anger destroys and kills. Maybe the myth is that only men are allowed to express anger. Maybe the myth

4. Sigmund Freud (May 5, 1856–Sept. 23, 1939): The creator of psychoanalsis and the first person to scientifically explore the unconscious mind.

is women sublimate their anger. Maybe the myth is that men overtly hold the power, but women subtly hold the power. So family myths are extremely critical.

Now we have the collective or transpersonal, the social and the family myths, plus your own innate material that you bring into life on your own. You see I do not believe, as many of the psychoanalytic schools would have it, that we are formed entirely by our environment or necessarily, even by our heredity. As an astrologer, I have to believe that we come in with an essential something of our own that is colored by and magnified by our interaction with these collective, social, and family myths. So, let's add all of these together. Take the collective myths, the social myths, the family myths, and the innate essence of what we ourselves bring into all of this, and out of that very early on, forms a mythos that you might call a *personal mythology*. And that is the stuff that inhabits this basic ground.

Now the problem with this is that, for most people, all this stuff is unconscious. They simply say, "Well, that's how it is." Instead, people see it reflected outward. They see problems in terms of events: "I've lost my job." They see problems in terms of relationships: "I've been divorced three times, why can't I find the right man?" or, "I'm having trouble with my children." They externalize it and by echo it reverberates inside again and you have people who will then say, "Gee, I have a health problem, although this has nothing to do with my psyche." And we, as astrologers, certainly must understand that psyche and soma are absolutely interconnected, aren't they? Body and soul are part of one great process. So this basic ground, surrounded in a way by a kind of psychic barbed-wire, is a place where we live and, although we may not be happy living in that place, at least it is secure.

Archetypally, this material may have some horns on it and that's Taurus-Land. That's archetypal Taurus-Land because the fundamental importance of archetypal Taurus is safety and security based on that which is familiar. It isn't necessarily that which is good. You see, Freud talked a lot about the pleasure principle. He said the most fundamentally innate thing that we have going on for us is the desire to go toward pleasure and avoid pain. I don't believe that. I did for a long time, but now I don't believe it. I think there's something more basic than that. I think more basic than that is that we keep our basic ground intact—that our belief systems about who we are, and who we are in our relationships to the world and to the universe, are kept intact. And to break that myth is a psychic dying. That's why Taurus and Scorpio are complementary opposites and that's why we connect the archetype of Scorpio with death. It isn't just your physical death; frankly I connect that more with Pisces and Neptune, with the ultimate dissolution. Scorpio is like a roller-coaster. It's the constant pain of awareness and realization that forces us up against our boundaries, up against the wall. It forces us up against our boundaries where our backs are pressed up against this barbed-wire. We can't go forward without pain—we can't go back without pain. And very often this is the point where a person comes for help into psychotherapy.

You cannot force a passage through this wall for another person. You simply can't do it. But what you can do is be the Virgil to the Dante and say, "Here is how this labyrinth proceeds," or, "Here is how the trip down the Amazon is. I know because I have been there myself, but I cannot take your voyage for you, I can only hold up a light. There's the cave of the Dragon and you must go in and slay it, I cannot do it for you." So, you see, the first step in both astrology and psychotherapy, I do believe, is identifying the nature of this basic ground—these myths that comprise our world of reality. And I like to see it in terms of myths rather than facts because myths are numinous, they're loose, they're mutable. You can work with them. You can shape them. But if it is a *fact*, if somebody comes to me and says, "Listen, I was an unloved, abused child. That's the way it is and that's that!" well you can't much argue with that. The statement may be a value judgment, or it may be true, and I might intellectually listen and say, "Yes, you had a bad deal." It is not a myth that is workable toward change. Do you see what I'm saying? The myth may then go on saying, "Since I was abused as a child, I can never trust anyone again." So what happens is that becomes part of the basic ground and defines your boundary. Now, if we see that as a fact, "people are dangerous," then there's no working with it. But if we say, "I have created a myth that people are dangerous out of the experiences I had as a child and out of the essential thing that I am," what happens is you soften the boundaries enough so the person can begin to move and change.

Does the astrological chart tell us about the collective myths, the social myths, the family myths? It tells us a lot about it. It also tells us about what the person is innately bringing in into the system. Yes it does. Does the chart tell us how the person has put all of this together and made his or her own mythology? No, it does not. So how do you find that out? By dialoguing with the person, because each individual is an incredibly unique, creative, original entity that has its own way of putting all of this together. What the astrologer who has a psychotherapeutic background, or the psychotherapist with an astrological background can help do is move toward the process of deeper, faster insight. Get to the nature of these myths, these "things that go bump in the night," and name them. Did you ever wake up in the night, especially when you were a child, and something went "bump" or went "scratch-scratch" in the closet? And you lie there paralyzed with fear and say to yourself, "As long as I don't open my eyes, they're not going to eat me." But if we put light on the subject and name what it is, then we are free to begin moving ahead in our process.

Many of you know the myth of Psyche and Eros. Very briefly, Psyche, the most beautiful princess in the world, whose very beauty and purity not only causes the tremendous envy and enmity of Aphrodite, but also the lust of Aphrodite's son Eros who steals Psyche away. He is told that this beautiful princess, having enraged the goddess, must be thrown off the cliff and she is indeed thrown off the cliff, but Eros with his wings comes and gathers her up. In the dark he carries her off to his palace and the one rule is that she must never look at him. He only comes to her at night and no light is ever lit. Then she begins hearing these rumors. Her sisters come and drop poison in her ear that this must be a terrible monster and, even though she's never been happier in her life, finally she breaks the rule and lights the lamp to see what it is. She finds that instead of a monster, it is the love-god, himself, the most beautiful of all the gods on Olympus, and she sits there transfixed looking at him sleeping. She drops hot oil on him and he wakes up cursing her, saying that it is the end, their relationship is over. Interestingly enough, he runs back home to his mother, so there's an Oedipal connection in here. (Incidentally, as Aphrodite is to her son Eros, so is Demeter to her daughter Core—there's one of those umbilical numbers going on.) At any rate, Psyche goes to the mother, Aphrodite, who now is in the role of wicked-witch, and Aphrodite says, "In order to earn this relationship back, you have these tasks to perform," and so Psyche begins her hero's journey. But you see, it was the desire to put the light on the subject, to illuminate it, that not only caused the pain, but led to her enlightenment and a true relationship with Eros. Because later she did win him back, she became immortal and lived in perpetuity in Olympus as a goddess. And, although the myth of Psyche and Eros is always thought of as Psyche's myth, which it predominantly is, there is important transformation for Eros in there, too. Of all the gods, he is the only one that ever fell in love and he is the only one that deeply transformed, and it was Psyche who helped him do this.

There's a very interesting tale there, for in some ways it is easier to live within this Taurean, Eden-like place of unconsciousness where everything is accepted as it is. Don't make waves—don't turn on the light. However, once the light is turned on, pain comes as an immediate result. Pain and light and enlightenment come at the same time. Now some people flee back into the darkness and some people push on. That's why, in this particular story, Psyche is a heroine. She is a heroine because she took the tasks that led her on to whatever her particular goal was. We all do the same thing. There are opportunities. The gods are rap-tap-tapping on the door all the time saying "Let me in," and we're saying, "Who? What god? What door? Nobody home. Excuse me, the TV's too loud. I need to distract myself. I don't hear anything knocking."

So enlightenment is a double-edged sword. It's painful and there's a kind of death that goes with it. Jung refers over and over again to what he calls the *psychically twice-born.*[5] By that he means the people who have been able to turn on the light, to bear the light, to bear the intense pain of the light and to move forward. Does this happen only once in a lifetime? No. To the person who is in process, it's constantly happening and there is a tremendous, perpetual desire to regress. "God, let me go back to Eden, to the safe place where I don't have to be confronted with myself, with my myths, with the pain and with the necessity for transformation." So there is always

5. C. G. Jung, *Alchemical Studies, Collected Works, No. 13,* Bollingen Series XX, Sir Herbert Read, *et al,* eds. (Princeton: Princeton University Press; 1970) p. 73.

that desire—this entopic desire. The word is entopy. It's our ata-
vism, our desire to return to the great cosmic soup from which we
emerged. The zodiac begins at Aries, but behind Aries is Pisces, which
is chaos and the great cosmic disorder. Out of that disorder we come
and to that disorder we must again return, but through a lifetime
process. There is some entopic process within us that yearns to go
back to that nothingness, so maybe food will do it to us, or a relationship, or whatever our particular addictions are—to simply go
unconscious.

What I want to begin sharing with you now is my shortcut
method of looking at the astrological chart from the point of view
of pinpointing some of these things we're talking about. I think you'll
find this method very useful and let me explain a little bit about
what I do. As I said before, the chart is loaded with so much information there is a tendency to have too much, rather than too little.
So what I do is distill the information down into what I find are the
most psychodynamic parts of the chart and I call what I'm doing
here the *legend*. Remember, in geography class there was a key to
explain the little dotted lines are railroads and the little stars are
capitals? That legend interprets the map for you. So this is a legend,
a kind of rough draft. Astrology, as an artistic model of the human
condition, ought to be like other arts in which we are allowed a
rough draft.

Isn't it interesting that we astrologers put an astrological chart
together, study it for two or three hours and think we should be
prepared and ready to give a person a reading or a consultation? It's
much like Aphrodite springing forth fully-formed from the sea of
our collective unconscious. But it doesn't really work that way. I see
the chart in a different way. I like to build it up layer-by-layer outwardly, just like an artist works at a rough sketch. The material I'm
going to be sharing with you now is how to build a rough draft of
the chart—the artist's sketch. This is not material to share with a
client, but this is a way to focus yourself. These are the beginning
steps of following the magic thread down the labyrinth. Trust me
that if you follow this magic thread it will guide you right to the
heart of the labyrinth and will save you a lot of time and sweat.

The legend is made up of a number of different things in the
chart. These things are finding what it is that stands out, what is

different or unusual, so what we're looking for is abnormalities. I don't mean abnormality in terms of sickness, but different from the norm, and it's made up of various functions. I extract the information from the chart that becomes part of the legend and then I put the chart away until the client comes. I don't want to look at it because there is a tendency among astrologers to over-prepare. We over-prepare so much that we stop listening. We've already formed our mind and it's like a finished product. I remember I took an acting class in New York with a marvelous director named William Ball, who is brilliant in terms of directing the classics. Each of us had to bring in a scene and I worked my tail off to make sure that my scene was absolutely right. I would do my scene and the class would say, "Wow!", but the teacher would only comment "Very nice, thank you, next week do something else." I was chagrined. Never any praise or any criticism. Finally I confronted him on it and he said, "Your work is so finished that it stifles the creative part in me. There's nothing that I can do. You bring in a completed performance." I think we astrologers tend to do that. We have completed our performance before the client arrives. If we can remain looser, keep our thread looser to follow it down to the heart, I think we'll do much better.

The highlights of the chart are made up of several things. The first is what I call the *functions*. I have my own interpretation of Jung's functions and I'll go through that at some length to explain to you what I mean. Pure Jungians are probably going to be horrified, but pure Jungians would have horrified Jung, so that doesn't bother me. We begin with the functions and then we look at other things in the chart that stand out. Things like major configurations. Things like planets elevated. Things like planets on their station and you know what I mean by that, it's planets without apparent movement or very slow movement at the time of birth. Specific aspect configurations, which I will go into, and a few more things, like degree significance, and so on. It's like making a stock for soup. The stock is basic. Once you have this legend you've got your stock, this basic thing which is your structure. Then you add in the chart and you can make almost any kind of thing out of that.

We begin with the use of functions. Now, what functions are we talking about? First of all, everything in the chart has *polarity*.

Let's talk about the twelve signs. We have six *Yang* and six *Yin*, masculine/feminine, positive/negative. I prefer using the terms Yang and Yin because they don't apply any value judgment and they don't apply sexist connotations. So Yang equals masculine and Yin equals feminine, at least in my terminology. So we know we have polarity and also we know we have m*odality.* Modality means a kind or form of motion. All signs have a characteristic motion which we call Cardinal, Fixed and Mutable. Cardinal is *centrifugal,* going out from self toward a goal. Fixed is *centripetal,* going inward from the periphery toward the center. Mutable is a *pulsating, fluctuating* back-and-forth function.

After polarity and modality we have *elements,* which I sometimes refer to as type. Fire, Air, Water, and Earth are elements roughly correlated to Jung's functions, but not exactly. The Earth function clearly is equated to Jung's Sensation function. Air is clearly the Thinking function. We run into trouble with Fire and Water, just like Jung ran into trouble with the same thing because he, himself, never clearly defined to his own satisfaction what he meant by intuition anyway. Feeling seems to go with Water, but is Intuition really the right word for Fire? Jung himself never could quite decide.

Finally, we have one other category I like to use which I call *orientation.* The orientations are three. I call them Personal, Social, and Universal. Here we go back to the business of the eye of the beholder. Each sign archetypally perceives time and orients itself in time and space differently than other signs. Aries, for instance, orients itself to me-here-now, "I want what I want when I want it." Libra says, "I don't know what I want until I hear what you want," or "I want whatever it is that you want." So Libra orients itself toward "you" and Aries orients itself toward "me." Pisces says, "Not me, not here, not now," or, "Everybody, everywhere, all the time." Now you see the difficulty in the dialogue that goes on between the signs when you see they orient so differently in time and space. Have you noticed how time seems to shorten as you get older? Remember when you were young, waiting for your birthday or Christmas, how time seemed to drag? Isn't it different subjectively? If you're having fun time goes quickly, and how dreary and slow it seems to go if you're having a miserable time. So each sign orients differently in time and space.

Beginning with Aries, the first four signs I call *Personal*, and
when I talk about these, please remember I'm speaking of them
archetypally. I don't talk about signs as people. I don't believe in
"Virgos" and "Sagittarians." These are archetypal principles. So when
I talk about signs, what I am really referring to here is the signs as
principles of process that go on with all of us. So Aries, Taurus, Gemini
and Cancer are oriented toward "me first." They are the signs of
awakening. They tend to be primitive and primeval, without any
negative pejorative comment in regard to that. There are some very
beautiful qualities that have to do with primeval and basic. If there
is such a thing as instinctuality, it's probably connected with Aries
and Taurus, the first two signs. The concern is "me," and "me" in
time and space orients to the immediate, toward now. The environment is small in its circle.

The second four signs, Leo, Virgo, Libra, and Scorpio, I call *Social* signs. Here the orientation is "me *and* you." Other concerns
come to the fore now. The world is widening. Just as in a developmental sense, the baby becomes a toddler, becomes a child, becomes
an adolescent and eventually becomes an adult, our world of perceptions widens, not only externally in what we see, but our internal world also widens, or at least it should. The social signs are
concerned with interconnections, social relationships, validation
from other people. The four signs go about it in different ways, just
like the four Personal signs go about it in four different ways, but
they're still concerned with the same thing. I call the four Social
signs moral signs, not because their morals are good, but because
morals are the glue that binds a particular social entity together.
Morals and taboos bind us together within a social community.

The last four signs, Sagittarius, Capricorn, Aquarius, and Pisces, are *Collective* or *Transpersonal* signs. Now it's "me and the universe." Even finally to the point in the last two signs, Aquarius and
Pisces, where "me" disappears and it's just "the universe with the
universe." So the concern now is with causes, theories, ideas, great
concepts. Things widening and further away from the individual,
the personal and even the social, which is why, although the textbooks often say that Aquarius is a social sign, it isn't at all. Libra is
the social Air sign. Libra is the one that enjoys parties and mixing

with people, not Aquarius. Archetypally, Aquarius says, "Let me join together with the entire world on some great cosmic level, or leave me alone." Gemini, the other Air sign, says, "But what does all this have to do with me?" So you see how each of the signs has a very different kind of orientation.

Now I'm going to show you a numbering system using Elizabeth Barrett Browning as an example, and who, as you will see, has a very unusual looking chart. (See Chart 1 on page 22). We will be looking at both signs and houses in our evaluation. Incidentally, I do not feel that houses have either modality or element. So I do not feel that houses are Fire, Earth, Air, or Water houses. I know that some of you may think so and use that and it's perfectly all right with me if you do. A little later on I may go into why I feel that way about it, but for the time being, let's just say I don't.

I use a weighted counting system to determine *dominant* and *inferior* functions. I give one point to each planet and one point extra for the Sun, the Moon, and the planet that is the Ascendant ruler, so you should have thirteen points in all by the time you're done. In Elizabeth Barrett Browning's case, what planet gets the extra point? Mercury. If Leo were rising, how many points would the Sun get? Three. The Sun always gets two points and it would get an extra point as the Ascendant ruler. By the way, let me tell you this is a very subjective system and I am constantly varying it. There are times when I'll add an extra point for a stellium dispositor, or an extra point for the Midheaven ruler. But what I've done is refine it to its barest bones for simplification. Once you have the system, it's yours. Many of my students have taken this system and done their own developmental themes on it. It's not mine, it's yours, so use it any way you like.

Let's begin by counting planets in Cardinal signs. Two for the Moon, one for Uranus makes three, one for Saturn is four and one for Jupiter is five. So we write Cardinal = 5. Now count planets in Fixed placements. None, so write Fixed = 0. There should be eight in Mutable since our total must be thirteen, so just count them to make sure. One for Neptune, two for Mercury as the Ascendant ruler, makes three, one for Mars is four, one for Pluto is five, two for the Sun is seven and one for Venus is eight. So we write Mutable = 8.

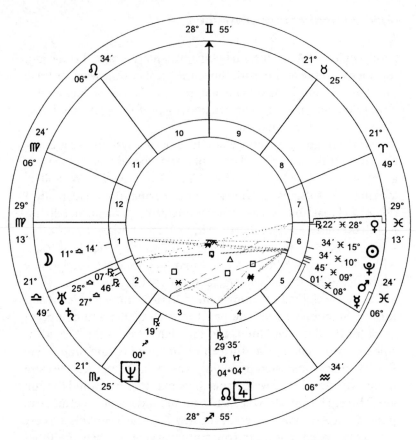

MODALITIES	MISSING	ORIENTATION
Cardinal 5	FUNCTIONS	(Houses)
Fixed 0	Fixed	Personal 6
Mutable 8		Social 7
	STELLIA	Universal 0
ELEMENTS	☿	
Fire 1 (♀)		ORIENTATIONS
Air 4		(Signs)
Water 7	SINGLETONS	Personal 0
Earth 1 (♃)	♀ Fire	Social 4
	♃ Earth	Universal 9
Yang 5		
Yin 8		

Chart 1. Elizabeth Barrett Browning.

Born March 6, 1806, Kelloe, Northumberland, England, 2W18, 56N20, 7:00 P.M. LMT. Placidus houses.

Source: G. Hambate's biography, *A Life*, listed in Lois Rodden, *Profiles of Women* (Tempe, AZ: American Federation of Astrologers, 1979).

Audience: Don't you count the Ascendant?

Richard: No. I'm not counting anything for the Ascendant itself, I'm only counting planetary placements. The reason for that is I see the planets as psychodynamic energies. They are the middlemen between the archetypal collective of the signs and the grounding in this world of houses. So I only count planets. I don't count Nodes, I don't count Parts, and if you use asteroids, that's up to you, but I don't. I don't count the Ascendant, at least in this part. The Ascendant is extremely important and we'll be talking about that separately.

Okay, now let's count planets in Fire placements. We have one point for Neptune. Here I write Fire = 1 and in parenthesis I put the symbol for Neptune, because I call that a *singleton.* I'll be talking quite a bit about singletons. The singleton is one planet of a kind in any category. Neptune is the only planet in Fire in this chart, so it becomes a singleton planet. Now, count Air. Two for the Moon, one for Uranus is three and one for Saturn is four. So we write Air = 4. Now if I add Fire and Air together, I will get points Yang or positive, so I have Yang = 5. Now let's look up Water. Well, you can see she's loaded. Two for Mercury, one for Mars is three, one for Pluto is four, two for the Sun is six and one for Venus is seven. So we write Water = 7. To total 13 points there should be one in Earth and that is Jupiter, so Earth = 1. That gives us another singleton. Jupiter is the only planet in Earth in her chart. Do you all follow me? Now, adding Water and Earth together we get points Yin or feminine, and that's Yin = 8.

Now let's count placements in Personal, Social, and Universal signs. Begin with Personal. None, so we write Personal = 0. For Social there's two for the Moon in Libra, one for Uranus and one for Saturn make four. So Social = 4. Universal will have to be nine and they are two for Mercury, one for Mars, one for Pluto, two for the Sun, one for Venus, one for Neptune and one for Jupiter. Universal = 9.

Now, we'll do the same thing with houses. Starting with Personal, we'll count planets in houses 1 through 4. That's two for the Moon, one for Uranus, one for Saturn, one for Neptune and one for Jupiter totals six, so Personal houses = 6. Social houses are planets in houses 5 through 8, and they are all the rest because there are

no planets in Universal houses (9 through 12). So Social houses = 7.
These are all *functions* and this information gives us so much data
about this individual that, even with this alone, we can start to do
our rough draft analysis of the chart.

∂

CHAPTER TWO

DOMINANT AND INFERIOR FUNCTIONS

N ow we're going to talk about dominant and inferior functions. In my system, as opposed to the Jungian system, any dominant function can have any corresponding inferior function with it. In the Jungian system it's quite fixed. In other words, if your dominant function is Sensation, then your inferior function must be what? Intuition. If your dominant function is Feeling, then your inferior function must be Thinking. This is not so in my system. Not only can you have a dominant function, you can have a co-dominant. Not only can you have an inferior function, you can have two inferior functions and, as you will see later, these shift by progression. So here's where you see, not only a typology that I think works, but one that also moves in time.

How can you tell what is dominant? Where the numbers are high in comparison to the other numbers, that will be a dominant function. So let's look at our legend for Elizabeth Barrett Browning. Among Cardinal, Fixed, and Mutable we see that Mutable is a dominant function because it is 8. In the elements, Water is a dominant function with seven points. Now, what we're looking for is how dominant the dominant functions are and obviously, since there are only 13 numbers to be divided up, the more dominant one or two functions become, the more inferior the others become. So, let me describe what I interpret dominance in terms of functions to mean. Dominance is a place where you are comfortable, you're at home there. Generally speaking, this is a normal, natural, and easy-flowing way of expressing yourself. This is home-base for you. There are exceptions to this. There are cases where the dominant function is forced into an inferior position, and very often when that happens, you get severe psychopathology. How does that happen? It happens when the dominant function is so at odds with the social or family myths and conditioning that the dominant function goes underground, and eventually becomes pathological. There is no way of looking at a chart and knowing that. Any questions so far?

Audience: In therapy is a dominant function that is repressed easier to work with than if there's a lack in the chart?

Richard: A repressed dominant function is very difficult to work with. An enormous amount of psychic energy has been put into it. For instance, if Elizabeth Barrett Browning lived in an environment where her dominant Water function was not permitted, look how much energy, how much psychodynamism is involved here. If this is repressed, what is she left with? It becomes a severe situation when that sort of thing occurs.

Here's another example of social conditioning. What about a woman who has a high dominant Yang or masculine function? Do you see already she's in trouble with the social mythos? But, in what society is she living? That is the important thing. Is she in India? Is she contemporary? Is she a black woman? Is she white? Is she living in the North or in the South? What is her family background? And who is going to be in more trouble, a woman with an overly developed Yang, or a man with an overly developed Yin? Psychologically, who do you think is going to more likely repress in our culture today? The man. Why? Because just in the last fifteen or twenty years it is becoming more socially acceptable for women to live out and actualize their animus or Yang function than it is for men to live out their feminine, anima or Yin function.

The inferior function is more interesting to me. The inferior function is an area in which the numbers are small, or one, or zero. In Browning's chart we have an inferior function in Fixed signs because they're zero. And in the elements, we have an inferior function in both Fire and Earth (in the Jungian system you couldn't have that). In terms of signs, the inferior function is in Personal signs, and in houses it's in Universal houses. Trust me, I will explain what all those things mean. First of all, the inferior function is an area that creates an enormous amount of stress. It is something that is difficult to integrate. It becomes what I call *psychosensitive*. It's an area where we seem to struggle to compensate for, to integrate. It's often an area that is unconscious and carries with it unconscious material. Or, put another way, it is an area that often falls into *shadow*, out of which complexes may be formed.

There are various ways of living with and working with these inferior functions. Very often they manifest creatively and they can manifest both creatively and neurotically at the same time, or interchangeably. The interesting thing about the inferior function is it's a place of perpetual discomfort. I call it the itch that cannot be scratched. There's something always wrong there that you can't ever quite get to. When you get an itch, that's the part of your body you'll focus on, not the parts of your body that aren't itching. How about a pain, a toothache, or a sprained toe? You can't think about the fact that your face feels perfectly fine when your toe is throbbing—all your energy is forced down there. Well, inferior functions often act like that.

The inferior function is of two kinds. The first is the *singleton*, which is one planet of any category in a given group that does not include the Ascendant or the Nodes. Now, you may not be able to go strictly by the numbers to catch a singleton. For instance, what if the Sun is the Ascendant ruler and it's the only planet in a Fire sign? I would show it to have three points, but it's still a singleton. When you're counting and come upon a singleton, put the symbol of that planet in parenthesis alongside the count, as we did in this chart with Neptune. Then every planet you see enclosed in a parenthesis will remind you that it's a singleton.

The singleton is of particular importance. I love finding charts with singletons because it makes my work so easy. *Singletons are areas that focus.* They are a point of nexus, of problem, of stress, of potential neurosis or complex based around what that planet archetypally connects with. We all know what the archetypes of the planets are. Mars has to do with anger, assertion, Yang or masculine energy, and libido. Saturn has to do with authority figures, structure, father, etc. I'm not going to spend an enormous amount of time here going through interpretations of planets, because I think it's not appropriate in this setting. Whatever your interpretation of planets are, those are the things that will be emphasized one way or another. Is there any way to tell what *way* they will be emphasized? No. How can you find out? Talk to the person. How are they living their life? In this case, with Neptune a singleton in Fire and Jupiter a singleton in Earth, the question we would ask is how has this lady mythologized the singleton energies of these two planets. What has happened in her life?

The more skewed a chart is, the more the numbers are wildly at variance, the more potential maladjustment you will find. However, the potential for creativity runs parallel with the potential for maladjustment. Now everybody's thinking, "Oh my god, where do I fall in all of this? Am I a nut? Am I a neurotic?" Well, I hope so, or you probably wouldn't be here. With the chart that has all the numbers nice and even (at least on the face of it, since there may be other things we'll find later on, like a powerful T-Square to Pluto), you find a person who is rather easygoing, a kind of trine-like personality. He or she may not be terribly ambitious; there are no strong pushes and pulls and tugs in life, so this person tends to be rather passive and accepting. Now remember, I'm talking about generalities here. Remember the whole is greater than the sum of its parts, so don't generalize any whole from any of the parts that I'm talking about. I hope you can all think in that kind of compartmentalized way.

In Elizabeth Barrett Browning's chart, since singletons focus on the archetypal interpretation of the planet, we know she is going to have issues around things archetypally connected with Neptune. Chaos, mysticism, sensitivity, imagination, fantasy, intuition, poetry, mood swings, psychosomatic stuff, highly developed psychic energy, extraordinary empathy, compassion, sympathy, self-destructive urges, and urges toward chaos. We could go on, but you get the idea. Same thing with Jupiter, and her issues are going to be around what Jupiter stands for—expansiveness, the desire to include, religion, hierarchical structures, cosmic order of some kind, philosophy, belief systems, wisdom, truth and long distance travel, not necessarily in the mundane sense, but psychological long distance travel. Those are going to be issues for her in life.

The singleton becomes a psychological sore-point. It's either the runt or the pig of the litter. In a litter of puppies, one is the pig that gets all the attention and all the food, and one is the runt that is very often left out. Another term I like to use to describe the singleton is Cyrano's nose. You know Cyrano de Bergerac, he had everything that could possibly be wonderful in the world. He was a poet, a cavalier, a sensitive playwright, author, and the most famous duelist in all of France. But he had a preposterous, long nose out to here and his entire life was colored by that nose. If you've read the wonderful play of Cyrano de Bergerac, you know he lives his life in love with a woman whom he feels could never love him because of his deformed nose. Well, the singleton acts like that. It's something that so obtrudes itself into our life that it tends to devour psychic energy that ought to be distributed equally. So what we see with the singleton planet is that it can be a psychic, psychological vampire. It consumes an enormous amount of psychic energy.

One more thing about the singleton. It not only brings the archetype to the quality of the planet, but also to the house that it's in. Obviously for Browning, because of the placements of singletons Neptune and Jupiter, the 3rd and the 4th houses get dragged into this syndrome and take on those characteristics because they are the domicile of these singleton planets. So, if we've got the vampire, now we have the vampire's castle. This is where the thing lives. And more than that, because every planet rules a sign, it drags another bit into it as well. Neptune rules Pisces, so Neptune is going to rule the house that has Pisces on the cusp and in this case it's two houses, the 6th and the 7th. So the 6th and 7th houses are drawn into the 3rd through this singleton planet Neptune. But there's more! Neptune is the dispositor of this whole cluster of planets in Pisces, isn't it? By ricochet, Neptune is the dispositor of all the houses these are connected to. So you see, it's not just that she's a Neptunian lady—you can get that from the stellium in Pisces—but this is a singleton Neptune. Count the houses the singleton Neptune eventually disposes of and you'll find it is 6 and 7 and 8 and 9 and 10 and 11 and 12 and 1 and 2 and also 3, because Neptune is in 3. Jupiter takes care of 4 with its own singleton and the 5th is ruled by Uranus, which is disposed of by Venus, which gets back to the Neptune, which gets back to the Jupiter. So every house is hooked into the singleton energy.

Now we have the basis of a true complex and you will see how she acted this out in her life. You know her poetry certainly, and I'll tell you a little bit about her story. She had a classic father complex and who did she find to live this out for her? Well, she found the most famous Sagittarian poet of all time. Robert Browning came along and rescued her from her Capricorn father. Her father was a sun-sign Capricorn and Robert Browning was a Sagittarius, so there's no accident about how these things tend to work themselves out. By tracing this, suddenly you see what an enormous, towering figure this Neptune becomes in her chart and you haven't even looked at an aspect yet!

Audience: Did I hear you say that whatever has a singleton in it is often exaggerated? In her case, the 3rd house, and she was a writer.

Richard: Yes, she, herself, was a writer who married a poet who went overseas to Italy (a long distance journey), where they did most of their writing. Right. She married a Sagittarius (Neptune in Sagittarius), and of course her illness, which we might describe as hysterical paralysis or psychosomatic paralysis, comes out of her inability to break her bond with her very devouring father. We'll talk a little bit about her father in a minute, but now I want to talk about the *missing function.*

If there's anything I like to find more than singletons in a chart, it's missing functions, because they tell me an enormous amount. A missing function is zero in any category—there's nothing there. What tends to happen with a missing function is that there is, on some level, a sense of great inner lack. In many ways it acts just like the singleton psychodynamically, but with this difference. The singleton at least has a place to focus itself because there is an entity there. Neptune in her chart is doing all of her Fire work in a way, and Jupiter is doing all of her Earth work. There are houses that they're in, they are planets, they are psychodynamic energies. There is a place for them to go, no matter how exaggerated they may be. A missing function, on the other hand, is, "Where do I go to grab hold of this? I don't seem to be able to hook onto it anywhere."

It's no accident that there is a kind of round-road that goes between the mad house and the ivory tower of the genius, because they're built on the same material. And the more skewed these numbers are, the more eccentric the person will seem, the more out of step with time and place, and often, the more difficult time within the family. Unless the family has the same kinds of off-balances, this person is going to come out like the odd duck. If your family tends to run among the balances and you come along with everything skewed, then nobody understands you. Unless you have a very conscious family, who really understands how to make space for somebody different, there's going to be a problem. Remember that Jung said the unindividuated tends to think everybody is either like they are, or should be. So how many parents who feel they are replicating themselves and solving their own future problems by creating this new entity in the world can let go of that child saying, "Okay, it's fine. I'm Mr. Joe Businessman and I can have an hysterically paralyzed, poetical daughter who wants to live in sin with a man she's not married to in this Victorian England. Sure, I'll go along with that."

So the missing function is a powerful dynamism. Why is this? Well, I believe the astrological chart, with all the planets and all the signs, shows us that no matter what the combinations are, they all must be lived out in one way or another. I call it a *sacrifice to the gods*. Each planet and sign is not only literally connected with an Olympian god or deity, but with an archetypal psychodynamic force. They are part of the world, of the universe, and must be part of us. Each planet and each sign is part of the archetypal process that we must have. It doesn't matter whether we have a planet in the sign or not, it's still archetypally ours. So, as far as I am concerned, it means that our most psychodynamically motivating is not what's *in* the chart, but what *isn't*. Because for us, on some great level, there's a hunger for integration, a desire for wholeness. *E pluribus unum* — out of many, one. That's what the astrological chart shows. We cannot have one at the expense of the many because then we do not develop. If we have the many at the expense of the one, we fracture and we become schizoid. We have to have both the many and the one, and that's the paradox. This paradox is very difficult to live with in our monotheistic, linear, rationalistic, dualistic society.

So, as the Greeks used to say (and you are probably forever hearing me quote), it doesn't matter whether you believe literally in the gods or not. "The sacrifice must be made to the appropriate God in the appropriate place," because Gods are archetypal energies; they are entities that exist. It's the same with these functions. The three modalities exist in the universe. It doesn't matter if you don't have any planets in Fixed signs in your chart, it is a concept that exists in the universe and you must find a way of honoring it. But if you've got no fixed planets, how can you grab hold of this energy to know how to honor it? That's the problem. Or if you have a singleton in something, do you go askew in some other direction in the attempt to honor it? Or maybe you're honoring this one too much and ne-glecting the others. See what I'm saying? So there is on some level a deep inner desire for integration.

It is the absent functions that I call the *uninvited gods*, and it's these uninvited gods that often end up turning the trick. You know from the story of Sleeping Beauty that it's the uninvited fairy who makes the story begin to move. She casts everybody into uncon-sciousness because she wasn't invited, and why wasn't she invited? Because she was disagreeable. The disagreeable one was not invited in and cast everybody into unconsciousness. Only Eros was eventu-ally able to awaken Sleeping Beauty. The same story comes out of the Iliad.[1] There was a banquet for all the gods and goddesses, and the only one who was not invited was Eris, the god of discord. He crashed the party, threw the golden apple down the table, where it stopped, midway between the three goddesses Hera, Aphrodite, and Athena. On it was inscribed, "For the Fairest," and three hands went out. Well, Paris was trucked in from Troy to make a decision be-cause Zeus says, "I'm stepping out of this problem!" He brought in Paris, the shepherd, the son of King Priam of Troy, to make the decision. The three goddesses trotted their wares out in front of him and made him an offer. Aphrodite gave him the offer he liked most, so he awarded her the golden apple and today, she is still shown on most Greek statues with the golden apple clutched in her right hand. (By the way, you've probably only seen Venus de Milo with-out her arms, but originally they were in a classical Aphrodite pose, with one raised high and the other lowered. The raised hand held a mirror in which she is admiring herself, the narcissistic Aphrodite,

---

1. An epic poem by the blind poet Homer set in the tenth and last year of the Trojan War. Believed to be the earliest surviving example of Greek literature.

and clutched in the lowered hand is that golden apple.) Back to the story, Aphrodite promised Paris the most beautiful mortal woman, and that woman was Helen. Helen was married to King Menelaus of Sparta, and he was not very happy that his wife got stolen away by Paris of Troy, and up came the whole Trojan War, where, for fourteen years, people died in the thousands, and the entire Trojan civilization was destroyed.

There's a message here. We don't want to invite discord to the party; we don't want to invite the unpleasant, but it crashes the party anyway. And that's what happens with singletons, with missing functions, with inferior functions. They tend to be areas that we are uncomfortable with, and because we're uncomfortable, we'd rather avoid them. But they come in anyway. That's why the Greeks used to say that you never pass by the shrine of the god without leaving the appropriate sacrifice, because you never know. The god comes and extracts the sacrifice anyway. Let's put it this way, as Buddha would say, "Everything is Maya." Everything must eventually be given back to the universe and it's not the desire world that gives us pain, it's our attachment to it.

Inferior functions, singletons, and missing functions constellate in what we call *psychological defense mechanisms*. What do we call up to help us deal with these lacks, these missing things, these areas that make us so desperately uncomfortable? I use five of these defense mechanisms—*denial, repression, projection, sublimation,* and *compensation.* (Compensation is sometimes referred to as overcompensation and sometimes as reaction-formation, but it amounts to the same thing for our purposes here.) So let me give you a brief impression of what they imply.

Denial says I am going to deal with this thing by refusing to acknowledge that it even exists. "What Neptune? I don't know what you're talking about." "What anger? I don't know what you mean, I don't feel angry, I've never felt angry." So denial is a bottom line refusal to admit the possibility that this particular archetypal energy exists at all.

Repression is one step up from denial in terms of consciousness. Repression says, "Yes, I know that it's in there, but I'm not going to let it out because it's dangerous." Denial and repression have two things in common. They tend to manifest most severely in the world of events or in physical health. Let me explain what I mean by events. We all know that dreams are symbolic of inner process, don't we? They're symbolic. We understand that most of what we dream is not literal. If I dream I ate a house with my mother in it, I don't literally think that I probably want to eat up that rose-brick cottage and Mama at the same time. You learn to see it symbolically. I see events in waking life in the same way. They are symbolic; they are dreams. As Calderon[2] said, "La Vida Es Alsueño," life is a dream. The world of events is a dream, just like the world of our nighttime sleep is a dream. The event that happened to us ought to be seen in a symbolic way. "What does this mean metaphorically to me and my process?" So denial and repression are like a deep *psychological constipation* that eventually explode in terms of psychic or physical problems, or in what we call events. The car crashes, the house burns down. We constellate it, we pull it in from the universe, from the collective in some way.

Projection says, "I realize that's happening, but it's not me that's doing it, it's you." Or, "Yes, I admit that I'm doing it, but that's only because you make me do it." I said to one client, "Gee, you seem so angry." "Well yes, that's because everyone in the world is so irritating to me. Why does the whole world irritate me like that?" So projection goes in both a positive and negative way. We often project outwardly in a positive way and we want to import material that we think we lack, but when we get it home and unwrap the package, we may not like it very much. That's why, interestingly enough, in synastry it is the inferior functions that are so psychodynamic in showing who we are going to be compulsively attracted to. It's because we want to "import" the material from that other person, but when we get it home we take one look at it and recoil in horror. It's the man who likes the sweet, passive, helpless woman because it makes him feel strong. We can also project out collectively. It's "all those people out there." Perhaps those with missing Earth functions become obsessed over people's sensuality, "All those sensually over-sexed people out there," or, "All those materialistic people out there." And "those people" can be either very attractive or very repulsive.

This brings us to an important concept. It is the tendency of

2. Pedro Calderón de la Barca; Spanish playwright whose philosophical play *Life is a Dream* is a masterpiece of world literature. Pedro Calderón de la Barca, *Calderón de la Barca: Six Plays* (New York: IASTA Press, 1993), p. 287.

things to become their opposites. There is a vacuum caused by what is missing in our charts. It pulls us in; we attract the opposite first and then there is an inner urge to become or envelope that opposite. One way we do that is in our erotic love relationships. We all know the kind of relationship that is so intensely passionate that we can't live with that person or live without them. There is something compulsive. We don't know whether we want to kiss or bite the person. That kind of relationship, on one level or another, is often based on a projection of inferior functions. And often what happens is that when one person reclaims the inferior function, the relationship starts to die because the balance is thrown out, the contract has been broken.

Sublimation says: "Yes, I do acknowledge that I have this energy, but I'm not going to let it flow in the channel *it* wants to. I'm going to make it flow in the channel *I* want it to." So for instance, as the Catholic church says, "Yes, I can acknowledge that I have sexual feelings, but it is not acceptable within the setting of the church, so I deal with it through prayer, teaching, and good works." I sublimate the energy. I meditate, I do yoga, if I'm of an Eastern orientation, and therefore I don't waste my Kundalini, or my vital essence is not wasted. It's okay to have the feelings, but I do not allow them to come out. I put them into another direction. Many psychotherapists sublimate their own psychological problems into their practice, into their work.

Compensation says, on some inner level; "I'm so afraid of not being able to function in *this* area that I go all the way over in the *other* direction and I over-function. I am so afraid on some level that I am missing something because of this lack that I'm never secure with it. So I go all the way over in the opposite direction, I become a super-functioner in that particular area." It's a compensation reaction.

For instance, if I have nothing in Fixed signs, I become super-fixed. And indeed, did not Elizabeth Barrett Browning become super-fixed? How did she do it? She made herself hysterically paralyzed for twelve years so she couldn't get off the couch. Her legs wouldn't work, she couldn't make her legs work, but she got up off the couch pretty fast after she met Robert Browning. And why didn't she want to get off that couch? Because she was tied to this father whom she both loved and hated, and who needed her. Her mother died and in a way, she became not only the father's daughter, but the father's wife. To leave him was to break this basic territory, to break out of it. She knew she had to leave it to survive. If she stayed she was going to die; if she left she was going to die. She couldn't deal with that. How did she deal with it? The missing function came and she said, "That's it! That solves my problem, I can't walk, so how can I leave my father?" And what did her father say? "My poor helpless, delightful daughter, I will keep you here with me all the time." And he became the ogre at the door to chase away all men because she was too fragile, helpless, and vulnerable, and he was going to protect her.

Can you look at a chart and see which of these defense mechanisms the person will be using? No, it's not possible. We're always in process, and they shift all during our lifetime. We can do some of each all at the same time. Is there anybody who is perfectly integrated and doesn't use any of these? No. When we're under enough stress we regress. We do that, not only personally, but collectively. Societies also regress when they're under enough stress. Look at Germany and Hitler and all of that business; you see it can happen. Look at the McCarthy era right here in this country. Societies themselves can regress. When we are under enough stress, we regress to the basic way we learned to function and any one of these defense mechanisms can begin to come popping up.

Denial and repression are a far more severe situation. This requires a trained therapist. Here's where the astrological interpreter runs into problems because the astrologer says, "Well, I just told him what I saw in his chart." But the person is not ready to hear that and will respond, "No, I don't do that!" The astrologer says, "You have a lot of sexual energy with Moon and Mars conjunct Pluto in the 4th house; you've got Oedipal feelings toward your mother." "No I don't!" "Yes you do, I see it right here in the chart. You suppress them, but they're there." So denial and repression are warning signals. The person is putting up the armor because there is something so fragile inside that he can't face it. This is why the person who is going to be an astrological practitioner needs to get counseling training in order to deal with issues like this when they come up.

Projections are easier to see. Why? Because people all tend to project outward in relationships. What they *don't* see is that this has anything to do with them. They say, "How come I always get these infantile men in my life?" Or, "I always get these dominating, devouring women and I don't see what I have to do with any of this at all. So look at my chart and tell me." The traditional astrologer will say, "No wonder you've got dominating women in your life; you have Mars conjunct Saturn in the 7th house!" But what does that tell you? It doesn't tell you very much.

Sublimation and compensation are, on the surface, a little easier to live with because they tend toward qualities that are acceptable in our society—achievement. First of all, our predominant religion, Christianity, *preaches* sublimation. Paul, himself, who was really the founder of the Christian church, said, "It is better that you do without (what he means is sex and marriage) even as I, but it's better that you marry than you burn." He would prefer that you sublimate. So we live in a society where, after we encourage a sublimation, we're also a capitalist society that encourages individual achievement—"making it" out there—and that encourages compensation. So the person who has learned to sublimate and compensate gets a lot of support from society and friends. "Great, good, you've built a new condominium, wonderful." "You've lost another ten pounds, Miss Anorexia? Great, you're even more in fashion than you were before." "You made more money. You've had another success. You cut another record. You put on another conference? Isn't that wonderful? Let's go on and have even more." So what happens for the person who is sublimating or compensating when you can no longer do that? The super-mom's children grow up and move out of the house and her husband dies. The man who compensates through achievement and corners the market on everything is now 65 and forced into retirement. He can't be Mr. Executive any more. Beethoven loses his hearing; the poet goes blind; the artist loses his eyesight. What happens then? It's like a house of cards. The house of cards comes tumbling down when great crisis happens. When the compensatory or sublimating mechanism is withdrawn, crisis comes up.

Audience: When you were talking about projection, you said that when a balance is achieved, you don't need the relationship any more. How is the balance achieved?

Richard: No, I said when *one* person has achieved an inner balance, then the original out-of-balance-contract that may have set the relationship going must now be renegotiated, and one or both of those parties may not be able to do that.

Let's say the woman is Miss Traditional Woman and she marries Mr. Traditional Man. Then she finds her power. She becomes more assertive, she wants a job, she gets more education. That may be fine for her, she has now collected some of her animus, some of her Yang energy, but how is the husband going to handle it? In order for the relationship to go on, he'll have to shift. He'll have to get in touch with his anima to the same extent she has integrated her animus. Then he'll have to say, "I'm going to take care of the kids some of the time. I'm going to have to cook for myself, do my own laundry, not have a servant running around to take care of me." If he can't do that, either she must regress, or the marriage is broken. Or he goes off and finds some sweet young thing who will do that for him. Do you see what I'm saying?

Audience: It seems on some level that all human achievement may be attributable to these last two, sublimation and compensation.

Richard: Freud would agree with you, because he believed that creativity comes out of sublimation and compensation. But I think that sublimation and compensation make a particular kind of creativity. Let's put it this way. There's an intense, obsessive kind of creativity. There is a frantic, passionate, erotic connection with one's creativity that's different from the dominant function creativity.

So that leads me into another point. Can a person create through the dominant function? Yes, but it's usually relaxed. It's easy-going and it flows smoothly. The person gets up to talk and out it comes, it just flows so naturally. With a dominant Air function it's just easy to communicate. But how about the creation through the inferior function? Its a compulsion, it eats at you, it's obsessive, it drives you, it possesses you. And out of that comes *thanic* material—thanic or thanos, coming from the Greek word for the underworld. It fetches up material from the underworld, it comes from the groin, it comes from the crotch. This is the stuff that comes from blood and excrement and vomit and the womb and death and all of that kind of stuff. That kind of creativity brings it up, and you see it clearly in the works of writers and musicians and artists.

I'm going to show you some of these so you'll see exactly what I mean. An example is Beethoven with no planets in Water, who was one of the most intensely and passionately emotional of our composers. Somebody once told him that a reviewer said he found his music cold. Beethoven wrote back scrawled all over the review, in red ink, and said, "Anyone who has the ears to hear, which God in his wisdom has deprived me of hearing my own music, will know that every note I have written has been in blood and tears." As opposed to Chopin, a dominant Water composer, whose emotion and feelings flow so beautifully. I mean it's watery all the time. But it's not that kind of wrenching emotion. You can hear the difference. Listen to the difference in the quality of the music.

Take artists, for instance, like Renoir, who is a dominant Water sign artist, or Monet with his lovely *Water Lilies*. It's serene, it's lovely, the feeling flows through. You're touched, you're moved, but it's not like watching Vincent Van Gogh and Toulousse Lutrec, who are low in their Water function and whose work grabs you and shakes you just as it did them. There's passion, there's horror, there's pain, there's angst, there's hurt, there's hunger, there's everything in that kind of work. That doesn't make one any better than the other, but it's a different kind of thing. See what I'm saying?

Audience: Won't this change by progression?

Richard: It does change by progression, yes, indeed. We'll be spending time talking about that. It's moveable just like the chart. Remember though, that the natal chart is the "given." This is the early thing and it progresses and grows within what the natal promises. But yes, it does move. The functions shift as you grow older. What was a dominant function suddenly shifts to inferior. Singletons suddenly disappear and move into dominant functions, while other planets show up as singletons. And watch the psyche change as this is happening. It's amazing; try it and see. Progress your own chart and you'll see the absolute shifts happening. So your point is well taken, and that leads me into what I want to talk about now, that compensating mechanisms really do work.

I want to begin by talking about the elements. Let's take Earth for a starter. Earth inferior function normally means that the person is going to have some kind of problems with *soma*. By that I mean with the body. Sexuality and sensuality become an issue; food is an issue; sexuality, sensuality, touching, food, all kinds of oral gratification. Oral satisfaction is the fundamental Earth pleasure center. I call it the Taurus center. It is *taking in*, dealing with money, dealing with objects, things, the earth, trees, nature, and reality— reality, at least in terms of the things that your five basic senses can see, smell, hear, touch, taste. How is it going to be dealt with? We don't know. Is it going to be denied? Projected? Sublimated? Compensated? All of the above, or some of the above? The answer is yes. We don't know. How can you find out? Half an hour with almost any individual will tell you.

If I have the chart and see a missing Earth function, my questions and the way I approach a consultation begins to shift by what I see in this legend, these first steps. I want to know what that person has done with that Earth. I might say, "How's sex for you?" "Oh, I don't like sex. Well, I do it to please my husband." I'm saying this because this is a client I had recently. "I do it to please him." "Well, have you ever had pleasure with it?" I asked. "I don't know what that means. I mean I like to please him." I continue, "Do you like the closeness or touching?" "Yeah, well, I don't know." Now, interestingly enough, this woman was a prostitute before she got married.

So what happens is you get a wide swing of variations with the missing or inferior functions and elements. Often the person doesn't know. For instance, people with a missing function in Earth don't know when they're hungry. They may go for hours and days without food and suddenly feel weak, and then gorge, or become anorexic. Why? Because they don't like their body, they're not comfortable with it. Or they'll become hugely overweight. Why? Because they never feel satiated. "I never know when it's enough." The same thing with sex. Same thing with money. Same thing with touching. Or it may be compensated for. The person may become a sculptor, like Michelangelo with missing Earth, who was very Catholic in the Renaissance and, being homosexual, repressed his sexuality. He probably repressed it and projected it or sublimated it into these great creative works, and compensated for it by creating outside of himself these divine works of art. All we have to do is look at Michelangelo's *David* in the Academia in Florence, which he did when he was 19 years old, to see that projected Earth function. You sit there and look at it and say, "I saw it breathe, I know I did."

Okay, an inferior function in Water—the feeling level of psyche becomes problematical. "I don't know what I'm feeling," or, "I don't know how to express it." It's like the faucet's all the way on or all the way off, and it comes out at inappropriate moments. Feelings are frightening. I connect Water with the capacity to deal with pain, and there's a lot of reasons for that. Cancer, Scorpio, and Pisces sit on the line between the three orientations. Remember, Aries, Taurus, Gemini, and Cancer are the Personal signs, after that it switches to Social. Then with Leo, Virgo, Libra, and Scorpio, Scorpio sits on the line before it switches into Universal. It's the Water signs that bear the burden and pain of transformation, of moving from one orientation to the other, so it's the Water signs that give us our capacity for pain.

People without Water may not understand or deal with pain at all, or may go in the other direction and become obsessed with pain. Now, they may become great healers or great villains, like Hitler, who had no planets in Water. In some way they are unable to be compassionate or hurt, either inwardly or outwardly. A kind of projection and compensation combination is going on simultaneously until they are obsessed with creating intense pain.

You might see a compensation reaction and have someone who is super-sensitive, intuitive, empathetic, and who has difficulty letting go of boundaries. Water is boundary-lessness. It tends to want to flow and join and merge. So a person with inferior or missing functions in Water often has trouble with boundaries, tending to merge and flow at inappropriate times and places. And sometimes, very appropriately, but compensated for, the person simply disappears. Maybe he or she becomes schizophrenic and simply disappears into imagination, fantasy, or into another inner individual.

Missing Air. Well, Air is the ability to stand back, detach, and observe. So again this gets thrown into extremes. People with missing Air find that the ability to stand back and look at things objectively is difficult. They're like water—they have boundary problems, except in a different way. Water's tendency is to merge, and Air's tendency is to separate. When Air is an inferior function, the person separates at the wrong moment, just like the Water people merge at the wrong moment. And that's why Libra, which is the sign of marriage, is an Air sign. It shows that the proper marriage includes a kind of separation, not a merging. People with inferior functions in Air often feel very helpless in one area of the rational mind and maybe compensate in another, where they become geniuses. You might find a super-intellectual like William F. Buckley with no planets in Air. But you really see the compensating mechanism coming through him don't you? I mean there's an obsessive kind of crazed intellectuality going on there. Not a planet in Air. Or you get the kind of person like one of my students who has three doctorates and speaks about twelve languages, and says, "I'm so sorry to ask this question. I'm so stupid. I never understand anything. Please, let me ask you this one more time. I'm so dumb." No planets in Air.

Fire as a missing or inferior function. Fire is the life-force, the prana force of the universe. It makes us feel at one with the universe. It gives hope, enthusiasm, joy, creative force. It gives great libido energy, both in the strict Freudian sense of primal sexuality, and in the more Jungian sense of the quality of life force—*joie de vivre*. It's the idea of life being beautiful and I am capable of dealing with it. I am at one with the forces of the gods; they flow through me; I am connected. Temperament, passion, energy, vitality are all connected with the Fire signs: romance, creative stuff—creativity as coming from the heart—the *passion* for creativity.

Now, I am going to mention some people that are super-achievers whom you would never guess have either a singleton or a missing function in these qualities, and you'll see how they're of a particular type.

Earth people: How about Adele Davis with her diet books and her obsession with eating the proper foods? Gloria Swanson who became obsessed with sugar and wrote books about diet, nutrition, renewing the body, and so on. Mozart, who is the typical archetypal dominant-in-Air function, has missing Earth. He was ungrounded completely. He ended up starving to death. He never knew how to make any money out of anything he did. How many of you have seen the movie *Amadeus?* He was obsessed with body functions, doing "poo-poo, ca-ca" talk. He and his wife called each other "poopy," "shitty," and "ca-ca," and seemed obsessed with smelling bottoms and body odors. It's quite bizarre and odd. How shocking it was that the man who makes this sublime music talked this way and didn't know how to make any money in his lifetime.

Marilyn Monroe, the divine body, the Aphrodite, has the missing Earth function, but she had Taurus on the Midheaven, so she projected outward to the collective something that internally she didn't feel and didn't have. That, in itself, creates great crisis. When I was driving a cab in Hollywood in my young actor days, Marilyn Monroe got in and I took her out to Malibu. She was very warm and wonderful. We had a lovely conversation and I told her that in six months I was going to New York to study acting. I knew that she had just returned from studying at The Actor's Studio, so I said, "I'm really scared, going to New York, it's such a big, lonely city." And she said to me, "When you don't know who you are, every city is a lonely city." That burned a hole in my consciousness and I got the feeling of this poor woman trying to live up to carrying this load of archetypal Aphrodite, Taurus on her Midheaven, when she's getting close to 40.

Another quality that happens with missing Earth is the tendency to deal with the uncomfortableness of the body through drugs or alcohol. That's why you find people like Rita Hayworth, Vivien Leigh, Judy Garland, Joan Crawford, Jackie Gleason, and Richard Burton. All of these famous alcoholics and drug users have nothing in Earth. They don't feel grounded in the body. They need something to get them out of it, or even back into it. Tennessee Williams was another alcoholic and drug abuser; so was Dylan Thomas and F. Scott Fitzgerald.

Mark Twain, interestingly enough, was condemned in his life for being so earthy. Do any of you know what his last work was before he died? It was published posthumously because it was so scandalous. It was called *Letters from the Earth*, in which he has a dialogue with the devil. Emile Zola also was condemned for the earthiness of his writing. Then there's Billy Graham, and here is a perfect example of some heavy-duty stuff going on with things of the flesh and the body. Graham said in his autobiography, "When I was a young man driving the back hills of North Carolina I used to take girls out and we'd kiss and kiss. I'd come back with my lips so swollen that I'd be like a Ubangi. That was before I got saved." So you see a compensating mechanism, how the thing begins to shift? Now, of course, flesh becomes evil. When Billy Graham is talking about sin, he's not talking about financial or political corruption, he's talking about sex. He's talking about touching those things in those places and doing that kind of stuff. That's what he means. Also think of Hugh Hefner, publisher of *Playboy* magazine, and Larry Flint, publisher of *Penthouse* magazine.

There's a clutch of astrologers—Rob Hand, Marc Edmund Jones, Dane Rudhyar—I'll let those go by without comment except to say Rob is a wonderful cook. Michelangelo, Velikovsky's *Worlds in Collision*,[3]—huge, theoretical, transformative ideas about how the earth was formed. Joseph Campbell, the mythologist, goes back to the archetypal, Taurean, primitive world and brings it out. Ingemar Bergman, Norman Mailer, and Zsa Zsa Gabor, with her singleton Venus in Capricorn in the 4th house. "Dahling, you never love a man who does not give you diamonds." Rodin, the sculptor, had a singleton Mars in Virgo in the 8th house. Cellini, who was the most famous artisan of the Renaissance, and other artists like Renoir, Rafael, Corot, Gauguin, Surat. Many artists are compensating through their work. There is Nijinsky, the dancer, and you find, interestingly enough, a lot of athletes, and body–builders—Arnold Schwartzeneger, Charles Atlas, Johnny Weismuller. A whole clutch of Olympic stars and people like Jackie Robinson, O.J. Simpson, Hank Aaron, Ray Campanella and Jack Dempsey with no planets in Earth who manifest an obsessive need for making the body do its maximum, and Charles Darwin with his *The Origin of the Species*.

Earth also gives us boundaries. People without Earth do not feel grounded. Olivier says in his biography that his wife Vivien Leigh was in love with Blanche DuBois from *A Streetcar Named Desire*.[4] To play Blanche DuBois, he says, she disappeared into the part and never came back. She was actually consumed by this character, who obviously was carrying around something from her own unconscious, and the play was by Tennessee Williams. Who was Blanche DuBois? Blanche DuBois was one part of Tennessee Williams, also with missing Earth, so it's interesting how these things tag in. The author deals with his compensating functions by creating a character who taps into just the right actress who was destroyed by it. Isn't it amazing how these things happen?

3. Immanuel Velikovsky, *Worlds in Collision* (New York: Dell, 1967).
4. Tennessee Williams, *A Streetcar Named Desire* (New York: Signet/Penguin, 1947).

I want to pursue this business of inferior functions a little bit more and talk a bit more about Water, Air and Fire. A special quality of the inferior function is that it acts archetypally and very often, archetypally in a *shadow* form. In other words, especially with the missing functions and the singletons, they constellate archetypally into mythical forms that come directly up out of the unconscious. With inferior functions, at moments of crisis or deep change or transformation in the lifetime, they come erupting (my favorite word) cathartically from the psychic underworld. So inferior functions often erupt from underneath at moments when they are least expected, and they tend to manifest in several ways.

They operate like the trickster, archetypally. In other words, the trickster yanks the cosmic rug out from under you, so you land hard on your bottom with a jolt of awareness of some kind. I call it the humpty-dumpty effect. It's the egg that falls off the wall and shatters, but by shattering it opens and reveals the yolk. It also acts archetypally in the form of the Hindu god Shiva, the Destroyer— the destroyer who creates again. The sense of it is *dissolution,* falling apart. And it often acts as the annihilator. This is Hades, himself, who comes and drags you off down to the underworld. He erupts from the underworld as he did in the famous story with Core, the daughter of Demeter, who was then seduced and taken down on into the underworld where she became Persephone, queen of the night, and a power in her own right.

These shadow figures, interestingly enough, can archetypally be connected with Uranus, Neptune, and Pluto. Now that's not saying that inferior functions are all necessarily of a Uranian, Neptunian, or Plutonian nature. But when they come erupting from the unconscious, if they have not been integrated, then the effect is shattering and transpersonal. So, one of two things can happen. It can be an enormous creative breakthrough, or it can be a tremendous psychological crisis, and sometimes both. Usually the crisis first before the breakthrough. So when the inferior functions erupt from underneath, it can act as a creative catalyst. It can bring great genius and insight. It's the "AHA!" the great gestalt that brings a break-through. Remember we talked about the basic ground surrounded by the barbed wire, psychically protecting it? This is the thing that pushes us up against the barbed wire and through it onto the other side, very often rending and tearing us while it's happening.

It can also have the opposite effect. The inferior function as trickster, as chaos and annihilator, likes to lurk in hiding, waiting for the dominant function to go to sleep. Then it comes slinking out of the corner and grabs you. So in a moment of crisis it drags all the unintegrated, psychic material (this is again the uninvited Gods crashing the party, isn't it?) and they choose just the right moment. There they are, all the Gods sitting around the banquet table in Greece, like the story about the golden apple, and in comes Eris, the goddess of discord. Doesn't discord know just the appropriate moment to come in and toss that magic golden apple down the table? So the inferior functions erupt into this marvelous feast. It's the same thing with the wicked fairy in the story of Sleeping Beauty. Again, she erupts into the scene, just at the appropriate moment to do the most annihilation.

On the other hand, there's a creative function in it because this force, this inferior function—dark, repressed, coming from the underworld—releases things in stasis. When Pluto (or Hades) comes erupting up from the underworld and kidnaps and rapes Core (*Core* in Greek means "maiden"), he breaks the unnatural umbilical cord between Core and Demeter, the great mother-goddess, the goddess of the harvest. It's an unnatural, narcissistic bond, or relationship, between mother and daughter. And what god or goddess was it that set this whole thing in motion? One of the gods or goddesses sat up there in Olympus and said, "This is an unnatural relationship. This mother-daughter bond includes no man, no lover." Who was it who set this all in motion? Aphrodite again. Yes, she of the earth, of fecundity, of breeding, of archetypal sexual erotic, especially of man-woman relationship, looked at this and didn't like it, so she set things in motion. She went down to her great-uncle, Hades-Pluto, and said, "There's a lovely, innocent maiden up there. I really think you ought to take a good look." Aphrodite, the instigator, gets things out of stasis, and this is the gift of the inferior function.

When the inferior function comes erupting up, it's often quite archetypal in its way of operating. Let me explain what I mean. Taken by element, when Earth, as missing or inferior function, comes erupting up, it will come sometimes as a form of a Demeter. Remember what happened when Demeter was deprived of her daughter, when her daughter was removed and taken down into Hades?

Demeter went into a sulk for seven years and we have the first case of involutional melancholia in mythology. She went to her sanctuary in Eleusis, a small coastal town near Athens, and disappeared. She forbade the crops to grow and the trees to fruit, so for seven years the world starved. Of course Zeus and the other gods and goddesses on Olympus looked around and said, "This has to be corrected." But Demeter tore her gown, sprinkled ashes on her head, went into mourning for her daughter, and would not let go. Eventually, of course, this was resolved. The gods and goddesses said, "If we do not resolve this problem, human beings will be wiped off the face of the earth." And it's not that they particularly cared about people, but they said, "Who will worship us? Who will make sacrifices at our shrines? We had better do something." So they struck a deal with Hades, and Core (now Persephone) returned to her mother for the six months of the year when the earth blooms. During the time of the autumn and winter when the earth went to sleep, she would go down again into the underworld. And that whole cycle of rebirth and death, the cycle of renewing itself, was part of the Eleusinian mysteries. So one of the qualities of the eruption of Earth is depression, melancholia, withdrawing, becoming cold and icy, holding back. Demeter, in her depressive state, the sorrowing mother, the withdrawn, says, "I'm not going to get enough of what I want, poor me, poor put-upon me," so we get this hunger. Not only that, but she cuts off nurturing. She cuts off the food in the world. Earth, erupting from its unconscious state, gathers all physical blessings and holds back, refusing to release them. It becomes psychically constipated; it goes into depression; it becomes withdrawn; it holds back.

Earth has another function. Cronos (Saturn) is also an archetype, and although he has many faces, one of Cronos' faces when he comes erupting from the unconscious as an inferior function is tightness. In Freudian language we call it Super-Ego. Guilt, pressure to perform, the constant awareness of lack of perfection, this kind of self-blame that we in the Judeo-Christian world are so apt to do. It's a kind of self-flagellation, "This flesh is somehow evil or wicked, I must suppress this flesh." There are many ways that this can happen. Anorexia and bulimia are one way. Sometimes it's Demeter, cutting off all physical nurturing because of the refusal to let go of something umbilical going on. And I believe in many cases that anorexia and bulimia are, in part, problems with the adolescent separating from parents on an umbilical level. There are a lot of issues around nurturing and feeding—it's not just a culturally derived thing.

Audience: Why is it increasing so drastically?

Richard: Well, I'm not entirely sure it's increasing drastically or whether we're just noticing it more. Sociologically the family is breaking down. Many children now are living in a one-parent home, or living in a four-parent home. Partly with mother and step-father, and partly with father and step-mother. I do attribute a lot of it to the fracture of the family system. I think that has a lot to do with it.

To go on, Water erupting from the underworld, tends to come in overwhelming waves of feelings. The crying jag, hysteria, falling apart. The face is one of dissolution, of falling into chaos, of drowning. And it's interesting, by the way, that these inferior functions show themselves in dreams. One woman that I worked with had no planets in Earth and her inferior function was beginning to emerge into consciousness. She was having dreams of huge, inevitable boulders rolling slowly after her, about to crush her, and she couldn't run fast enough to keep up with them. Dreams of the emerging Water inferior function often have to do with drowning, creatures emerging from the sea, deep wells, dripping Water, drowning dreams, being overwhelmed by tidal waves. Very common, and it often is a symbol of the inferior function about ready to emerge into consciousness. Sometimes these dreams go on for years before it ripens enough and gets up to the level where it's able to be absorbed. It may be Mermaids with their siren call, these elusive figures that are not quite one thing or another, half fish and half maiden. These creatures that kind of lure and seduce us, the kind of witch-bewitcher, the enchantress figure Circe, the lady from the Odyssey, who seduces us away from our path. She seduces the very practical Odysseus into a kind of state of madness so that the Water function, the intuitive, emotional function can reemerge.

Hades loves Water, the Water element; he lives in this kind of swamp and murk. He loves pulling down into something that is not quite earthy and not quite watery. Persephone and Inada, the goddess who went down to visit her sister Arishkegal, was, for her pains, hung on a peg and left to rot. But she renewed herself with the help of her earthy friend and came up from underworld. So the Water function, when it emerges from the unconscious, can be experienced in a devastating tidal wave of emotional feelings. One feels drowned or sucked into the quicksand of being submerged, of being annihilated, of being drowned in feelings.

Air, as an inferior function, has a number of faces. One of them is the trickster. The trickster, since it's the function of Air to consider and to jolt one into intellectual, cognitive awareness. Air loves the aha! experience of, "Now I understand!" which is the idea of Uranus. Astrologically, it's not a completely satisfactory figure for the planet we call Uranus. I would rather call him Prometheus, or Lucifer, The Light Bearer. He's the one who shocks into awareness and at the same time is destroyed, losing his place among the gods for having given this gift of awareness. This is the figure of the trickster. The trickster who, out of love for mankind, jolts us into a kind of awareness. This is different from the prankster, which is more of a Mercury figure.

Prometheus and Lucifer are trickster figures, and by the way, how many of you know the Carlos Casteneda books? Don Juan, himself, is a classic trickster figure. The trickster keeps chipping the parameters. As soon as you think you have everything understood, the rug is yanked out from under you again and says, "No that's not what it is; it's this whole picture." The prankster is different. The prankster is Hermes. In one of his faces, and Hermes has a great many other faces, too, he loves pranks for the sheer mischief of it. These are things that happen from fate, they seem fated; the slip of the tongue, the unexpected experience that removes us from our structure. So Hermes, himself, is the prankster, and the trickster comes out in an airy experience when Air comes erupting from the underworld.

Often when Air comes erupting, the feeling is madness. It's like, "Now I see things so clearly, but I do not have a framework to put them in." Suddenly, it's like a veil has been removed and the brain is conceiving things in such a wide-ranging function that I am lost, I am annihilated by the vastness of it. One of the consequences is often agoraphobia. I cannot deal with this spaciousness that suddenly has emerged—the possibilities, the enormous complexity of relationships. Since I'm now beginning to see so much, I must retreat back into my territory and withdraw. So a panic reaction, an anxiety reaction comes erupting when Air emerges from the unconscious. Another thing that happens when Air erupts from the unconscious is that relationships are shattered, because Air is the quality that gives us the ability to understand space between people.

People with Air as a missing or a singleton function have difficulty understanding space in relationships. They move too close when they should withdraw. They withdraw at the times that they should be too close. Their timing is off. At the moment when you should move forward to meet somebody, you miss the time because you're saying, "Gee, maybe I moved forward too quickly, this time I'm going to hang back." By that time you've missed the opportunity because they've gone off with somebody else. And you say, "Oh, well, my timing's off again." Next time it's too fast. She withdraws, it's not ready, it's not the time. "What have I done? Well my timing and sense of space isn't right." So the eruption out of Air often manifests itself in terms of relationships, feeling lonely, feeling devastated by people moving out of your life. It's the sense that I am alone in this great void. It can be an extremely annihilating feeling. The anxiety attack.

Next is Fire when it comes erupting out of the unconscious. I'm reminded that I didn't go into how Fire works as an inferior function, so I can combine the two things now. People with a missing or singleton function in Fire often, if they are denying or repressing it, become depressive. They feel a lack of energy, they feel helpless in the face of the world, melancholic or withdrawn. They lack fire, they lack the vitality of the universe, and the sense of such people often is there's a kind of clammy, swampy feeling about them. When you're with them the sense is, whatever the obvious agenda, you feel they're sucking life force from you, I even call them "sucking ghosts." How many of you do counseling or astrological readings? Most of you. You know instinctively when one of those arrives for a reading, don't you? It's not that they want any information from you, it's not that they're ready to open up emotionally, it's your life force they're after. It's vitality they're after, and if you let them get to that, you feel it when they've gone because you're drained. Interestingly enough, a lot of people who themselves have a singleton in a Fire function, or imbalance in their Fire function, seem to attract that kind of person. They will marry someone who sucks that energy from them and constantly feel a depletion of their energy, or vitality, or life force.

Fire, when it erupts from the unconscious, can come out in terms of aggression and rage. Here's Aries, this terror figure, this mindless destroyer that lives only with passion. His lust is to kill and rend and tear. To win, to triumph at any cost. He's an incendiary Fire when it comes erupting from the unconscious, but in its creative sense, it is the brilliant flame of creativity. Here is Apollo. Apollo has an Aries side, but he also has a fiery side because he is the god of the Sun, and the Apollo side can, in a positive sense, be an eruption of this creative flame. "I don't know where this came from!" This burning, creative inspiration comes erupting from the unconscious. Often, the feeling is of being consumed, "I'm burning."

You see it in the poetry of the romantic poets. It's romance or passion, it's being "in love with love," and it's very different from Eros. Water kind of love is the sense of, "I am losing myself, I am dissolving and merging into this other person." The fiery kind of thing is, "I am elevated, I am inspired and awakened to the full potential of who I am by the love relationship." Interestingly enough, what often happens is that when we are ready, when the inferior function begins to want to emerge, we constellate it into another human being. We project it onto another person and we attract this person into our life. The other person becomes a kind of catalyst, the alchemical catalyst that forces the precipitation within us. Then often, when the job is done, the person moves out of our life and this may be the person that we think is the most consuming passion of our life. There you are, happily married you thought, living your life in an ordinary way and along comes this person erupting out of nowhere in your life, who destroys everything around it. And you may give up everything for that person. Isn't it interesting how many of the romances and the gothic novels are full of this kind of thing? The "other" who comes along to shake and quake and transform me. However, in the gothic novels these people always end up happily ever after, married forever. In truth it doesn't work that way. That person moves through our life like a flame, an acetylene torch scalding us and moving on. And it can come in a number of ways.

In an Earthy function, it's like, "My God, I've never been into my body as much as when I've been with you." An Airy one is, "My God, I've never had this kind of communication. Nobody has understood me or sensed what I am going to say before I say it." Water is, "I don't know what's happening to me. I'm losing myself. All my self-control is gone, I'm merging into this puddle." Read some of the romantic poets. Read Elizabeth Barrett Browning with her dominant Water. "How do I love thee? Let me count the ways."[5] Browning goes on to say she loves with all the dreams of her lost youth, her hopes, her past, her future, her all, her past life, her next life, her everything.

When Fire comes erupting in the relationship, the sense of it is, "I am consumed. I am enlightened, I am awake." How we know when we're in a romantic love is, "I like who I am when I'm with you. I feel alive, enlightened, glowing, inflamed, hot, alert, creative. Something about being with you makes me feel I can do anything." So the fiery person often erupts into the light as that kind of sense of, "My God, I see my creative potential now that I'm with you. I believe in myself and that I can do more than I ever have done before." Now, the crash comes when this person moves out of our life, and he or she inevitably does. If we marry this person, the projection has to fall apart because a projection falls apart, once we've taken the package home and unwrapped it. This projected archetype that we have put into human flesh cannot live with us on a day-to-day basis, with dirty underwear and toothbrushes left on the sink. So, one way or another, this archetype must destroy itself. It is at this point, when we come up against the boundary of what I call our basic ground or territory, that a chance for an emergence onto a new level of consciousness can take place. And if we can't do that, we withdraw, regress back into a safer world, and sit there waiting for the next catalyst to come along. See what I'm saying?

Audience: Will you elaborate on what happens when the projected archetype falls away?

5. Elizabeth Barrett Browning, *Sonnets from the Portuguese and Other Love Poems* (New York: Doubleday, 1990), p. 53.

Richard: Scott Peck says, in *The Road Less Traveled*,[6] That people only learn to love when they fall out of love. That is the paradox, because *falling* in love is not *being* in love. They are two entirely different things. So the process of falling out of love means the projection has been broken.

And what happens in our society is that when we fall out of love, we look to fall in love again. So we throw away the old person and look to have that next feeling of elation, which often is triggered into our own inferior function. You see, *any* kind of stress-related experience (and falling in love is a very stressful experience), will invoke the inferior function. It summons it out of the underworld. So that's one of the reasons we feel, "I'm some way complete in a way I never have been before." It's like having somebody fill in the missing leg of our T-cross. In some way, something has come along that has completed us in a way that has never happened before. But we can't live with it. It's the other person's planet completing our T-cross; it's not our planet. And eventually, that realization has to soak in. So, that's the point of falling out of love, but it's the potential point for *being* in love where we can build relationships. However, we live in a society that worships the ideal of romance. We're not only supposed to fall in love with this magical person, but live happily ever after, and it is a quincunx. It's a paradox, it doesn't work that way. That's why in astrology the 5th house and the 7th house are different. The house of romantic love and the lover is not the same as the house of the marriage partner and the life-mate.

Audience: It sounds like the person with the inferior function will always go out to find it in a partner.

Richard: Oh no, absolutely not. It's to the degree that the person has begun to capture his or her own unconscious material, in other words the stuff that has come up, and if he or she got it. It's like it has erupted there and I've managed to contain it and hold it rather than pushing it away. At that point then, the person can move on within the relationship. The projection falls away, and it's a painful period in any case, but it does not necessarily have to destroy the relationship.

6. M. Scott Peck, *The Road Less Traveled* (London: Hutchinson, 1978; New York: Simon & Schuster, 1988), p. 118.

Audience: The whole thing about relationships is that we do projections.

Richard: Of course. To some extent we're always bringing our projected material into relationships. But the point that Jung makes is that the relationships we form, as he calls it, "in the morning of our lifetime," are built upon projections. And he says, as we mature and individuate, or become more full and complete, at that point the material we're projecting is less and less. We're more and more conscious of it, so we're not trapped and compelled by the projection.

I have to tell a little story of how the so called Freudian slip is usually when your inferior function, something that you're expending a tremendous amount of energy holding back, comes out. The story goes that a woman, when she was a very little girl, was to be visited by grandfather. The grandfather had an enormous amount of money and had not drawn his will up yet. His money would be divided among a number of grandchildren, and grandfather was taking one last look at all the family. Now this little girl was 4 years old, extremely precocious, and tended to notice things. Her grandfather had a huge nose and was extremely sensitive about it. As a matter of fact, he was so sensitive about this nose that any mention of it could mean being eliminated from the will completely.

So grandfather is coming over for tea and the little girl is going to meet him for the first time. The little girl is instructed for six days ahead of time. Not only is the word n-o-s-e not to be mentioned, not only are we not to look any place above the Adam's Apple, but no word beginning with n is even to be mentioned. So the little girl has been told that right after she greets grandfather and kisses him, she is to leave the room. Everything goes like clockwork. Grandfather comes in, the little girl is perfectly mannered, looks at her hands, smiles at grandfather, never looks at this enormous nose standing out there, kisses grandfather and walks out of the room. The mother breathes a sigh of relief and she says, "Well now, Grandfather, do you take cream or lemon in your nose?"

So the moral to that story is that there's an unconscious sense of inner dishonesty that the inferior function knows and, as trickster, loves to yank the rug out from under you. There is something within us I think, that desires wholeness and growth and integrity and truth and honor. And it is those parts that very often will come sneaking out at the last minute, in spite of all of your best intentions. It will come out and make you honest at the last minute, even at great loss. So what happened? She was pushed out beyond her barbed wire. She may lose the inheritance, or she may have to confront grandfather about the nose. (Or get a sense of humor, right?)

I want to give you a few more examples of some people with inferior functions, but I don't want to spend a long time doing it. People with inferior functions in Water signs include a number of musicians—like Grieg, Haydn, Beethoven, Debussy, and Richard Strauss. I think music in and of itself seems to constellate around Water. Beethoven, with his eruption of passion, is almost archetypal for me. There are artists, like Toulouse-Lautrec, whose work is so deeply and passionately emotional, and writers, like Virginia Wolff—how did she die, by the way? She drowned, did she not? Katherine Ann Porter, who wrote *Ship of Fools* [7] about these archetypal people afloat on this ship at sea; the poet Shelley—how did he die? He drowned; Swimmers Mark Spitz and Johnny Weismuller. Isn't it interesting how often we constellate in the world? You see here's where the world of dreams and events move. Dream symbology and waking symbology emerge into the same kind of thing. Why is it any accident the person with the missing Water becomes a famous swimmer or drowns in the water? I don't think there are accidents about things like this.

Okay, missing Air. Well, with missing Air we have this incredible catalog of geniuses and great thinkers. I'll just run through the list: Thomas Jefferson, probably the most intellectual of our American presidents; Schiller; Sir Walter Scott, the prolific English writer; Spinosa, the philosopher; Tolstoy, probably the greatest Russian writer; Oliver Wendell Holmes; Edgar Allen Poe; Swinburne; H. G. Wells; Edgar Rice Burroughs; Dostoyevsky; de Maupassant; Alexandre Dumas; Flaubert; Goethe; Hemingway; Hesse; Bertrand Russell; William Soroyan; George Bernard Shaw; and you can go on and on. All these people with no Air, I mean the great intellectual geniuses of our life. So when Air erupts from the unconscious, it can bring genius. There's a specialized genius that's involved, but the shadow side of it often is an inability to function in other areas of life. Einstein is a perfect example. He had a singleton in Air,

7. Katherine Anne Porter, *Ship of Fools* (Boston: Little, Brown, 1962).

Jupiter in Aquarius in the 9th. He was a dominant watery person and Einstein literally could not figure out how to tie his shoelaces, but in the one area in which he was overly specialized, he was a genius. That often happens with inferior functions. There is tremendous compensation in one area and tremendous helplessness or repression in another area.

Here's Air on another level. There are a lot of actors with missing functions in Air and they tend to be of two types. One is of the extremely exquisitely articulate school and here we have, what I would call, the *compensating Air*, like Rex Harrison, Laurence Olivier, Peter Ustinov, and Richard Burton. The other kind of actor is what we call "the scratch and mumble" school of acting. This is the person who seems tormented by his inability to communicate and something about that attracts us. We want to say, "Yes, I'm with you, I know how it is a struggle, let it come out." I'll give you an example. Montgomery Clift and all of the actors who constellated around The Actor's Studio. There's Monte Clift, Sun singleton in Libra; James Dean, Sun singleton in Aquarius; Marlon Brando, nothing in Air; Paul Newman, Sun singleton in Aquarius; Warren Beatty, Robert Redford, and Jack Nicholson. Isn't it interesting? What these people are known for is not their brilliance of communication, but the struggle to get this stuff out. So we're attracted to that erupting inferior function when it comes out in that way.

Let's talk about some inferior functions in Fire, which is a little bit elusive and hard to get hold of. Nevertheless it comes out among romantics—people who consume themselves for a cause. A certain kind of martyr gets consumed by flames, so you have people like Joan of Arc, who managed to find her fire, and Vanessa Redgrave, a firebrand. You see, it's one who gets involved in polemics and passion and is carried away by a belief system. Patrick Henry was called the spark who started the Revolutionary War, and that's literally the term used to describe him. He was called "the passion that ignited the war" by any number of generals and martial people like George Patton. Our dear friend Ronald Reagan has no planets in Fire and there the unconscious quality of the missing Fire is the incendiary. The fact that on a collective level worldwide, people say this man is a match looking for someplace to strike, is exactly right. Let's have a small fire here. There's something of the psychic arsonist in the person without Fire. Great passionate lovers like Valentino. The two great romantic poets, Byron and Keats—no Fire. Great romantic figures like John Barrymore and F. Scott Fitzgerald—no planets in Fire.

Lots of psychotherapists are short on Water and that's the way they compensate. People like Alan Ross and Rollo May. Freud himself was low on Water and Jung was low on Water, as I recall, I don't have the charts at the moment. So yes, these are the people that delve and dig into the psyche. One of the best psychotherapists I know, who has a missing function in Water, says, "I never have experienced an emotion in my life. I don't know what people mean when they talk about it, but I am excellent at evoking it in other people." So they bring it out to complete the therapist, and that's when therapy becomes a mutual process! We attract toward us.

As I was discussing with a friend the other night, I think there is no accident why a particular therapist is attracted to a particular model. And why a particular client is attracted to a particular therapist who is practicing a certain model. No accidents with that. It's no mere accident that Tennessee Williams created Blanche DuBois out of some anima figure within him which sent out a beacon around the world until along comes Vivien Leigh who says, "Yes, that's me," gets sucked into it, and becomes destroyed. Vivien Leigh actually acted out and consumed herself in the anima of Tennessee Williams. Now, how about that! Wouldn't that be an interesting chart comparison to do? So, as I say, there is no accident as to what we're attracted to in terms of the therapies.

All right, in terms of modalities, singletons and missing functions are a little harder to see, because, although we can see element clearly, we have to intuit modality. Basically speaking, when they are erupting from the unconscious, inferior function, Cardinal often comes out as impulsiveness—an eruption toward sudden action. These are often people who find it difficult to either make beginnings or endings. It's hard starting something and it's hard finishing something. When Cardinal is inferior someone will suddenly bring things to an end. He's been married twenty-five years, has fourteen kids, and suddenly one day he's standing at the door with suitcases, saying, "I'm leaving. Bye. I'm bored with you." You never knew anything was wrong. Or you may have a sudden urge toward beginning or starting something, so you pack up and out you go—the pioneer. Or the impulsiveness from the unconscious can destroy everything that you've set up. The person who has the impulsive love affair or makes an impulsive money investment.

Again, here's the trickster, the annihilator coming from underneath that wishes to jar you into consciousness. Naturally what happens is, if you're low in Cardinal, then you've got to be high in Fixed or Mutable, so Cardinal says, "Oh, I'm going to yank you out of your inertia-fix," or, "Now, Mutable, I'm going to make you focus." When Fixed is an inferior function, of course *inertia* is a key word. We saw a very good example of how that was lived out by Elizabeth Barrett Browning, whose shadow function of Fixed came up from underneath. Her inability to connect with that archetype hysterically paralyzed her. Inertia can also come out as excessive behavior, or excessive and compulsive as well. In that case, it suddenly attaches itself to something and psychically, like a barnacle, will not let go. An *idée fixe*. Obsessional material that very often manifests itself in intense sexual passion—an obsession with a person who may be completely unavailable, like with a rock star. Or a consuming desire to master all of the information about something, "I'm going to know everything about Greek mythology or astrology," and it becomes devouring. It's like this maw, this hungry maw that is forever consuming.

Remember the symbology for Fixed. It's this vortex pulling in and it's often Aphrodite-like. Aphrodite herself is a nymph. She's a goddess of "fill me completely," if you read her earlier form. How many of you have read the lovely book, *Descent to the Goddess* by Sylvia Brinton Perera,[8] a Jungian who lives in New York? She talks about Inana, the Sumerian original Aphrodite figure, who stands leaning against the pole describing the beauty of her vulva. And she says, "Come man, come beautiful man, fill my lovely vulva." The desire world pulling in. Aphrodite was a little raw even for the Greeks, but of course, by the time she became Venus in Rome she got very aestheticized. Although Aphrodite, herself, has an aesthetic function, as she goes back into history she becomes more and more primordial. Finally you see her in those ancient statues where she has

8. Sylvia Brinton Perera, *Descent to the Goddess: A Way of Initiation for Women* (Toronto: Inner City Books, 1981), p. 18.

no head, great breasts, great belly and a huge bottom. She is the archetypal Earth Mother that takes in seed and brings forth life. That's her function.

Mutable, when it comes erupting from the unconscious, comes off as hysterical, schizoid—it falls apart. On an extreme level, it can be a schizophrenic break. It's like all of these denied, broken parts, suddenly come erupting up all at the same time, or one of the parts that has been missing for a long time erupts as a separate personality. Perhaps the feeling is a nervous breakdown, "I'm falling to pieces," is the feeling a person might have. Disorder, chaos, and the archetype is Shiva, the god of destruction and rebirth, who has six hands with the weapons of death in them. And literally, the dance of Shiva is the dance of death and life. One has been thrown into chaos when unconscious Mutable comes erupting. An interesting example of that is Jimmy Carter, whose dominant function is Cardinal, so you have a very directed, planned kind of personality. But he has a singleton Mercury in Mutable and at the moment of crisis he became indecisive—that whole business of the Iranian hostages. Why? Because mutability sees so many sides, suddenly you become paralyzed by seeing all the possibilities.

Okay, now I want to talk about inferior function in orientation—Personal, Social and Universal. First, inferior function in Personal. What often happens is that people may compensate. Let's say no planets in the first four signs. They may find it difficult or impossible to say, "What is it that I want?" "Who am I? What do I need?" They may compensate for it and become extremely self-centered. These may be the people who see all other people around them as objects, things to fill them, to complete them. They become de-personalized. Again, is it denied? Is it repressed? Is it compensated for? You often see denied people in therapy. There will be a singleton or no planets in the first four signs, and they'll say, "I don't know what I want, or who I am, or why I'm here, or what I feel. You tell me." It's kind of an empty void here and they try to fill it up. Or, out of the fear of that, they go the opposite direction and compensate for it and say, "I know what I want, I've got to have it this minute and you better give it to me immediately or I'm going to kill you or abandon you."

I used to counsel and teach in the prison system in California. I taught astrology there and found that a lot of inmates who had an inferior function in Personal found it very difficult to take "no" for an answer. The minute the urge emerged, that urge had to be fulfilled. The other side is the people who direct all their energy into Social and Universal. They're constantly giving to other people and they are involved in causes and ignore everything around them on a close, personal level. They often neglect their physical appearance. They neglect their health, they won't eat right, they don't get enough sleep. Their relationships are falling apart, but there they are, their outward world seems so wonderful and the inner world seems so bleak.

A couple of interesting questions came up during the break. The first thing someone mentioned I think is very right. She said, "I know someone who is very fiery, full of energy, who seems to be all over the place, or someone who might have a dominant Water sign who is always wallowing in emotions and feelings. How is that different from the inferior function?" And the difference is that people with a dominant Water sign *like* where they are. They're used to it, that's normal for them. They may say that they want to not do that, but the chances are they do want to continue doing that because that's their basic ground. They may learn eventually how to live better with it than they do. Now, let's say their dominant function is Water and their inferior function is Air. When the Air function begins to emerge from the unconscious, it will help that dominant Water function. The inferior function will help the dominant. Why? Because the inferior function emerging from shadow begins to tell them, "It's okay to have some space. I don't have to disappear totally. I have Air down there that will enable me to separate. I won't have to lose my individuality." But when the inferior function is erupting from the unconscious, it's cataclysmic in its feeling to the extent that it is denied or repressed. The more familiar you are with it, the easier it becomes. I mean if you've looked at the face of the dragon, and although he shifts his face many times, if you've looked at the face of that once, then it's not so difficult the next time.

Another question came up. A mother was saying that she has a son who has dominant Mutable and nothing in Cardinal, so how can this young man get focused in his life? I said that I would suspect that she, the mother, was being his Cardinal function for him. And, indeed, she said yes, her Saturn is on his Sun. There's a danger when the parent tries to replace the child's inferior function. And sometimes you get it the other way around—the child tries to replace the parent's inferior function. In that case, you get a state of total dissatisfaction. The parent is dissatisfied with the child, the child feels the dissatisfaction, imports the inferior function from the parent, and it cements the umbilical cord. The child now becomes attached. There's a love-hate relationship because the child says, "I need to separate from you, my parent, but if I do that, it's at the total loss of this function, since you're doing it for me."

Here's an example: a child, someone with an inferior (I sometimes call it an *impacted*) Earth function. Let's say the parent does all the Earth function. The child doesn't clean his room, doesn't learn to take care of himself, never takes a job during the summer, and the parents provide everything for whatever reason. It may be out of guilt or obligation, or they're compensating for their own youth when they didn't have a lot. So the child is showered with things. Out of this we get what we call the classic Jewish Prince or Princess who feels born to be special and catered to. All this giving from the parent interferes with the separation function, the natural separation function between the child and the parent. The child says, "If I leave my parent, which I must do, I also leave my Earth because I can't provide for myself." The parent subtly (and here's Demeter in her other force) says, "I don't want you to be independent, I want to keep giving you money because that keeps you tied to me." It's a kind of symbiosis.

So a parent does a child no favor when the parent, out of the desire to rescue, lives out the inferior function for the child. The child who says, "I don't understand this, help me with my homework, do my homework for me." Missing function in Air. The parent does no favor by doing that. The parent does a favor by saying, "Let us see how we can go about doing this together or find another way," but not to rescue. Because later in the life, before the inferior function comes out, the harder it is for the child. So parents, out of love for a child, try to rescue the child from pain, and very often do that by being the inferior function for the child, which is ultimately no favor. What happens is the "oneness" in us very often resists the "multiplicities" in us and those multiplicities are often the things we relegate to shadow. These multiplicities wish to come up and be part of the party, too, the oneness resists that, but the multiplicities want to come up too. And it works the other way around. The multiplicities resist the oneness. I know this is a little paradoxical, but do you follow what I'm saying? The oneness itself says, "I wish to make unity." We see this paradox in the chart. Here is the oneness all contained within a circle, but here also is the multiplicity of it. How can we be both many and one at the same time? That is the divine paradox we live in and the United States is a perfect model of that. How can we be a Federal and a Republic and a Nation? Well, our motto says *E Pluribus Unum*, out of many, one. So we honor both the many and the one, and it's not an easy thing to do on the level of psyche.

Audience: If a person has an inferior function in Earth, will a strong Saturn in the chart make up for it?

Richard: Not necessarily. Because in my judgment of astrology, one thing does not equal another, nor does one thing replace another. A liver does not replace your kidney, though one kidney can take over the work of two. They are different things entirely. The missing Earth function may put added pressures onto Saturn in some way, but it may not be the earthy part of Saturn that's going to be working.

I think that a lot of you probably are hearing this missing function as a terrible thing to have, and it is not. It is not. Please don't see it that way. Out of the creative juices in Fire comes consciousness and creativity. I mean, if I had to choose, I would rather have a chart full of missing functions and singletons and T-crosses, rather than the classical "nice" chart. Because nice chart equals nice people, and God knows, we don't want to be that! So there's a tendency to think in "good" and "bad," and it isn't that. That's why I say let's remove our value judgments from these kinds of things. *The chart that you have is the most perfect you!* Your task is to learn perfectly how to live with that perfect you.

Audience: Is it because it is so strangely familiar that it comes up in a very primitive way?

Richard: Yes, it comes up in archetypal forms. It comes up raw, simply because you're not used to doing it. How many of you saw

"Tarzan"? It's like all his social functions had never been developed, because he's an ape-man living in the jungle. When he's suddenly forced into dealing with society, he is in no way prepared to do it, and it comes out in very odd, peculiar and sometimes beautiful ways. His kind of honesty and openness in ways of dealing shocks people. In other ways it's extremely awful and embarrassing and uncomfortable.

Audience: Inferior really means that it is in a low place, where it is not an act of consciousness?

Richard: Yes. Yes, inferior doesn't mean worse. Please don't think of inferior as worse. Words are tricky and they're loaded with other meanings. Inferior doesn't mean bad, it means *underneath*. It's from Heraldry.[9] A superior position is up and available and inferior is below.

The inferior function in Social often indicates people who are extremely uncomfortable in social interaction with others, or they compensate in another way and don't like to be alone. These people literally panic if they're not on the phone with somebody or don't have the TV on. They have to be married, have to have a relationship going, or they feel like they're going to be annihilated and fall apart. Or, they become the recluse. They can be people who find it totally uncomfortable to be around other people and relate to them on a one-to-one basis.

For example, Howard Hughes had no planets in Social signs. And yet, in his early life he did not compensate because he was the great seducer and escort of all of the beautiful Hollywood starlets. He was running for political office; he was involved in everything. Later on in life the shadow emerged in a different way and he became this odd recluse who had food left by his door. Queen Victoria is another example of no planets in Social signs. Early in her life it went projected out to Prince Albert who was her social function and with him she was able to be social. When Albert died, she turned back in and became a recluse. Another example is Richard Nixon: no planets in Social signs, and his absolute uncomfortableness, not only with being around other people, but also the seemingly

9. Heraldry is a system of hereditary identification using visual symbols called coats of arms.

peculiar inability to understand the rules by which people play. His stuff is all in Personal and Universal. It's "let the history books decide" on one hand, "what I want and need" on the other, and the stuff in the middle doesn't seem to count.

Now finally, Universal signs. People with nothing in Universal signs often tend to not be able to see the broad picture. It's hard for them to see fate or great encompassing theories. Very often it's simply a lack of interest. Their orientation in time and space is toward the immediate, me and you and me and me. The collective, or what's going on in the future, does not involve them or possess them much. Or, again, you might get a compensating reaction and people whose lives are all *causes*. It sucks the energy, like Cyrano's nose, and it pulls everything into it. These are people who will compensate and live a collective or universal life. They become the martyr, the teacher, the guru, the servant, and so on.

In addition to missing functions and singletons, dominant and inferior functions, which we've talked about, there are some other things to add. Of first importance after the functions are major configurations. I'm not going to go into them and describe them until they start to show up in charts, but at least I want to list what they are. So we start with the functions and from there I like to look at major configurations. Major configurations evoke archetypes and they often come out very raw. They form complexes. I'm always happy to see one in a chart because it makes my work so much easier. There are different kinds and they combine the energies of the planets into dynamic and often mythical tales. So, whereas the planets as singletons or missing functions come across as archetypal *figures*, major configurations come across as archetypal *themes* or *stories*. Here's where we get a dance.

For example, let's say someone has a T-cross between Moon, Venus, and Pluto. Here is the dance between Moon as mother, Venus as the nubile maiden, and Pluto as the erupting force that separates the mother from the daughter. I actually have worked with a number of cases where it exactly shows that. Moon and Venus in opposition and Pluto as the focal point of the T-cross forcing the break between this umbilical opposition between the Moon and Venus. Here's where knowledge of myth, fairy tale, and archetypal stories enrich your work so greatly—the drama, the theater.

Because, as it's been said, there's nothing new under the sun, so every time you see these planets in complex, what happens? You say, "Aha! I hear this person's story and it sounds familiar. That's exactly the relationship between Blanche and Stella and Stanley in *A Streetcar Named Desire*. I know what this is."

Freud hooked onto one particular little drama. Specifically the drama of Oedipus and his relationship with his mother Jocasta and the father Laius. Why did he so particularly hook onto that, although it's certainly a valid archetype, and is it part of the human condition? Certainly it is. But why did he universalize it so greatly? Look at his chart. Mars singleton opposing Venus, the Mars alone on one side of the chart in Libra. The phallic thrust goes toward the mother and Mars is in the 8th house. I can't do his chart off the top of my head, but I know it hooks into 4th house mother significators in his chart.

So major configurations are very important; there's the yod, the T-cross, the grand cross, and the grand trine. Certainly there are other major configurations, but I focus mainly on these and especially what I call lop-sided major configurations. Of those the most important are the T-cross and the yod. The T-cross and the yod I call *open systems*. The reason for that is that they are out of balance, they have a planet at a focal point. In the yod, of course, two planets are sextile each other, let's call them A and B, and both are quincunx a third planet we'll call C, which is the focal planet. That planet becomes full of psychological drama and in many ways acts like a singleton, except instead of operating alone it now is pulled into a complex. Why? Because it's in a dance now with A and B. The T-cross is the same thing. Here you have A opposed B, both square C and C is the planet that is the pressure.

So here is the difference in a nutshell between these two things. I'm not going to spend a lot of time on aspect theory, but I want to give you the psychodynamics as I see it in these. A and B create a tension. A and B are in opposition in the T-cross. The energy is dumped onto C as a resolving force between the tension in A and B. You often see this in marriages and families. A and B very often are the parents, but not necessarily. A and B have this tension in between them and it's often the child who will act out the unresolved tension between the parents. So, symbolically, I see the T-cross as a bow and arrow. When you string a bow you have to get a lot of tension to get the bow strung, and once it is, the bow is taut. And what happens is, in order to make the bow work, you pull it back and now you've got a T-cross. Then there's an enormous amount of tension and a desire to release. The release point comes out opposite and the outlet point is often the area where the projected action takes place. The pressure is on the focal point and the release point is in the sign and the house opposite. These are very dynamic configurations and often form complexes that become consuming life issues.

The yod is a different kind of dynamic, and let's go again to a family theory. Here is A and B now in perfect agreement. Here's mother and father that continually support each other in their own version of reality, and poor C down here at quincunx is odd man out—odd child out. Partly because A and B are threatened in their kind of lovely little sextilian dance by the pressure that comes up from this paradoxical, dangerous, quincunxial C, A and B agree that C is crazy. When A and B agree that C has a bad problem, then C comes to agree that it has a bad problem. Again, you often see this in family dynamics don't you? The parents are smoothing everything over, "Let everything be nice, we have a perfect relationship," but the unconscious stuff comes out, the shadow stuff in the marriage gets acted out in the child and then you have a schizophrenic child, a drug abusing child, the delinquent child. The parents are constantly saying things like, "We can't understand dear little Sophie. We come from such a happy home. How could she have gone so wrong? We've given her everything. She's never heard her mother and father raise their voices in quarrel, only in song. We attend church regularly every Sunday. How could she have gone so bad?"

Now I'm setting this up as a drama in a family setting, but can you see how this could also go on internally? The archetypal figures in A and B, whoever they may be in your chart, collude to find C nuts. And the planet at C, then, is carrying the load of the fact that some part within you at A and B have agreed to say C is crazy. Why is that? Well, that keeps us sane. So in family therapy we have a work called IP, the *identified-patient*, and in every family dynamic we always have an identified patient. The "poor alcoholic mother," or "depressed father," or "drug-abusing son," or "delinquent daughter," is the problem. And if we could only fix this person wouldn't the whole family be wonderful? Well, astrologically, focal point planets often become this kind of identified-patient and they often carry the weight of the problem. However, the problem is not necessarily there, although it's *felt* there. Frequently the problem is the tension in the opposition, or the collusion in the sextile, that creates the problem.

The grand cross and grand trine are different. The grand cross is a complete square, the grand trine is a complete triangle. There's no opening into them and the psychodynamics of them is that they tend to be *closed systems*. Grand trine says, "I'm all right, Jack. This is the best of all possible worlds. It's quite Zen. It is the way it is and if it wasn't supposed to be that way, it wouldn't be that way, so why should I make any effort? When it's supposed to be different it will be, and in the meantime, let's just boogey!" So, frankly, I find of all the major aspects, the most difficult one to work with and intervene with is the grand trine, because it doesn't see that anything is wrong. And if anything *is* wrong, it's a self-completing system.

Once again, the grand trine is a collusion. "Yes, yes we are all in agreement and nothing is wrong and we have our closed little world where nothing can intrude." I often call it *the greased pole*. Everything is easy, no stress or difficulty or unpleasantness is allowed to intrude at all within this magic system. So what happens when the grand-trine-dominated personality is faced with eruptions from the unconscious? They are thrown by it. They often get it in extremely powerfully and painful ways because they are not used to having to deal with it. Like the expression we used to use in the 70's, they "shine it on." It's an expression that means "let it go, it's all right, it doesn't matter."

In the pathological family there is a scapegoat, that's the identified-patient, the wounded one, the crippled one. And it's often interesting to see how these roles will shift and how the family will collude. The alcoholic father, who is the identified-patient, goes for therapy, joins AA and gets off the bottle. The family will then begin to collude to get him back on the bottle because it's like musical chairs, something's missing here. "If *he's* not the identified patient, it might suddenly become *me!*" That's why family therapy is such an important process, because, like a major configuration, you're not going to solve the problem by dealing with one end of a grand cross. You've got to deal with the whole system.

Okay. So the grand cross is another closed system and it says, "The world out there is tough, so I build a fort to protect myself from that. And, man, I'm going to survive within that and you're going to be outside—I'm a survivor!" So there is a quality of surviving in the grand cross. There's an enormous amount of toughness there, and it's very difficult to intervene. Because, just as the grand trine normally carries the myth that "Everything ought to be easy so don't intervene and tell me about difficulties," the grand cross says, "Everything is a struggle and don't intervene to tell me that there's any other way of being. I'm going to be in there and fight it." So both of the closed systems are more difficult from the point of view of the astrological counselor, because the inner sense is, "I contain all of this within me." There isn't an opening. In the open systems, the T-cross and the yod, there is a *focus-itch* that needs to be scratched. There's a hurting point. So when the person with the focal point at the T-cross and the yod comes in, he or she knows something is wrong. Often the grand trine or the grand cross doesn't know that anything's wrong. There's a general feeling of malaise. "Something is wrong but I can't focus on what it is."

In addition to major configurations, I also like to look at what I call *planets in weird places*—like stationary planets and planets without apparent motion. You look in the ephemeris and you see that the planet doesn't seem to have moved much during the day. The faster the planet normally moves, like Mercury which is a fast planet, the more potent it becomes when it is on its station. For instance, Mercury on its station, tends to evoke the shadow side of Mercury. It evokes the deep, frantic parts of it that normally don't come out. You get Mercury-to-the-nth-degree, depending upon what sign you find Mercury in. Archetypal figures begin to come up. There is something that burns. It's like a laser energy of the planet because it comes out in such a pure, crystalline, archetypal way. What happens if you were to pass your hand through a laser beam quickly? Probably nothing. But if you moved it slowly in front of the beam, what would happen? You'd get scorched. And what would happen if you just left your hand there, stationary in front of it? You'd have a hole right through your hand. So stationary planets also constellate in archetypal ways.

Another thing I find important are planets at the 29th degree. The closer to 29 degrees 59 minutes, the more unstable the planet becomes. It is a planet in a rather *schitzy* situation—about to change and transform by sign, modality, element, polarity and, in certain instances, also its orientation. If we can personalize here for a moment, it's like the planet, sensing this, is backing off from the inevitable. Or, like The Fool in the tarot deck, it's toppling forward and going off the precipice. So very often there is something erratic. Again, it can have a brilliant kind of creativity, so don't see this in any way as a negative thing. And, by the way, this includes to some extent the 28th degree—we're not going to just draw the line at 29— because, as we're beginning to shift, it's a "twilight zone." There is something magical and numinous about this and I think it has a rather Neptunian nature to it. There's impending chaos and change—Shiva is coming and something is destabilized here. The ground is shaky underneath my feet. You'll find that complexes can begin to build around planets that are in that degree.

Also the zero degree is a zero-and-change, as I like to call it, and is also a position of potential instability. But here we have a different quality. Something new has just been born and I'm not quite sure how to do this yet. A zero degree really is, in many ways, much like Mars. It's kind of raw and bumptious. Mercury at 0 degrees is, "Boy, I just open my mouth and out it comes. It may be completely off the wall but, I just got it from there and here it is!" Sometimes it's brilliant and sometimes it's whacko. So the zero degree and the first degree have this sense of new birth—it's the awakening Aries-lamb in a way. And the 29th degree brings in this Neptunian quality of entropy, of merging back into the chaos. Look for both of them, they're very important figures.

Another thing that you want to look at is aspects. What aspects are dominant? Are there ten squares in the chart? Fourteen quincunxes? Are there no trines? And you can have missing aspects, too. What happens to the person who doesn't have any squares? Again, you get an inferior function, because the major aspects themselves are archetypal. There is something about the impact of the irresistible force and the immoveable object that's part of the process of evolution. How does the person deal with it? It may be a person who can't stand disagreement or stress. Or maybe the person projects it and finds somebody who will provoke a scrap. I've seen lots of charts with no squares, and I tell you, it ain't easy. I would rather give up all my trines than give up my squares, because the person without squares is not prepared for struggle. Forget about this marvelous thing in traditional astrology that the best thing to have is Sun and Moon trine in your chart, maybe with Jupiter making it a grand trine. No way! Give me a Sun-Moon square any day rather than a Sun-Moon trine. Why? Because the so-called "hard" aspects are what I call the aspects of *resistance* and it is through resistance that struggle toward evolution comes out. The so-called "easy" aspects, like trine and sextile, I call aspects of *acceptance*. There is nothing there provoking them toward making the step toward evolution. Now most of us have a mixture in our charts, but it's important to check the dominance when you're looking. So, what aspects are dominant, what aspects are missing? Is there a singleton aspect in the chart? Often a singleton opposition, square, or quincunx will define the primary psychodynamic that's going on within that individual. Check it out and if you have one, it's very useful for you. Another thing, is there a planet that is a *nexus link*, a planet that connects two major configurations? That planet becomes hooked into a double-complex, as it were.

So this is the material. There are other things you can look at, too, but keep it as simple as you can. This is the material, the building blocks out of which you're going to build your rough draft of the chart. Remember, as an artist, what you may be doing. Here is your canvas and you might say, "Well, okay, I think I'll have mountains here, and maybe these will be trees. And, I don't know, I think I'm going to suddenly turn the tree into an elephant." And you build up layer by layer. So, as you interpret the chart from this point of view, you'll begin to see it in process. It's like building a body from the marrow to the bones—to the muscle tissue—to the organs—to the skin and finally, to the aura. We're building from the inside out.

Audience: If by progression a planet goes into a missing element, does that take the charge out?

Richard: Well that's often the time for the inferior function to begin to work. There's an opportunity for it to emerge at that point.

Audience: Do you also look at patterns of planet distribution overall in the chart?

Richard: Yes, I would add this to the list; it's a very valuable thing. Is there nothing in the North, South, East, or West of the chart? Yes, look at that. In this first look at the chart we're looking for what stands out and is different.

Audience: You said the T-cross projects out. What do you mean?

Richard: Well, the pressure is felt at the focal point of the T, but the *action* is often projected out to the opposite sign and house.

Audience: What about retrograde planets?

Richard: Planets in retrograde I do not give a lot of importance to. I think it's important if you have a lot of planets retrograde, but what *is* important is when planets shift direction by progression. That I consider a very critical thing, especially when by progression a planet goes onto a station. I used to give far more emphasis to natal retrogradation than I do now. I do think there is a quality of inward turning, but I hate to put any value judgment on what that means. For some people it can mean a suppression, for other people it can mean going in and doing inner work, so I certainly do not put it in this first category of things to look at.

Audience: Does it make any difference if aspects are out-of-sign aspects?

Richard: Yes, it does make a difference. If they are trine by sign then they find the qualities within them that are most agreeable to each other. But if it's a trine aspect that turns out to be quincunx by sign, then they select to work another way with each other, which is to find the things that are most difficult to resolve between them. However, for the purposes that we're talking about here, it doesn't make any difference.

Audience: Are stelliums important? What makes a stellium and could an unaspected planet be part of a stellium?

Richard: Oh yes, as I've said before, stelliums are important. For me, four or more planets in any one sign or house is a stellium and yes, unaspected planets could be part of it, too, absolutely.

CHAPTER THREE

෯

FOLLOWING THE MAGIC THREAD: STEP-BY-STEP INTERPRETATION

L et's take a look at a chart (see Chart 2 on page 74). I won't identify the person for you for just a moment. The game is not to guess who it is because I'll tell you who it is afterward. I think it's probably somebody you know of and probably someone whose chart you haven't seen, but if you think you know who it is, please keep it to yourself for just a minute.

Let's look at a few things from the point of view of what we're talking about. At this point try not to do a chart interpretation—let your eye wander all over this very complex system. Let's go step by step and just look at it. This is the chart of a man, and first of all, what do we see? We have a stellium of Mars, Mercury, Venus, Moon, and Saturn in Capricorn. I am particularly intrigued by the Moon-Saturn conjunction in Capricorn in the 8th house. That draws my attention as a particular area of focus. I see a grand trine in Fire between Sun in Sagittarius in the 7th, Jupiter in Leo in the 3rd and Uranus in Aries in the 11th. You see that I've drawn a little antenna coming out from Jupiter? That's my signal for myself that I have a singleton (only planet in Fixed), and you'll see it noted on the chart under "singletons." So the two little lines outside mean singletons and the box around a planet means focal point of a T-cross (see Uranus).

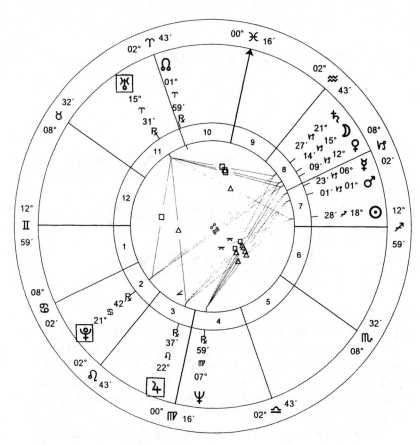

MODALITIES	MISSING	ORIENTATIONS
Cardinal 9 (T)	FUNCTIONS	(Houses)
Fixed 1 (♃)	Air	Personal 3
Mutable 3		Social 9
	STELLIA	Universal 1 (♓)
ELEMENTS	♑	
Fire 4 (△)		ORIENTATION
Air 0		(Signs)
Water 1 (♀)	SINGLETONS	Personal 2
Earth 8	♃ Fixed	Social 2
	♀ Water	Universal 9
Yang 4	♓ Universal Houses	
Yin 9		

Chart 2. Example chart.

Birth data cited in footnote 2, on page 83.

Normally I do my charts in many colors and this chart in black and white is taking away one dimension for me. In any case, there's a grand trine between Uranus, Sun, and Jupiter in Fire. There's a T-cross between a singleton Pluto in the 2nd house (only planet in Water), opposing Saturn, Moon, and Venus in Capricorn in the 8th, all forming a T-cross to Uranus in Aries in the 11th and out-letting itself into Libra in the 5th house. Those are the major dynamics. There are a few smaller aspects that I did not put in so we could get a clearer picture of it, so that's an overall impression.

The first thing I see when I look at this is a highly unusual person, a very lopsided kind of personality. The archetype connected with Capricorn is going to be emphasized. It doesn't matter where we start, my eye can go to the stellium first. Here is the final dispositor of the chart, Saturn in Capricorn in the 8th house. It disposes of everything else in the chart, so there is something of the archetypal figure of Saturn here that is going to be extremely predominant. And what do those issues mean for me? Well, it means Senex, it means the wise old man. It means the authority figure. It means the super-ego. It means Cronos in either his most ordering, loving, wise old man face, or in his devouring of his children face. You all know the story of how Cronos ate his children. Why? Because he is the father that cannot be supplanted by the young that grow up. These obviously must be issues somehow or another that are tied up here. Notice that, except for the Sun, all the personal planets are involved— Mars, Mercury, Venus, and Moon—so here is a consuming archetype that's going to be involved for this man. When a person manifests a stellium like that, the archetype comes in and possesses you. And it's very easy not only to identify with the archetype and say, "This is me," but it's easy for the world to project upon you and say, "Yes, you are this archetype, you are living Capricorn."

So let's look at the functions. The dominant function is Cardinal. Here is a person who normally and easily functions beginning things, starting things, is an initiator, a person with drive; he's goal-directed, he reaches out from himself toward some goal outside himself. We might say he is ambitious, pushy, dynamic, forthright and outgoing. Mutable—well, let's leave that alone because we want to go for just the big pieces now. We find a singleton in Fixed, so an inferior function in fixity. What does that mean? Something of the stability, inertia, gathering, hording, bringing in together, , is going to be an issue for this person in his life. Pretty going to tell you who this is. Are you getting curious or would you rather not know yet?

Audience: Let's find out more about him first.

Richard: Okay. So what we have here is something of fixity. It means here is something from the unconscious that erupts and wishes to gather, to hold, to become inert, to obsess, to hang on. Will this erupt from the unconscious at a critical time to break through in terms of a new consciousness, or will this undermine and form in the way of the trickster? We don't know yet. The singleton is Jupiter. Now that means that already Jupiter, itself, which is the dispositor of the Sun anyway, and part of the grand trine, becomes an archetypal figure. Who is Jupiter? Who is Zeus? We talked about him earlier. Jupiter has this very warm, benevolent, Guru, teacher, friendly-father side, but he also is a great manipulator. He loves power, he likes to look good. As we talked about in mythology, Zeus can be very sneaky and he gets other people to do his dirty work for him. He always shines. If he needs something done, he sends Hermes, or Apollo, or Athena, or someone else to stir up the trouble and he sits there, bathed in this effulgent glow. He often gets his wife to do it for him. Hera actually gets thrust into the role of "royal shrew," because Zeus, himself, is constantly going out and impregnating all these ladies. It is his function to plant the seed, but he doesn't want to have all these mortal and semi-mortal nymphs and demi-goddesses hanging around saying, "How could you abandon me?" His function is to give birth to the Hero. The woman doesn't count, unfortunately, in this situation. Hera comes along and turns her into a cow, or a swan, or a piece of wood, and Zeus says, "Well I'm sorry—nothing I could do—where's the next lady?"

So Jupiter has the desire to shine in effulgent glory and the shadow side of this Zeus is a kind of tricky manipulator who projects all the shadow and the dark side, and finds people to carry that role for him. Now, it's in the 3rd house, this Jupiter, and 3rd house, of course, has to do with communications, thinking, learning, and ideas. We have Jupiter, which archetypally connects with the 9th house of wisdom, religion, ethics, theory and it's in the sign of Leo.

It's the only Fixed sign, so here we have someone who's kind of royal and we now invoke the archetype of the king. We could have the philosopher-king, the philosopher-entertainer, the philosopher-showman, the one who is a communicating system, but what we know is that Jupiter constellates into something archetypal. Look at you in the audience, all debating who it is now. I knew that wouldn't take long.

Let's move on to the Elements. Grand trine in Fire—Sun, Uranus, Jupiter. What do those three planets all have in common? They are all *Yang*, outgoing, extroverted, fiery, passionate, and although Uranus, itself, is normally connected with Aquarius, it is extremely extroverted in nature. The grand trine is in Fire, so here we have enthusiasm, prana, creativity, vital energy flowing all over the place, but it's a closed system. What we have here is the *eternal optimist*, "Everything is all fine with the world, isn't it a brilliant Candide? [1] It's the best of all possible worlds and aren't we lucky to be part of it? There's great beauty and tranquility and harmony and peace and joy and love and light." Emphasized again because one leg of this is already the Jupiter singleton that has begun to form a complex.

Okay, let's go to Air. Nothing! Now isn't this interesting? What do we get here? Missing function in Air, except the Ascendant is Air, but remember the Ascendant does not make up for the missing function. Now what do we know about missing function in Air? We said if it's compensated for (let's assume compensation, but we don't know), what kind of a person will you get? A great or brilliant communicator on some level and yet something may be missing. Or, the inferior function may come up from underneath and then what happens? Coming up from the communications function, it can be great impulsive creativity or destructiveness. The annihilation, the agoraphobia, the loss of space and boundary and territory can also come up from the Air function. Can it be both simultaneously? It sure can. Can they alternate at different points in the life? Yes indeed. Now the interesting thing about this is that here we have this Gemini on the Ascendant with nothing airy. What does this mean?

1. *Candide;* Voltaire's most famous philosophical tale satirizing the belief in providence and reliance on the optimism that "all is for the best in this best of all possible worlds." Voltaire, *Candide and other Stories* (Oxford: Oxford University Press, 1990), p. 1.

The persona, the mask, the face is of this communicator. Here is a person with brilliant ideas who has it all down, who sees things clearly, who communicates so facilely, who says everything in such a lovely way, but there's nothing on the inside to back it up. What you have going on is an awful lot of other stuff. You have a lot of fire and brimstone, passion, excitement, and optimism, but when you really think about it, are the concepts there? We don't know yet, let's see.

One planet in Water—we have a singleton Pluto. What is this archetypal figure that begins to emerge? It's the Pluto in Cancer in the 2nd house. Okay, let's go with it. We have Hades, we have the tempter, we have Lucifer from the underworld. We have he who comes and rapes us from our innocence, drags us into the unconscious of our own experience, shows us that from true pain comes enlightenment, someone who is erotic, someone who invokes sexual energy, someone who evokes healing, danger, death. But it's in Cancer and that's the only planet in a Water sign. What does that mean? Well, there's something nurturing in a way and it brings in qualities of the family and love and umbilical stuff—breasts flowing with milk, the womb, the net, the family all being held together. "Make a community. Join the family." In the 2nd house that has a lot to do with security, basic ground, things that are valuable, that which we need in order to survive. On a mundane level, it's money, things, and objects, because of course, money is just a materialized object that enables us to buy the things that give us emotional or physical security. So here we have this singleton Pluto. Watch whenever you see a singleton Pluto in the chart that some of this archetypal Luciferian, Plutonian influence is bound to rear its head up into the chart, just as with Jupiter you're going to get the Guru, the teacher, the implanter of the seed. We'll get to the singleton Uranus in a second.

Earth has eight planets, so the dominant function is in Earth. Very clearly we see that. Here is a person who naturally longs for, accepts and absorbs the material world. Things come, money comes, body things are in some way acceptable, physicality is an important thing, money and objects. The real grounded world is the natural element in which this person moves and yet, it's a very Capricornian kind of world that he lives in. Now, what is the difference between the Capricornian aesthetic and the Taurean or the Virgoian? Capricorn says you have to be one way or the other, "It has to be perfect or I'll do without." It's the gourmet. Virgo wants it broken so they can fix it. Virgo wants to improve it, Capricorn says its got to be perfect to start with or don't bother me. Taurus says I don't care, if it feels good do it. If a little food feels good, a little more will do. I don't care what I need, just give me food. It's sensual. If it feels nice and warm in my mouth, I don't care what it is. So here we have either the Capricorn gourmet who wants everything perfect, or the other face of Capricorn. And the other archetype of this figure is the Yogi, the one who is working on the perfection of the physical plane by doing without. Can these figures exist within the same person? You're darned right. Absolutely.

Going on to orientation, the dominant function is Universal. Just look at that for a moment. Here's a person who naturally functions in the world of the collective—that's home base for him. Ideas, theories, the divine, the way we connect with the universe is his home ground. Both the personal and the social are, in a sense, undeveloped because, although there's two in each category, they are both inferior functions which may be overcompensated for. What is he to himself? How does he relate on an interpersonal level with people? Is he carrying this load of universal, collective energy at the expense of his personal and social life? Or is the personal and social realm going to erupt from the unconscious at some point and undermine this collective thing that he has set up for himself?

Finally, Universal signs and Social houses are dominant. Now isn't this interesting? Universal signs and Social houses. To borrow from a theatrical image, I see the astrological chart very much as a kind of drama going on. For our purposes, what if the planets are actors, they're the energy, the signs are the roles that they're playing, the houses are the set or the stage on which they are operating, and the aspects are the dialogue that goes on between them. In this case then, the houses are the setting in which the drama is going to be acted out, but the signs here are the archetypal principle that needs to be evoked. So the energy that needs to be evoked is universal and collective, but where is it going to be acted out? In the interpersonal realm. This is not a person who, on the face of this, will be in an ivory tower. This is a person who is out there in the throng, mixing with the people. Except, the paradox is singleton Uranus sitting up there in Universal houses. Look at that planet, sitting there all alone, and focal point of the T-cross!

So now, let's look at Uranus. What does Uranus evoke? The trickster, the magus, the magician, the genie in the lamp, your Carlos Castaneda's Don Juan, your Prometheus who brings the fire and the enlightenment. Here is the eccentric, the genius, the bohemian, the iconoclast, in the 11th house. As I see it, the 11th house is the area, not of friends, but what I call *joint endeavors*. Here's where people come together in such a way to accomplish something together that cannot be done by one person. So I make a differentiation. For me, the kind of friends that we talk about as "my bosom buddy, my best friend" is the 5th house. These are what we call "friends of the heart." The 11th house is much more abstract. The 11th house says, "Everyone who believes in democracy is my brother." It's a woman saying "Everyone who believes in women's rights is my sister." It's that kind of friend by *brotherhood* and *sisterhood*, rather than the more immediate.

So here is the kind of thing that lends itself to causes. Notice that the Uranus resolves the opposition between the Capricorn and Cancer planets, between the Saturn-Moon-Venus opposition to the Pluto in the 2nd. The Uranus is the arrow in the bow, ready to go. So here we have something very *Yin* and withdrawn. All these kinds of archetypal Yin, feminine, unconscious, dark figures—Saturn-Moon, Saturn-Capricorn, Moon-Capricorn, Venus-Capricorn—and Pluto in Cancer, more of these feminine, underworld, rather dark issues. Then here's this glaring light coming out of this. What more brilliantly, inflammatory thing is this dazzling, laser-like Uranus in this pure flame of Aries coming out? And where does the outlet fall? Into the 5th house. I'll leave that alone for the moment. There's still so much we haven't looked at, but I'd love to explore this Moon-Saturn quality and say that it's the next thing my eye would go to.

We've looked a little at major configurations, there are no stationary planets, I don't see anything at 29 degrees or zero, aspects we've looked at a bit, hemisphere emphasis not first look, stellium we've talked about, unaspected planets, none. So then my eye would go to this Moon-Saturn and my experience of Moon-Saturn is that normally it constellates in an innate feeling of *the deprived child.* There's never enough, I'm not going to get what it is I need and the myth that comes out of that is what I call the myth of the hungry child. No matter what I get it's not going to be enough and if I get it, it might be taken away from me. So how much is enough to make me feel secure? Never enough. It also certainly does things to the anima. The mother now becomes constellated with the parent— the feeling of not enough closeness, or denial from the mother—a longing or hunger for the nurturing milk and love of the mother. Or, the tendency to internalize that and become that myself. Moon-Saturn in Capricorn brings in the idea of the Cronus, of something hardening there and the danger of a hardening. If I cannot get my emotional needs met, as Moon in Earth sign often does, do I sublimate it into things, into objects, into food, into sensuality?

In terms of talking about the Moon, I think that of all the positions most likely to compensate or sublimate, Moon in Capricorn is number one. Why? Because Capricorn is the sign of material perfection and can we achieve material perfection on the emotional relationship level? So very often people with Moon in Capricorn or Moon and Saturn mythologize mother letting them down. There wasn't enough money, she liked little sister better, she didn't feed me, one time I had hurt feelings and she wasn't there for me. There's a danger of Moon-Saturn becoming an injustice-collector. And the myth that is carried into the world is that the world owes me something to make up for what I lost and lacked. The deeper belief than that is I'm not going to get it, and if I get it I'm not going to be able to keep it.

Another thing, look at the close Moon-Uranus square. For me that's the archetype of the classical *fear of abandonment.* Moon-Uranus says, "Something unexpected is going to happen. I'm going to build up my emotional expectations and you're going to pull the rug out from under me and I'll be alone." So often what happens is the person with Moon-Uranus, and here they are square, finds intimacy and personal one-to-one relationships very scary and threatening because the fear is, "You're going to leave me." So how do you deal with it? You leave *them* before they leave you and then, of course, you can project it out in the world and say, "The whole world is made up of instability and impermanence and there's no hope for me anywhere." This is the person who loves to go out and be the awakener. Archetypally his Uranus wishes to awaken the feminine. His own? Other people's? We don't know.

Moon-Pluto. Here is *the devouring mother*, the erotic mother who is giving sexual, erotic, power messages. Here is the mother that in some way is going to annihilate me and strangle me, and yet I am hypnotically and mysteriously attracted to her just as well. So what would I say, looking at this very problematical, difficult Moon? His anima, his internal mother, his nurturing function, his internal child, which I connect with the Moon, is in sore distress. It's going to be a critical issue for him and, as far as I'm concerned, Moon is a planet of fundamental importance. Here it is conjunct Saturn, square Uranus, opposed by Pluto, and yes it's also conjunct Venus, but those are the main dynamics happening to that Moon. I don't like to use the word affliction, but if I did use it, I'd use it here. However, since I don't use it, I won't.

What we've done here is a rough sketch. I've pulled the highlights out of the chart. Obviously it's easy for me because I know who it is and you don't. But you can do this, I guarantee, with any chart. What I suggest you do is copy down all the highlights and then turn the chart face down. Otherwise your eye gets pulled into seeing, "Yes, but on the other hand, there's Mars and the Sun, the Moon and Jupiter, and the ruler of the 5th, and so on." Then the kitten is lost in the ball of yarn, you begin to become an astro-mancer and find anything you want. Extract the information, turn the chart over, write it down and analyze what it is you've got. Is that the final thing? No, it's not the final draft. It's your rough draft and that is the basis of the structure of what we're looking for. I'll take a few more questions before we leave.

Audience: What about Moon trine Neptune?

Richard: I think Moon trine Neptune is not necessarily positive or good. I find the Moon difficult when it is making any aspect to the three outer planets, because we have the most personal with the most transpersonal, and what it gives is the soul hungering to rise to the light.

Here is the person that can never settle down in Eden because the collective and transpersonal is calling him. I would like a show of hands. How many of you in the room have Moon in close aspect to Uranus, Neptune, or Pluto? Look around, almost every hand in the room is up and that puts you on the cutting edge where accepting things as they are is not enough for you. There is no home, is what it's saying, "There's no home for me in this world that I can live in," and it doesn't matter if it's a trine. A trine simply means there's more acceptance. So what it does is, on one level, bring great personal pain, especially early in the life. The earlier in the life it is, the greater the suffering because there's this feeling of the loss of this Eden-like, safe world. It's only later in life that there is an elevation for the person who begins to compensate and work through their projections, maybe having gone through a period of sublimation, and in some way transcends that. Is there always a sense of inner loss? Yes, indeed. Is the wound ever healed? No it isn't. What's the difference? Some learn to live with it and some don't. Some walk around perpetually being "poor, put-upon me and it's up to the world to fix me," and other people walk around and say, "I accept that. This is indeed a fate and my fate calls me up into the transpersonal."

Audience: What is he projecting?

Richard: It's interesting. Here's the Sun in Sagittarius, but what he's projecting out is archetypal father-figure Zeus and Cronos, Guru and teacher, and so on. Here is a double-bind. Here is a person who sets himself up as a Guru and says, "I don't know anything. You're the one who has all the answers."

This is the chart of Rajneesh. [2] Hold on for a moment because the Aha! you just got says, hey, this stuff works! You see for yourself how logically this system proceeds. I won't go back through everything, but you see how all the Rolls Royces, the emphasis on sexuality, free love, and the feeling of homelessness apply. Look where he is now, wandering from place to place where nobody will give him a home. He can't even go back to India because they threw him out of his own home there. He has financial problems. He had 100 Rolls

2. Bhagwan Shree Rajneesh; Hindu guru and author of *Meditation: The Art of Ecstasy* (New York: Harper & Row, 1976). Born December 11, 1931, Kutchwada, India, 2INIS, 77E23. 5:13 P.M. INT. Placidus Houses. Source: Letter from disciple quoting him.

Royces, but he wanted 365, one for each day of the year—the archetypal Jupiter. The Guru figure here in the 3rd house is the divine communicator. Pluto in Cancer in the 2nd is his emphasis on sensuality, sexuality, and money. And Sheila, his assistant who turned on him, look how he found the "wicked mother"—how he constellated the mother who turned on him to devour him. First of all, he created this Sheila, Ananda Sheila is her name, as his Hera, didn't he? He was the Zeus figure, she was the heavy. And I tell you, once you've constellated a Hera, never divorce her because she's got all the goods on you! So she comes back as this Plutonian, devouring figure to dethrone him. There's something extremely archetypal in the Hera and Zeus dance that goes on in that particular constellation.

Audience: Is there a dichotomy between the Cronus, Guru figure, and the Gemini Ascendant?

Richard: Yes, sure. Let there be all love and light is what I'm giving out to the world and the persona Gemini is the *puer* figure. "Hey, I'm just Hermes, I'm a little boy and I'm kind of helpless and I'm not very grounded in the world and I'm just kind of saying these things." When he was interviewed on TV and they called him a Guru, he said, "I'm not a Guru. Some people call me a Guru but they're their own Guru. I tell all my people you are the Guru." Here we go with the projection, here again is the missing function in Air, the magical communicator. Well, obviously a lot more can be said and gotten out of it, but this gives you some sense of how it works.

❦ ❦ ❦

Now we are going to have a look at this other chart (see Chart 3 on page 85), a person who, for the time being, will remain unknown. This is the chart of a man and we're going to take a look at it from the point of view of some of the things we've been talking about so far. We will look at archetypal and mythic themes, things of shadow, unconscious material, compensation matters, and if you want to, we can look at things about dominant and inferior functions, some of the highlights of the chart. I believe this is a good opportunity to start to digest and use some of the material that you've got and see if you can begin to apply it.

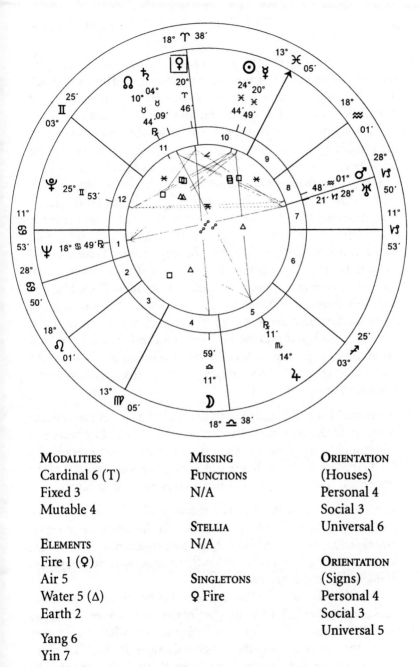

MODALITIES	MISSING	ORIENTATION
Cardinal 6 (T)	FUNCTIONS	(Houses)
Fixed 3	N/A	Personal 4
Mutable 4		Social 3
	STELLIA	Universal 6
ELEMENTS	N/A	
Fire 1 (♀)		ORIENTATION
Air 5	SINGLETONS	(Signs)
Water 5 (Δ)	♀ Fire	Personal 4
Earth 2		Social 3
		Universal 5
Yang 6		
Yin 7		

Chart 3. Example chart.
Birth data cited in footnote 4 on page 97.

We'll start the ball rolling with some dialogue about what are some of the dominant themes we see in the chart. There's so much there that, as you see, it's an extremely interesting chart. Let me just point out a couple of things to you that you might not have seen. There is a grand Water trine between the Sun-Mercury in Pisces in the 10th, Neptune in Cancer in the 1st and Jupiter in Scorpio in the 5th. There's another major configuration, and that's a T-cross in Cardinal signs from Venus in Aries in the 11th, opposition Moon in Libra in the 4th, squaring Neptune in Cancer in the 1st house. So the interesting thing to note is that Neptune is not only part of the grand trine, but it's the focal point of the T-cross, and that should mean things to you now. There is possibly another T-cross here. I put it in because, even though the orbs are wide, there's a potential and, when in doubt, I'd rather include than exclude. There could be a Uranus-Neptune opposition even though the orb is nine degrees. Some of you might use that as an effective orb and others may not, but let's include it just to see what happens, and that makes a focal point out of the Venus in Aries in the 11th house. So those are the major configurations. So what grabs your eye first? What intrigues you about this gentleman?

Audience: My eye is grabbed by the over-abundance of Water in the chart. With the Sun in Water, Ascendant in Water, Midheaven in Water, and Grand Trine in Water, there is water, water everywhere. But that Mars in the 8th house conjunct Uranus on the cusp of the 8th, which is in turn square Saturn, makes me a bit uneasy.

Richard: Yes, it's like there are two characters on the stage—one the lovely, idealistic watery temperament and the other has a rather brutal feeling about it with the Mars-Saturn-Uranus. So we begin to get the feeling of two different kinds of things, two different people living inside of this person.

We talked about not trusting grand trines to be all good because people can hide in them. They're so easy to use and things go so well that the person never really has to deal with other issues. That's the business about the self-containment. It's like, "I am unapproachable within these walls and everything is magnificent." The world of unpleasantness outside cannot encroach here. So you would think then, that on some level, the feelings are highly developed, but what in the world does that mean? Because a person has a grand trine in Water does that make it a sensitive, empathetic, caring person? I think there's a tendency for us to assume that Water, because it's sensitive, implies compassion and empathy at the same time, and that's not necessarily so. I know a lot of extremely selfish and destructive people who are very sensitive, but they're sensitive to *themselves*. They are a contained emotional system within themselves. Everything is observed from the point of view of, "How does it make me feel?"

Another dimension to what I'm saying is that Water is the feeling function and Air is the ethical function, so it's the element of Air which comprises codes of morality, ideology, and ethics. Water is extremely sensitive, but sensitivity without ethics becomes manipulation. Now, that's not to say that all Water people are manipulative, but sometimes if you get a very great weight in Water and the thinking side is not developed, it is not an ethical code by which the person lives. It's a very high subjectivity and often, what's *right* to them is what makes them feel good. I think that Water's sensitivity combined with a basic integrity is truly compassionate, but very often, especially when people have been deeply damaged, they lose that essential morality and Water becomes a con-artist. It can be immensely charming and seductive because it senses what the other person needs and produces it. And isn't it interesting that Air without Water can be cold, but ethical, while Water without Air is sensitive, but can be amoral? So here the Mars in Air is so separate from the Water trine that we wonder what it's going to do, don't we?

In addition to that, you see all that Pisces. Pisces on the Midheaven, Sun-Mercury in Pisces, the grand Water trine, and now we have the focal point of the T-cross at Neptune, which also is a part of that grand trine. So this Neptune stands out very powerfully in the chart—10th house ruler in the 1st. That much Neptune makes me uncomfortable because I always find something extraordinary on the numinous level. Remember we talked about chaos, and Shiva, and images of mermaids and sirens, and a kind of seductiveness in Neptune? I think not everyone has the capacity and the foundations to be able to integrate these highly developed transpersonal images, and the question is, what happens when Neptune is that prominent if there is a failure to integrate on a deep level? Where could that go?

Audience: Isn't it the archetypal messianic force and couldn't the person identify with being God the Redeemer?

Richard: Yes, and this would also make a wonderful actor because of the Neptunian, chameleon-like quality as well. I like the use of the image of the chameleon for Neptune—that multi-level shifting image—this can be anything. And notice it is sitting here so close to the Ascendant, which is already Cancerian. I think of people like Lon Chaney, "The man of a thousand faces," with Pisces rising— the elusiveness of that Neptunian mask to be whatever you need me to be. So there's a very seductive quality in Neptune and that's why I like the image of the siren and the mermaid. If you go back to *The Odyssey*, [3] remember what the sirens sang when they lured the mariners to their death? The song had a special meaning for each person who heard it. They sang of home and wife and mother and country and people who have died because they are away and people who love you and are longing for you to come home. So each particular mariner would hear his own message and throw himself into the sea.

Audience: What about that Pluto in the 12th house? Doesn't it seem rather ominous?

Richard: Yes, since the 12th house is unconscious, the repository of the collective, and not connected to the ego, there are mythic themes that are brewing underneath the surface that threaten to erupt. If a planet in the 12th is well integrated with the rest of the chart, then it can be immensely creative, but this Pluto is in a tight square to the Sun in the 10th house.

I think there are two kinds of people with Sun-Pluto squares. Those who are not afraid of it will express it consciously and be driven to power, while those who are terrified of that side of themselves and can't face it, will project it onto others where they act it out themselves, but are totally unconscious of doing it. However, they have a way of running into their Pluto *outside* as a force of evil, yet it really is inside and I think it takes a lot of courage to face up to and integrate a Sun-Pluto square. Here, with that Grand Trine in

3. *The Odyssey* is an epic poem by Homer, describing the long and perilous journey of the Greek hero Odysseus to Ithaca at the end of the Trojan War.

Water and all that Neptune, he's probably more likely to see himself as a compassionate, kind, and generous person (Sun trine Neptune). And what is interesting about this particular Sun-Pluto is archetypally I think we're dealing with the Sun, the power, going into the underworld. The God of Light, the Hero in a sense, having to deal with the forces of darkness, the part that wants to pull us down into the murky swamp where the Sun is the last planet that would want to go. So possibly here, we have the Hero facing the Dragon and the redemption of the going down into the dark place. But is it owned or is it going to be projected? Is it going to be denied in the 12th house? I'm as uncomfortable about the 12th house as I am with Pluto, because that is an area that becomes less accessible. Not only is it a transpersonal planet, it is in a house connected with the collective, and obviously it's going to affect him in a very personal way through the square to the Sun. How will this be resolved? What will he do with it? And how rough is it to deal with a Sun-Pluto square?

Audience: I would think that Pluto is quite unconscious and would work on the shadow side, but what I wouldn't know from the chart alone, is whether that shadow side would be repressed or acted out.

Richard: So if it were repressed what might happen?

Audience: If it were repressed, then it would get projected and he might be someone who saw evil in the world outside him and perhaps saw himself as one who was destined to cure it or redeem it.

Richard: Yes, I think so, especially with the 10th house Sun, the grand trine in Water and Neptune as the focal point of the T-cross. The T-cross tension is resolved here between that Moon-Venus, two archetypal feminine functions, with that Neptune in the center, which is itself of a feminine nature. So here we have the tension in the T-cross with Neptune carrying it, and I often get the idea of the *misunderstood martyr*. The suppressed Pluto in square to the ego (Sun) may be blocked, but the Sun is trine Neptune, and that's acceptable to the ego. So I accept the part of me that is Neptunian, sensitive, flowing, compassionate, and mystical, and I resist and struggle against the part of me that is Plutonian, the part that is demonic and dark, and wishes to pull down. And maybe the way I resolve all those things is to say, "Well, one may have to cause pain in order to heal."

One of the themes that I see so clearly is the whole idea of pain. Remember we mentioned before about Water having to do with pain? It's the Cancerian pain of the separation of the umbilical cord of the child from the mother, the erotic pain of Scorpio, the pain of compassion in Pisces—a kind of runaway quality of pain. So, on one hand, I get a bit of the savior, "My life is dedicated to saving and relieving the pain," and on the other hand, that Mars-Uranus-Pluto combination can be very ruthless and cruel in its method. Now, how do I resolve the cruelty with the compassionate part? Again, the Neptune is acceptable to the Sun, it flows easily in the trine, and it's so easy to reject the square to the Pluto. I'll tuck it into the 12th house and say, "That's not me, and if it is me, it's only out of necessity. The end justifies the means."

Audience: I'm curious, I have the feeling this man has many sexual problems because of the Venus-Moon and Neptune T-cross being excessively idealized, and some very deep parental problems as well.

Richard: Yes, isn't it interesting that midway between the Moon and Venus is this idealization of the woman? I often find that with Moon-Venus in hard aspect there is a problem dealing with the issue of woman-as-mother and woman-as-lover, and with Neptune there is confusion. So yes, I do smell some Oedipal things potentially. Now, how do I resolve that issue? Remember what we said about the T-cross and what resolves the tension of the opposition? The planet at the focal point, and there again, is that Neptune. Is it by idealizing both? Is it going unconscious? Is it setting oneself up to find an ideal anima figure? I mean what's the condition of his inner woman?

Audience: Wouldn't he both idealize his mother and yet associate her with disappointment and inadequacy?

Richard: I see the issue that often comes up with a Moon-Neptune contact is the merging of the mother and the child and that sense of being "drowned" in mother. There is a boundarylessness that makes it unsafe to separate or leave because mother is both chaos and the all-nurturing, entopic womb—this kind of Universal Sea that I can return to for all safety. And I find a kind of universal problem with Moon-Neptune, especially with men, because I think it makes the anima, the feminine function, difficult to reach. In this case, the paradox is, "If I reach my anima, if I get into my Moon (or my Venus, for that matter), then I'm touching it on my Neptune and to do that is to lose myself, to dissolve in chaos and I'll be destroyed." I think it's interesting about this Venus anyway. The Moon, disposed of by Venus, opposed by Venus, and square Neptune, which itself is disposed of by the Moon. All that lunar, feminine stuff. So, how then can I get in touch with the inner feminine function? Can I integrate that? Is it safe to do that, or will I disappear? Or, maybe I *want* to disappear. And another thing, too—Neptune in the 1st house. Ruler of the 10th in the 1st is that your destiny is to submit to authority, so I must become egoless in the face of authority and flow and do and follow the cause. It's the *true believer*.

Audience: I see some victims here.

Richard: Yes, there's an interesting theme of victimization. Who is the victim? Am I the victim? And what do you do with that victim quality? Notice the outlet of the T-cross, the focal point is Neptune in the 1st house, which would say, "I am the victim." Remember, we said the outlet of the T-cross often falls in the 7th and then who would be the victim? You! The other, the not-self.

Audience: Can you comment about Pisces and what to do with this? Pisces has the reputation of being deeply connected to the group and to the whole of humanity because of all the connections with Christ, the "victimized savior," but when you get this Pluto contact, might the "helpless victim" be projected in a cruel, brutal way?

Richard: Yes, I think there is a Shiva quality in Pisces. It's the undertow, it's the one who rends and tears and destroys. Remember, Pisces is the gateway to chaos. It's dissolution, and there can be a love of dismemberment and dissolution—the "falling-apart-ness"—the ultimate taking apart into its component parts. I think there is a face of Pisces that can be very cruel and it always is startling when you run into it because it's not the usual run of Pisceans, but it can happen when you get a Pisces with heavy Mars-Pluto-Saturn contacts.

I have another anchor to throw out, too. I think that Libra can be an extremely cruel sign. We think of dear, sweet, charming Libra lying on a chaise lounge eating bonbons. And then we wonder about people like Ghengis Khan, Alexander the Great, Napoleon and Hitler with Libra rising. One thing about Libra that impresses me is it's the only inanimate sign. It is neither fish nor fowl nor man nor woman nor child—it's a *thing*. And it's a kind of metallic, measuring thing, weighed and judged in the balance and found wanting. I get some of Athena out of this Libra, Athena herself who can be very cruel to be just. And if it is not fair, if it is not justice, it must be corrected at any cost.

So I think that Libra in a chart like this, especially when you have it connected with something like Neptune and with Venus, its dispositor, in Aries, we get our 300 foot creator of terror and death. When a Libra situation is connected with Neptune, it manages to mesmerize the self and I'm uneasy with it. I don't see a Libra Moon as necessarily "sweetness and light"—I think it can be heartless. The Moon in Libra is the tactful, charming diplomat and wonderful at organizing. If Aries is the ultimate subjectivity, then Libra is the archetype of objectivity with the ability to withdraw in order to be rational, but sometimes one withdraws so much that there's a kind of cold distancing there.

Audience: What about the Moon in the 4th house square Neptune? Is that a charming but weak, dependent, and needy mother?

Richard: The situation is very interesting. The ruler of the 10th in the 1st means that in some way there is an identification with the authority figure, and with Sun in the 10th and Neptune as the dispositor of the Sun, it must be the father. So both father and mother are tied in here because the Moon is in the 4th, archetypally maternal in its nature. So this man with Neptune in the 1st, is like, "It's *me* caught between the tension of my parents." Remember we talked about that bow and arrow? Here the unresolved tension between the parents focalizes out on me because it's *my* 1st house with Neptune there. But, who experiences it? Again, it's opposite to that 7th house where everybody else must somehow bear the burden of this stuff that has been uncompleted.

Audience: Something in this reminds me of Dionysus with the Maenads who went mad and ripped themselves and other creatures to shreds, devouring the pieces.

Richard: There certainly is something of Dionysus in the Neptune and I think this gets us closer to this dangerous part in Pisces and Neptune. That Dionysian desire to not only provoke madness in the Maenads, but to invoke that in others and sit back and watch it. Dionysus is a very cruel god with two totally different faces. On the one hand, he's a redeemer who offers ecstasy and cleansing, but on the other, if he's offended, he's the most vicious god in Greek myth. He's a seducer and he's cruel, like a cat playing with a mouse, and he doesn't just take revenge like Zeus, he torments and won't let go. Dionysus also is in a sense the god in love with death and dismemberment. Remember, Dionysus himself was dismembered, torn to pieces, similar to the Egyptian Osiris who is torn apart as a redeeming. And in that sense, Christ, himself, is a Dionysian figure who suffers and dies on the cross in order to redeem others.

So you get two qualities here. You get the martyr, gentle and compassionate, who loves mankind so much, this god, that he gives his only begotten son, and the Christ, himself, who surrenders and takes on the sins of mankind. But you get the reverse of that when projected outward, "It isn't *me* who needs to be dismembered and suffer, it's *you*, for a very good cause." So the reverse is the Inquisitor who says, "I am burning you at the stake, Jean D'Arc, to release your soul because it's your soul that is the important thing." Or, "This is going to hurt me more than it is going to hurt you," and the trap is *for a good cause.* Especially in Neptune and Pluto, I find people who have as one side of their nature an enormous amount of cruelty. The rapist in Pluto and the Dionysian-Shiva part of Neptune, who often transcends that, you see, but it's for a cause: "You see I am just a servant of the collective and I must do this." The holy warrior, where blood must be shed, but, "I bear no responsibility for it because I am just serving this higher force."

Audience: I look at that Mars-Uranus on the 8th cusp and I imagine he could incite people to revolution. You know, like putting the revolution out and inciting others to act.

Richard: Yes, I think so and just looking again at the Mars-Pluto quincunx, I am not easy with it myself and neither is Mars, but Pluto rather likes it. Mars is the dunce, this clunking, overweight boxer that is hardfisted and never can clobber-plan for a moment, but in the hands of conniving, manipulating Pluto can become quite vile. And I often find that Pluto has a tendency to suppress the overt expression of the vileness and undermine it. If you can imagine Hades erupting from the underneath and instead of grabbing Core, he grabs Aries and takes him down to the underworld, does something to him and then returns him up above and says, "Go to it, boy!"

Audience: There are very feminine dimensions in the chart that begin to look beautiful and then they line up with so many connections to the Ascendant. Especially since we have Mars conjunct Uranus, isn't he going to want to just be that and perhaps be gay?

Richard: I don't know. I don't think so. I don't think sexual preference has anything to do specifically with masculinity or femininity. It may be one of his options, but I don't think that the chart is going to say it will be. He has to do something about his "split," but whether that is particularly the way it's going to express, we don't know. It's a way to go, but one of many.

Audience: I would suspect that alcohol or drugs could be a big problem, or one way that he would try to split. And I would also think that maybe his father was an alcoholic because of that Sun in Pisces squaring the Neptune on the Ascendant.

Richard: Thank you, I think so and that is something that had slipped my mind. That is the Dionysian part that in the beginning seems so seductive and elevating and uplifting and then once it has you in it's clutches, begins to tear you apart. I'm thinking of drugs and alcohol and Neptune and the seductiveness of it. "It will be a most wonderful world and I'll float in this world of dreams, but I can stop at any time—I know my limits." So there's the Dionysian quality. Dionysus himself loves the drug legends, the psychedelic experience. "Lose yourself, abandon ego, flow, let go." But then what happens is, how do you find your way out of it? Again the Shiva part comes in, the submerged part of the personality comes up under the influence of the drug.

Audience: He might be an addictive personality, yet that grand trine of Jupiter trine Sun and Jupiter trine Neptune makes me wonder if something protects him, and I have the feeling that somehow he lands on his feet.

Richard: I think that Jupiter trine Sun is a nice way to protect the ego. It says, "I'm fine, I am an expansive, noble person and I come from only the best intentions." There's no resistance there at all.

Audience: He would be a skillful liar.

Richard: Yes. The greatest liar is one who has convinced himself first and, because of the *cause*, the revolution, the ideal (Mars-Uranus in Aquarius, and Mars square Saturn in the 11th), any kind of cruelty could become acceptable.

Audience: Shouldn't we bring in the issue of the home life here?

Richard: Yes, we have the extension of the mother and the family to the Homeland, the Motherland, the Fatherland and becoming the cause. So whatever must be done in terms of protecting and nurturing this homeland is perfectly acceptable and therefore resolves the square to the Pluto through the trine to the Neptune. It's to be cruel in order to protect the Homeland, the Motherland, the Fatherland or the Country. You can get the same thing when you think of the church as Mother-Church, for example, and with the Inquisitor. Above all things the Church must survive and individuals do not count—"I must be cruel in order to be kind."

Audience: With the Saturn square to the cause of Mars in Aquarius, will the cruelty be projected out to the Saturn?

Richard: Yes, probably the Saturn will become the scapegoat. Who is it out there that he is going to go for? What is the image, what does Saturn in Taurus look like?

Audience: Miserly, tight, conservative, earthy, rich, materialistic, hard working, physical, sensual.

Richard: Saturn is Cronos, the devourer, and what is he devouring? Things, objects, the land, food, money, pleasures, security.

Notice the Earth function is the inferior function and will be projected, so now let's extend this and look back again at the Saturn square Mars and Uranus and what does it mean? Instead of simply saying it's "bad"—two malefics in bad aspect to each other—what does it *really* mean? What's going on? What constellates around this "scapegoat" with that Mars? In this context at least, how is it working? One of the things Saturn tends to do is to suffocate Mars, so Saturn pushes the Mars away. What happens is, it *suppresses*, and there's a deep fury that often goes on with a Saturn-Mars, especially in an Air-Earth combination. There's no Fire or Water there to let it loose with passion, so there's a very constipated kind of thing. Another thing I find with the Saturn-Mars is, if you combine their elements, fire and lead, what do you get? You get steel. There's a steely, tough, hard quality that happens. There's an indomitability, "I am going to survive at all costs and no matter what happens I will make it through." Tough as nails. This is the person who comes marching down off the mountain in the face of a blizzard after everyone else has died. And when asked, "Why did you survive?" the person replies, "Because I wouldn't give in." But it's a paradoxical aspect because it's also impotent at the same time. With Saturn (where we feel inferior), in Taurus, he may believe himself to be ugly, and with the square from Mars, project it out. So the love of beauty and form and a kind of divine essence that is found throughout the chart must be had at any cost and he feels a repulsion and disgust for anyone ugly, so the physically inferior must be destroyed.

Note that Jupiter trine the Ascendant and the Midheaven indicates a rather charming person. You can get away with murder with Jupiter conjunctions or trines to the Midheaven or Ascendant. Zeus, himself, with all his multitude of cruelties, never seems to have to bear the brunt of being the "bad guy"—he got Hera to do that all the time. The thing I'm interested in here is the problem both around the sexuality and the anger with the Mars, as we were talking about before. I see that Mars is not only conjunct Uranus, but quincunx Pluto and square Saturn. So hard aspects to these planets, that of their own nature are difficult, combine with Mars which is so primitive in its nature that it adapts in a very difficult way to transpersonal energy. I think one of the paths of least resistance for it is the libido, and another is in terms of anger, so my guess is that Mars tangled up with Saturn and Uranus and Pluto could very well indicate a person whose anger devolves into outrage. "I'm not angry for myself. It isn't me, it's these other people out here (Saturn in Taurus in the 11th) that make me angry and my anger is a justifiable cause."

Well, I think it's time you need to know who it is. This is the infamous Dr. Josef Mengele, [4] and now no one will ever believe in Grand Trines again! Does anyone know what he looked like? As I recall he was a rather sour, sad appearing person with dark, intense eyes, a mustache, and he had a deformity. It was either a club foot or a hunch in the back, or something, I don't remember which.

Audience: Is this inevitable?

Richard: That's an interesting question. Does a chart show fate? Does a chart show destiny? If someone brings in the chart of a baby Josef Mengele, what do you say? Is that a "given" in the chart? Well, there are some sides of this that will have to be worked out. He has a great split in his chart that would be there from the start, but the way in which he deals with it you couldn't say. Would he be the same man if he were born into a different collective? Much of what he became has a lot to do with what was going on around him, and you can't separate strongly outer-planet-people from the time in which they live.

I think this chart shows us some of the things I was talking about before. What makes up a person's personal myth? What goes into his or her basic ground? How do you interact with the archetype from the collective—not only the collective that is limitless in time and place, but the collective of your time? What have you done with the myth and the social expectations of your time and the family mythology? How would you live in some way with your inferior functions? What work have you done? That's the thing that is the difference, and out of that comes the personal myth. I think another thing, too, that a person so strongly connected with the transpersonal planets is somehow used by the collective or the universe for its own ends, and it's hard to see those ends immediately. Those ends may be very painful both personally and collectively, it's something fated. However, *how* the fate will manifest is not something I think you can see within the chart. Probably the most you could see is that this man has an enormous split, and he is the sort

4. Josef Mengele was the notorious Nazi who was chief medical officer at Auschwitz concentration camp and called "the angel of death." Born March 16, 1911, Gunzburg, Germany, 10E16, 48N27, 11:45 A.M. CET. Placidus houses. Source: birth certificate according to Edwin Steinbrecher.

of person who would not deal with his split in a very honest way, so he would have very deep problems.

Imagine him living his entire life after the Second World War—eluding, running away, being deceitful, changing his face, having plastic surgery (there's that Neptune on the Ascendant), changing his name, disappearing and being found. Disappearing again, homeless, cut off from his country, cut off from his family, knowing he was hunted and living in a life style he never had to do before. But he had a grand trine and the fact that he got away links the grand trine with the T-cross, and nobody knows if he's alive or dead. It's believed that he recently died, but was this really him or wasn't it? Is he somewhere or isn't he? Did they get him or didn't they, or has he triumphed finally, and is he off living somewhere in a mansion enjoying himself? We're never quite sure.

Audience: It's fascinating that with his Saturn in Taurus square Mars in Aquarius he wanted to create a physically beautiful master race and Hitler also had a Mars-Saturn square—Mars in Taurus and Saturn in Leo.

Richard: Yes, of course, a lot of Mengele's so-called scientific research was to create the beautiful master race and he experimented with horrific things like, "How can I make a brown-eyed child a blue-eyed child because blue eyes are so much more beautiful." But the ability to do this, to split into this incredible cruelty in the pursuit of beauty, was all for the "greater cause."

Audience: It seems like his Mars got exploited by his idealistic urges and impulses to mutilate, cut, and sever in order to achieve this ideal goal of transforming this physical ugliness into something he thought was so beautiful.

Richard: Yes. And here's how Dionysus would rationalize it, "I rend and tear in the service of beauty and the destiny of my Fatherland, but I, myself, am a lover of beauty and harmony and I would never hurt a flea."

I thought this would be a fascinating chart to have a look at, but I think a point needs to be made here. We've focused in on a lot of the dark, and a lot of shadow stuff has come up here in this discussion. First of all, I think it's very important, *do not personalize what we have said.* Like, "Oh my God, I have Pluto in the 12th; I have a grand trine in Water; I have Neptune on the Ascendant; I have Mars square Saturn; I'm going to start chopping little children into pieces!" I think there is a tendency in astrology to do that. We all seem to bring it back to our chart and say, "Oh, horror, horror, what have I got here? What have I done?" Remember what we've said before, that the whole is greater than the sum of any of its parts. We have all reacted differently to the collective, the social and family myths, and we're living out all of our things quite differently. Everything has different sides to it. There are various archetypal themes at work in this chart, some of which indicate great gifts and others indicating destructive impulses, and they're not the marks of a war criminal, they're the marks of most people.

For example, take the chart of somebody like Abraham Lincoln. You see a lot of potential cruelty within the chart, "I have to be cruel in order to be kind. I have to see the country split apart, brother making war against brother," which obviously tormented the man terribly. But some kind of cruelty had to be inflicted in order to heal, and I'm sure in this man's rationale, he felt exactly the same way. There are certain epochs in history which draw these things out of people, and when the collective is in the grip of something, then individuals get sucked into it. H. G. Wells, in his *Outline of History*,[5] said an interesting thing. He said civilization is relatively new, but the veneer is very thin. He said, it doesn't take much for an entire race or nation to regress and when you regress, beneath all the powder and lace, comes the snarling, red-eyed, fang-dripping neanderthal waiting to come out. I think we have to understand that as a potential, and if we do not accept that, it's at our own peril because it can happen here, too. That's why I say that on a personal and on a collective level, powerlessness corrupts and absolute powerlessness corrupts absolutely. And if a people remains powerless, eventually that shadow gets constellated into leaders who will take that Pluto and Neptune and run with it. That's when the abyss opens up.

5. H. G. Wells, *Outline of History* (New York: Somerset Publishing, 1920).

CHAPTER FOUR

SHADOW ISSUES

D id you get any sleep last night? Maybe Josef Mengele was not a good chart to choose the night of the Full Moon. Anyway, before we get started on shadow issues, a couple of questions have come up and I'd like to take a few minutes to try and deal with them.

The first question is orbs of aspects. I use ample orbs. I err always on the side of generosity with orbs, and the reason for that is, as a born-again astrologer, I'm not particularly interested in prediction, and I'm not interested in events and timing events. If you are a predictive, event-oriented astrologer, then you need extremely tight orbs because what you do is based upon being right and timing events accurately. But I no longer feel the necessity for being right, thank God. What I'm concerned with is the human potential and process, development and growth, and because of that, I tend to say that if it's possible that there might be an orb, I'd rather include it. Now, later on, as I get to know the chart better and the person better, I might say, "Well, I don't know, maybe this is not working." But my choice is to err on the side of generosity in all orbs.

Now, naturally, you're going to ask me what orbs I use, so I would have to say roughly, I use 10° to 11° for a conjunction or opposition, and it doesn't matter between what planets, even the outer planets; squares and trines, roughly 9°; sextiles, 7° maybe;

quincunxes, 6° and I consider them a very major, very important, critical aspect. I do use semi-squares and sesqui-quadrates and I use small orbs for them, about 2°. I tend to find that the more confident we feel about an aspect, the larger orb we give it. When we feel we can interpret it, we want to find more of them. If I see an aspect that is *forming*, or wanting to turn itself into a major configuration, I help it because I think there is something that attracts the planet into these group dynamics that we call major configurations or complexes. So I'll extend one leg of a grand cross for instance, and sometimes if it's in opposition, 12° or 12½° . So it's an area in which I am not dogmatic and, hopefully, that's the development we all go through. Early on in our study of astrology we tend to be extremely dogmatic—"This house system is the *only* house system"—and how many angels can dance on the head of a pin? I think your relative values begin to switch, and as we get older in astrology, we become as we do as people—more tolerant. Okay, any other questions?

Audience: Does any given degree have special meaning?

Richard: I think the 29th degree on the Ascendant or Midheaven is important. We are, after all, talking about masks—interpersonal and collective masks. A little later on I'm going to focus more on the Ascendant and masks because I feel that they are critically important. So yes, I think there is something in a 29th degree on the Ascendant-Descendant axis or on the Midheaven-IC axis. What that says to me is that, perhaps, there is something unstable in the setting in which this occurs. We've talked about the 29th degree as a shaky degree that is in some way unstable and at the borderline of transformation. At the one extreme motile,[1] frangible,[2] labile[3] (lovely words I like), and on the other hand, there's something tentative, something is about to happen, to switch. I especially find it of concern with the Ascendant, since the mask is such an important thing. When it's on the Midheaven and 4th house axis I sometimes begin to cast this into the parental and home environment.

---

1. Motile: having the power of or demonstrating motion. In psychology: one in whose mind motor images are especially distinct.
2. Frangible: easily broken; brittle; fragile.
3. Labile: Liable to lapse or change; unstable.

That leads me to another issue. Some astrologers feel that the 10th house is more the mother, the 4th house more the father and I tend to reverse the two. I don't think it matters much, because it is the tendency of things to become their opposites, and opposites in astrology always are complements; they complete each other. Nevertheless to be more specific, what I would say is that on one level, the houses are settings. They are settings in which things happen, stages on which dramas occur. So the 4th house-10th house axis entirely, I would say, is the home environment and the home drama—the place where these things are acted out.

I see the 4th house as the inheritance from the family, the family collective. I actually see the 4th house as having to do with the source of family myths and taboos, and how we deal with them. The 8th house, the same for social myths and taboos, and the 12th for the universal collective. Now, I know other people see that in different ways, but to me Cancer is the last of the Personal signs, Scorpio the last of the Social signs, and Pisces the last of the Universal, Collective, Transpersonal signs. It makes sense to me. I think that we might say the 4th house is the setting in which we have experienced the family as nurturing, as nest-making, as providing emotional safety, and that can be either parent. In most societies, and in ours, normally we project that role upon mother, but it isn't always the case. The same thing with the 10th house as the parent, not so much in their nurturing role, but in their protective, structuring role. The disciplinarian, the authority-ness, takes on the Saturnian quality of the 10th. In our society, and in most societies at least nominally, that role tends to be given to the father, but not necessarily so. I think this gets around the issue of is the 10th the father and the 4th the mother? I don't think a house is a *person*, just like the 7th house is not your husband or your wife. The 7th house is the area of not-self, that which I wish to complete myself through, and it very often comes out to be exactly the kind of person you end up marrying. So the human being that we project into the house is not a direct consequence of the house, but is *a direct consequence of our projections.*

Now, in terms of one's subjective mythologizing about mother, I would go to the Moon. Who is mother to me, not who is mother to her, but the subjective mother whom I have created alive inside of me. Obviously, mother is a subjective thing. All you have to do is look at the Moons of your siblings. Sister Sue has Moon in Sagittarius conjunct Jupiter and brother Mike has Moon in Pisces opposed Neptune square Pluto conjunct Saturn. You get together and compare notes and you think you're talking about the same person, but you're not. So the Moon embodies the subjective mythos you have created about mother. From that, an extension to nurturing figures and finally to the internalized mother that you've prepared out of all that material to live inside of you. Now, Saturn as a parental significator is again a projection of the quality of parenting that gives us protection, authority, structure, and limits us. So a lot of raising the child is embodied in the Moon-Saturn complementation. The child must be loved, protected, nurtured, given to, loved in non-judgmental ways, given freely to on an emotional level. That is the area in which we do not need to *earn* love. It's given to us simply because we *are*. But polarized against that is, "Yes, but you must come along with this. You must grow. You must separate and break the umbilical cord." The whole Moon-Saturn axis is critically important in describing this function of parenting and nurturing, of limiting and indulging, of binding and freeing, of enveloping and autonomy. So, going back to the 4th and the 10th houses, we might say that the 4th is where we're coming *from* and the 10th is where we're going *to*. We start as child, an egg within the family nest, and eventually we move out from that, out into the world where we ourselves now are nest builders. So we take on, we internalize, the qualities of both nurturing and parenting, if you see the difference in what I mean.

I do think the Sun is a significator of father; it is a primary planet of *Yang*. We have polarized so clearly in our society between that which is Lunar and that which is Solar, and I think that the Sun is, in a sense, the ideal mythologized father just like the Moon is the mythologized mother. Saturn is the parent as an authority figure, but Sun is the father as the creative, inspiring force. This is the father as the ideal, the father who has said, "I have created you in my own image and I am well pleased" (or not, as the case may be). Here is the urge to reproduce as a desire to replicate oneself. So I think there are father qualities in the Sun and father qualities in Saturn, because nominally in our society, it is the father who is supposed to be the authority and disciplinarian. It doesn't always work that way.

I think what appears to be going on on the surface is not what is happening in actuality. The father is nominally the authority figure because that's the hidden contract between father and mother, but mother really does it. Mother very often does it by saying, "Wait till your father gets home," and very often there is jockeying in particular families for who gets to be the good guy.

It's clear, for instance, if you've read Patty Davis' book (the Reagan's daughter), that as far as I'm concerned, Ron and Nancy have a classic Zeus and Hera marriage. Zeus is the one who always gets to look good. He smiles and beams and winks and nods, and he's kind, optimistic, and occasionally he throws a thunderbolt when he gets mad, but then everybody says, "Oh boy, he really is a strong daddy after all." He never does anything devious, he never does anything bad, he has no dark side at all, Hera is called in to do all that nastiness for him. Hera has to carry the weight of all that. So Patty Davis describes in her book about how you could always get around Dad because Dad was easygoing and kind, or he'd say, "Ask your mother," and mother was the one who put her foot down. This is often a problem that I call the classical Zeus and Hera marriage, and you often end up with a very embittered wife. She feels, in a way, that this is part of her bargain. Usually the Hera kind of wife is attracted to a powerful man, then proceeds to psychically carry out his garbage and resents it. It's interesting how you find this a lot among political wives. Note the depression and alcoholism and breast cancer and things that have been endemic among the wives, such as Betty Ford, Happy Rockefeller, and Pat Nixon. It isn't easy. Okay, I'll leave that alone for awhile. You'll see it will come alive when we talk more about it later on.

Now, with regard to the Nodes, I don't know what in the world they mean, to be perfectly frank. Since I correlate all planetary energies with psychological archetypes, I find it difficult to give psychological meaning to the Nodes because they're not planetary places, they're imaginary places in space. I think there is probably something on a metaphysical level, a metaphysical meaning in regard to them. Certainly the signs that they run across, the sign polarities and the houses that they fall in, certainly indicate an area of polarity and of life tension that must in some way be worked through. It's as if the life constantly returns you to this axis to work something out. I don't do aspects to them from the other planets, yet I know other astrologers do.

Audience: The signs my Moon, Saturn, and Sun are in do not seem to describe my parents, my relationship with them, or the dynamics of my early life.

Richard: Check the aspects out. It isn't just the Moon in the sign and in the house, the aspects are so critically important. I think it's much more important to see that the Moon is square Pluto than that the Moon is in Pisces. Aspects are far more obviously dynamic than disposition. Moon in Pisces says simply Moon is connected with Neptune through disposition and that is an important relationship, but I think the aspectual relationship is much more obvious, so go back to check that out and see if that doesn't work.

I want to talk about *shadow* and I'm looking to see if somebody is here who particularly needed to hear this. The reason I say that is there was someone last night who was very upset by our discussion of Dr. Josef Mengele. I've found over and over again that people get into issues and they say things like, "But doesn't that have a positive side?" Or, "Why do you deal with such negative people, why couldn't you find a nice person to do their chart?" Then the next step is often the internalization and they say things like, "I have Pluto in the 12th and I don't think I do anything like that," but not everybody is that overt. I see you looking at your charts out of the corner of your eye when we're having these discussions and when we say things about the dark, evil side of Pisces and the hard, cold side of Libra, it's like the lights start going out in different places around the room. It's an interesting phenomena to watch. I see it happening and I care about it, but I'm not quite sure what there is to do about it except to bring it up and sort it through. I want to get into it a little bit now because we're talking about shadow issues.

A famous poet-philosopher said, "Nothing that is human is foreign to me." There is the tendency of things to become their opposites, and on some level we're afraid of that. We live in a dualistic, linear, rational, monotheistic world in which good and bad are so split down the middle that we have lost the circularity and have become linear along the line. So, it is in our mother's milk and in the blood of our culture that things are this way or that way. They are either works of the Deity or the works of Satan and there's nothing in between.

I was in Texas recently and went to one of those big revival meetings and the preacher said, "Forty percent of the American public now consider themselves born-again evangelicals." Four out of ten, forty percent. And this preacher was commenting on why he thought this was true and he said, "People in this country are tired of these grays, they want to go back to simple black and white," and I think he puts his finger right on it. Because gray is a combination of black *and* white and in our linear, Cartesian, rational, dualistic society we can't make a place for either and or. We don't live well with paradox. We don't understand the Eastern way of looking at something and saying, "It is this and it's opposite at the same time, and that's both okay and not." We say, "There they are, being inscrutable again." So we get trapped in this duality.

I remember the first astrology books said, "If Pisces is evolved, then you have the mystical, spiritual, loving, poetic, self-sacrificing person who is just at the right hand of God. On the other hand, the unevolved Pisces can be drug-addicted, nymphomaniacal, manipulative, sneaky, slippery, slimy." Well, nobody wants to be that, so what happens is we choose up sides and hope to go with the side that we like better, the one that is more approved within the mythology of our culture and our society. We shove all the dark side into the closet and throw it down to the underworld where it festers, and this is the material out of which shadow is made. So to the extent that we are not conscious, to the extent that we have not experienced our own dark shadow underworld material—experienced and learned to live with it—it is terrifying when it comes up. It's terrifying because we say, "I don't know what this is in me!" And that's why I say, if you are studying the art of the human condition, which is astrology, get into psychotherapy. That is the clearest, fastest, cleanest way to get in touch with your own shadow material. Otherwise, you're going to terrorize yourself every time you look at your chart and I know people who are forever doing that, "Oh my God, that Saturn; Oh, that Pluto; Oh, that transit; Oh, here it is coming out of the 12th house, it's going to cross my Ascendant and what's going to happen?" People absolutely terrifying themselves all the time. Well why? It's "things that go bump in the night" if the dark underworld is not explored. Remember back when you were a child in bed and something went "clunk" in the closet? So the idea is to light the lamp, like Psyche did with Eros, to light the lamp and see what that thing is in the dark. And one of the best ways to do that, though not the only way certainly, is through an experience of psychotherapy.

Now another danger comes among people who are attracted to metaphysics, like we as astrologers are. That is the danger of surrounding ourselves by "white light" and transcending the whole business: "This has nothing to do with me. I am an evolved being myself, I don't know about all of you." There is nothing of the dark, and you hear this all the time. What I say is that between Libra and Sagittarius comes Scorpio and you can't get there from here. It's like the revival song, "Too high, can't get over it; too low, can't get under it; too wide, can't go around it; you gotta go in by the door," and inside the door lives the dragon. People would like to transcend it, but you can't get around it.

I got into a bit of a disagreement one time with Dane Rudhyar, with whom it is not easy to disagree, as you may imagine, when he came to one of my lectures. Actually I was quite a new astrologer and when I saw the "gray eminence" come into the back of the room and sit down, I immediately went into catatonia. The jaw tightened up and I said to myself, "Oh God, the archetypal wise old man has just walked into the room." He sat there, listening intensely, and afterward he came up to me and said, "This is all very interesting, but I do not like all this emphasis on the psychology and problems and phobias and complexes. It is so negative. I think one should transcend ego." And I said, "But how can you transcend who you are until you *know* who you are?" And he said, "I did." So, end of subject. Well, maybe that's true and there is that school in astrology. It's not to say there is not a spiritual part of us, an urge toward lifting, toward rising, toward transcending, toward growing. But to paraphrase Scott Peck [4] in his wonderful book *The Road Less Traveled* (which I hope all of you will read because it's a true gift), we can't sacrifice something we don't already have, and we cannot give up something that is not ours to give. So, you cannot give up your

4. M. Scott Peck, *The Road Less Traveled* (New York: Simon & Schuster, 1988).

dark, evil, corrupted, jealous, passionate, manipulative side until you *own* that side in order to give it up. And that's the danger of shadow. That's the trap in shadow. We say, "Get thee behind me, Satan," but that's the last place you want him! Get him out in front where you can look at him.

Audience: When you have a chart like Josef Mengeles and you do not know who this person was, whether he had been in therapy, for instance, and where he was in his evolving, you can't determine what side of Pisces he was manifesting.

Richard: Exactly. Nevertheless, when we're talking about shadow, there is no way to look at the chart of whoever that person was without knowing he or she would have had that kind of shadow. Now would he or she necessarily have had to act out the shadow in that way? The answer is no.

So, when you take the pieces out of that chart and try to extrapolate those pieces into your own chart, you say, "My God, that can't be right. I do not behave in that way." But, what has happened is the door to where shadow lives has blown open a little bit and you don't like the smell of it because sulphur comes out of the door. It's sulphur and brimstone that comes out, it's the hot breath of the dragon, and we slam the door shut very tight. That's why we have these psychological defense mechanisms like projection, denial, repression, going unconscious, and addictions to keep us from looking at all that kind of stuff. I think of my favorite philosopher, Pogo,[5] who says, "We have met the enemy and he is us."

As an actor, I'll tell a more personal story about some shadow stuff. Actors have to face their shadows all the time, and I think if you have trouble getting into shadow, go into the theater. Take some acting classes. Do some improvisation. Get involved in your local community theater because, by golly, unless you want to play "Rebecca of Sunnybrook Farm" all the time, you had better get into some of your shadow. Otherwise, you don't get to play anybody interesting. So, as an actor, like all young actors, we tend to think of ourselves as good, nice, kind, charming, wonderful people. Every-

5. Newspaper comic strip titled *Pogo.*

thing Leo and Libra, nothing Scorpio and Capricorn or Pisces, nothing negative, nothing dark. So, when I was a young actor, I couldn't get angry. I could *act* angry, but I couldn't *be* angry. My first acting teacher was a wonderfully wise woman and she said, "You're *acting* angry—*be* angry." We were working on a scene together, the scene between the mother and the son, a very angry, violent scene, in Ibsen's *Ghosts*. The mother married a man who was a syphilitic and the son, Oswald, inherits the syphilis. He is going mad and has finally come to understand and know that he has inherited this degenerative disease, and he confronts his mother with this rage. We were working on the scene and nothing was happening. She said, "Get mad at me!" and I said, "I can't get mad at you, I like you." She said, "It isn't me, it's the mother. Now get mad at me." "I can't do it," and she said, "You're acting mad, now be mad." "But I like you, I'm afraid of hurting you," I said. "You won't hurt me, get mad." I couldn't do it and finally she said, "My darling boy, you know I care about you and you know I want the best for you and to be the best actor you can possibly be, don't you?" And I said, "Yeah, I think so." "Do you trust me?" she asked and I replied, "Yes, I do." She said "Okay," and WHACK! she slapped me hard on the face. I recoiled in shock and WHACK! one more time. And before I could recover from the shock she commanded, "Do the part!" I did the part, and at that moment the ego and the shadow connected. Do you see what I'm saying? It was okay for me to be mad because I had the channel of the role to do it in, and I never had trouble getting mad again. I had made a breakthrough.

I'll tell you another story that happened later because this doesn't happen all at once. It isn't just that you open the door, suddenly fall through and there you are in bliss—it's a lifetime process. The shadow world is like Dante's *Inferno*, Dante's underworld, there is circle after circle. It is a perpetual process of inward turning and downward spinning down to the heart. It is Ariadne's *Magic Thread* that we follow down to the heart of the labyrinth where dwells who, by the way? the Minotaur, the monster that must be faced. That's the whole purpose in going there in the first place, isn't it?

These things come in levels, and another thing that happened a little later in New York, where I was acting, was that I met this wonderful black man. He was a Jamaican director and he wanted to go

off to Jamaica to do an all-black *Othello*. He thought it was an interesting idea and in this case, only Iago was going to be white. He
himself was playing Othello, so he was casting the people to play
other parts. My agent, who sent me up for everything, sent me up
for the part of Iago. I was about 25 and I would never have thought
of myself for that kind of part, but you go for everything. I ended
up getting it and I couldn't believe it, because Iago is probably the
most evil character that Shakespeare ever created. He is bloody, he
betrays his best friend, he causes murder, he kills his own wife, and
he is a smiling, conniving liar. At the end they ask him why he has
done all of these things and he says, "I will remain silent. I won't
even tell you why. But I did it and I'm glad!" Not even repentance.
There were hundreds of guys reading for the part, all these dark,
swarthy types, and I thought, no way in the world will I get this, I'll
probably end up carrying a sword. But the director gave me the
part and finally I confronted him and said, "I'm scared to death I
can't play this part. Why did you cast me in this part?" He said, "I'll
tell you why, man, because you got a devil in you." Well, I went
around in shock for two weeks saying, "What does he see in me that
I don't see in myself?" And up until that time I had been in terror,
running to every acting teacher I knew crying, "Help me, help me,
help me find my way through this part!" My best friend and great
acting teacher in New York, Ruta Hagen, said to me, "Well, what I
suggest you do is climb into the shit and wallow in it. Get down
inside there and see where that person is." And boy, I tell you, I went
into instant psychotherapy with myself to get it and all that stuff
came out in rehearsal. I can't describe what happened to me, the
doors that opened and the depths that I had to get into! But out of
that (and I'll leave it up for grabs whether I did or didn't do a good
job), I got into my Pluto.

So my first teacher, by helping me with the part in *Ghosts*, led
me to my Mars, which is a shadow figure, and then this wonderful
man led me to my Pluto. Not only did I get into Iago, I loved it! I
loved it! I lied and cheated and betrayed with a sweetly smiling face.
I didn't have to do the Commedia Dell'Arte⁶ version of Iago where

6. Translated "professional comedy," the name given to traveling companies of actors that emerged in Italy in the mid-16th century and played in European theaters
and marketplaces. Unlike staid literary comedy, it was unique in its improvisa-
tional style, lively wit, obscene action, and overall vitality.

he's always walking around in a black cape and lurking. I played what is called a "good, honest Iago"—corrupt to the soul! So after that, part of my Pluto no longer frightened me, just like having released the anger in the *Ghosts* play, some part of my Mars didn't frighten me. But does that mean I solved *all* my Mars and Pluto problems? No. Because the dragon, the shadow, has many faces. However, having triumphed once, you can do it again. So, that's what shadow is all about. Theater was a vehicle for me and I've spent many years in psychotherapy. I go back, on and off, all the time because life for me is a psychotherapy.

Audience: Do you think psychodrama is a good way to do this?

Richard: Psychodrama is a wonderful way and there are many ways to go about doing this. I can only speak from my own experience that psychotherapy of certain kinds, depth psychology and drama, have been the things that have helped to release, but something else might be the path for you.

Audience: Can we return for just a moment to Mengele's chart? I couldn't see in the chart that Mengele had an ego, and you made an important comment just now that the ego and the shadow connected, and you could get angry because they came together. But in some charts you see there is not much ego, that's when one of the outer planets, particularly Neptune or Pluto, is right on the Ascendant, and the ego has a hard time and can hardly exist. Therefore, without ego where is the shadow? The whole chart is a shadow because there is no identity to confront.

Richard: Let me comment on that in this way. Yes, there are some charts that show more apparent difficulty than others. For instance, charts that have few aspects to the Sun, or an unaspected Sun, show indications perhaps, of difficulty in getting to the ego. Charts where the Sun doesn't make many aspects to other planets may show more difficulty, but it also may show more of an inner awareness to get there.

One of the most enlightened human beings I know is a woman with a totally unaspected Sun in Scorpio in the 12th house and it's been a battle for her; it's been a struggle. Other people I see with Sun aspected to every other planet in the chart and who have not even begun to take step two. Why? Because they don't feel the need for it. So, yes, every chart shows its own potential difficulties and traps and problems, but there is no way of looking at a chart and knowing what someone is going to do with it. I don't believe in a "difficult" or "easy" chart. What appears to be good—a chart full of trines—is not necessarily so good because trines don't push toward evolution. Okay, then do you say that a chart full of squares is good? Not necessarily. If what we're looking for is "good" or "bad" charts, where do we draw the line there? There is no good or bad, there is only one perfect chart for you, and that's yours. You can't go back and exchange it for another one, it is yours and what you have to do is accept the shadow quality inherent in every potential.

Do we all have a Josef Mengele living inside of us? You betcha! And if you can't acknowledge that, you're in trouble. You have an Iago and a Lady Macbeth—these are all archetypes and they are you. There is Hecate, there is Hades and Pluto and manipulative Zeus and bitchy Hera and tricky Hermes. These are archetypes, and this is what it's all about. Don't just leave them up there and say, "Oh, aren't they lovely archetypes and they have nothing to do with me. I'm all of these, but only in their positive sense." Own them. They have to become part of you and if they don't, then when they erupt they take you over. This is exactly what I'm talking about when I refer to the inferior function. There is nothing wrong with the inferior function, except that because it's frightening, we turn it into shadow—we lock it up. It's a thing we haven't experienced, so naturally we're frightened of it. Little children are frightened of lots of things they haven't experienced.

Once, when I was in New York, I went to Brooklyn and met a woman who was born and raised in Brooklyn. She never crossed into Manhattan, which is twenty minutes on the subway, and she said, "But there are strange things going on there." How many people are there who have never gone fifty miles beyond the place where they were born? Well, most people who live in a tribal situation have never gone that far. Think of that! Most of the people who have ever lived have probably never gone one hundred miles from home—never away overnight in some place where some family member is not. So "things go bump in the night" on a tribal level, too.

Audience: Won't people like Mengele acknowledge their power when the 12th house Pluto moves into the 1st house by progression?

Richard: Well, yes, but I don't think you really need progressions to help a 12th house Pluto. I mean, it's okay, it's all right, there are riches to be had.

Remember this, every dark side has a shadow and when you slay the dragon, the dragon is curled around the treasure. In getting an awareness of it, the dark side often shows itself first, and it's frightening; especially when it's children, it frightens the parent. If parents have not touched in on their shadows, they cannot accept the shadow of the child. Each family tends to pass its own particular family-shadow on down the line. Maybe it's anger—anger is never expressed, it's not spiritual. Sex is filthy—mother and grandmother and great-grandmother, when they had sex, closed their eyes and thought of England! So, it doesn't matter that you were born in the 60's and were a hippy-child, you've collected through those genes a collective taboo and shadow, and it's not easy breaking through that. That's what I meant when I was talking about the importance of these family myths and how powerful they are.

So family myths can constellate shadow, just like social myths constellate shadow, and we deal with these shadows by projecting them outward and finding scapegoats. In Germany it was the Jews. In the South it was the Blacks. Or it's the homosexuals, or it's women, or it's men, or it's bleeding-heart-liberals, or uptight-conservatives. And it's always epithets—it's always "them over there" who are carrying this collective shadow stuff. That's why I say over and over what happened in Germany was that people were devoted to the ideal of "let everything be comfy and cozy" and they forgot the Viking unconscious background out of which they came. They were one of the last countries to be Christianized so there was a Pagan thing that came erupting out. If you forget the Pagan and Neanderthal that is lurking inside all of us, that is the opportunity for him to come out and take you over. If you *live* with the Neanderthal, he won't take you over, and that is the story of *Beauty and the Beast.* When you love the beast, you see that the beast is the *other.* When you kiss the frog, it may turn into a prince, but you've got to kiss it first. And not the outer-frog—the inner-frog and all the little toads.

Audience: But just because I am aware of the shadow, I may not necessarily transform it. Maybe Mengele looked at it, maybe even had counseling, but didn't transform or change it.

Richard: Yes. However, I doubt that the man had psychotherapy. It's conceivable, but for me that is the example of an uninsightful life on one level or another. Yes, when you've taken the sword out of the sheath and you open the door and face the dragon, you can be slain. So the worst that can happen is you can be destroyed, you can be annihilated. Or, you can, yourself, be the destroyer. If you're a healer, if you're a psychotherapist, if you're an astrological counselor, you are in the role of "healer-destroyer," because they are two faces of the same thing. And you had better understand the Mengele part of you—the person who delights in dis-assembling people to put them together into something more beautiful. He acted it out in a horrible way, but there's also that part of us among astrologers and psychotherapists that delight in the same thing. We invade somebody's psyche, we get in there and love seducing them into consciousness. There's pain involved, transformation, with the hope that out of this pain and yuck, something much more beautiful comes out of it.

Now, here's a trap. When you ask someone, "Why did you become an astrologer?" and they answer, "Because I like people, I wish to follow a spiritual path and I find astrology interesting," but, are there any personal motives involved in it? You had better acknowledge your own shadow if you are going to be a healer, because the Pluto part of us wants to seduce, wants to take down into the underworld. And if you don't, then you fall into the trap. If you haven't faced the fact that behind every healer is a destroyer, a client may come to you and you may destroy that person, or the client may destroy himself or herself in the process that's going on. Can you accept and live with that?

You may destroy yourself by facing your own inner dragon and here's another paradox. We tend to worship life and sanity and pleasure, and we put into shadow death and madness and pain. Those are "bad" things. The Greeks didn't do that. Look at the Greek dramas. They're all about death and madness and pain. They had to collectively bring up the shadow and look at that by catharsis and by sharing. It was the whole function of the Greek drama. Aristotle said, "The function of drama is a communion." By the shared pity and terror of observing these mythic things happening, the community has catharsis. It purges itself and it blends together through the joint suffering and sharing. And that is entirely what the Christian communion is about, or ought to be, isn't it? Christ is sacrificed and dies on the cross—he has given up his life for your sins. Through communion, by symbolically taking in his blood and eating his body (a cannibalistic and vampiric act, if you take it literally), you have taken on some of his sanctity and he has taken on your sins. That is an enormously Plutonian thing. How many people really feel that? See what I'm saying? So there is a risk, always, and it's a perpetual process. It is a process forever unfolding, we don't suddenly *get there*. It's not just slaying one dragon, it's levels and levels of unfolding. We are always facing deeper and deeper levels of our unconscious.

Audience: I don't think there is any success or failure in this. I don't think there is any one point in this process where you can say, "I've succeeded," or "I have failed," and I think that doing that is a result of our Western consciousness, to look at something and call it a success or a failure.

Richard: Yes, I think so. As Gertrude Stein said of Oakland, I say the same thing of consciousness and enlightenment. "There is no *there* there." You don't get there. It's an unfolding process. I taught astrology in the prison system in California and I taught rapists, mass murderers, and child molesters. These people have souls, too, and they're on their path of redemption, and yes, unfortunately, they acted out their shadows in very terrible ways.

Audience: If somebody's aware of the shadow, say it's betrayal, but continue to act it out, is it still a shadow? And if it's no longer a shadow, then why continue to betray people?

Richard: Yes, it can still be a shadow, except I don't acknowledge that that's what I'm doing. I rationalize it. "Of course I'm betraying you, because you're making me do this." The murderer says, "Sure, I may have done this act, but it's not my fault or my responsibility. It has nothing to do with me, you goaded me into doing that."

Audience: What if the murderer says, "Sure, I have done this act, I don't see anything wrong with it and I'll do it again," what then?

Richard: Then what has happened is the shadow has taken us over completely, and what we're talking about now is psychosis, severe illness, and for that reason we put people away.

Audience: Are there people who don't want help or to change for fear of losing the self that they know and they won't enter into psychotherapy?

Richard: Well yes, and that's why I'm saying the dragon coils around the treasure. The famous German poet Rilke[7] knew both Freud and Jung, and in the 30s when everybody was going into psychoanalysis like crazy, people asked him why he didn't go into therapy, since he was a special friend of Jung's. And he said "I'm afraid if my devils leave me, my angels will leave me as well." Do you see the point of what I'm saying? As the lady in the audience so nicely put it, "The larger the light, the larger the shadow." If you can't look at the shadow, you can't have the light, and the shadow is always there whether we look at it or not.

Death, for instance, is an archetype of shadow. None of us ever likes death. We come more or less to accept it, or live with it, or tolerate it, or face it, but none of us *want* it unless there is indeed some psychopathology. That's why, for me, the symbol of Scorpio is so perfect, because it looks like a roller-coaster. It's not just up, down, face the dragon and back up to the light, thank you! It's up and down, and up and down, and up and down. That's why we have the symbol of the phoenix. It isn't that the phoenix just burns in flames, rises renewed out of its own ashes, and is then enlightened. No, it is forever doing that. That's the cycle, there are layers and layers. You think, "Oh boy, I got it *that* time!" And you didn't because there's another layer down there, and another and another. But with each release of the dark you release more light. There's always more shadow and you're never done. The more light that's released casts more shadow so it's a constant, ongoing process. Somebody here put it very nicely. We tend to think we're going to get

7. Rainer Maria Rilke (1875-1926): Most influential German poet of the 20th century and considered one of the guiding spirits of modern poetry.

"there," wherever "there" is—enlightenment, the Buddhist state Nirvana, the "there" of perfection. We will be saved and everything will be done with. But it isn't. Life is a constant, recurring circle and the circle gets wider and wider, and includes more and more. And as my circle expands, the more I must include, not only more awareness of the world, but more awareness of myself, and it's a lifetime process of moving into the light.

It's interesting that in Greek Pluto (Plutous) means wealth, so he is the god of the riches. The dragon that you slay sits on the treasure, or reveals the truth. So there are great riches coming up through this dark world, it isn't just all horrors. Please believe me, it is not. We only see it that way because we separate the dark from the light. We tend to think that pain should be avoided at all cost. We've got to love pain and that doesn't mean become a masochist, but you have to get into the pain and into the dark and enjoy it. As it has been put, climb into it and paddle around in it.

Audience: But don't we project it onto another person?

Richard: Yes, we're forever doing that in our relationships. We find other people to live out a lot of our shadow, and once we get it home, we recoil in horror and then try to fix the other person. How many women come into consultations and say, "Here's my husband's chart, fix it." Or men who say "I have this neurotic wife, fix her."

Audience: You have to live in hell to be in heaven?

Richard: Right. It's interesting in Dante's *Divine Comedy* there's a trilogy of Hell, Purgatory, and Heaven. Where does he start? He starts in Hell. From Hell he goes to Purgatory and from Purgatory to Heaven. It doesn't go the other way around.

⋆ ⋆ ⋆

Now, let's take a look at a chart (See Chart 4 on page 119). We'll incorporate some of the stuff we've been working at today into our way of looking at it and examine it from the point of view of shadow. So, if we talk about dark potential here, we're not going to say this person has to live that out, and we're not going to say if you have a similar configuration that you have to live it out at all. I hope we're clear on that, if one ever can get clear. I think you're going to find this is a very interesting person. It's a chart I've been after for a very long time and finally got it.

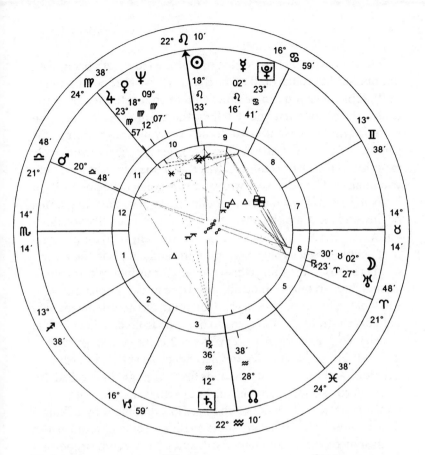

MODALITIES
Cardinal 4 (T)
Fixed 6
Mutable 3

ELEMENTS
Fire 4
Air 2
Water 2 (♀)
Earth 5

Yang 6
Yin 7

MISSING
FUNCTIONS
N/A

STELLIA
N/A

SINGLETONS
♀ Water
♄ Universal
   Personal Houses

ORIENTATION
(Houses)
Personal 1 (♄)
Social 3
Universal 9

ORIENTATION
(Signs)
Personal 5
Social 7
Universal 1 (♄)

Chart 4. Example chart.
Birth data cited in footnote 8 on page 136.

Starting with our way of looking at the chart, let's begin with our outline, our rough draft of the chart. When we are doing a rough draft, remember you can be quite wild in your interpretations because this is not what you're telling the client. This is your own material. And just as the artist doesn't show his rough draft in the gallery, and actors rehearse in private, you get the chance to be wildly experimental in all directions. Later you'll refine it level by level until you finally get it to the place where you are going to be presenting it to the client. And even then it doesn't come alive until the drama begins, and the drama begins in the consultation. Just like you don't know exactly, although you've rehearsed and rehearsed the play, you don't know how it's going to go until the audience is in the room.

Let's look at the things that come up for us first. We have four, six and three among the modalities and that doesn't attract my eye— I'm looking for stuff that's big and different. I'm now doing the very bold brush strokes, so I'm going to move on from that. Let's look at the elements. Fire = 4, Air = 2, Water = 2 (Pluto is a singleton but gets two points because it's the Ascendant ruler), and Earth = 5. Let's look at the dominant functions first. We might have called this a Fire-Earth co-dominant person, but Earth is slightly more dominant than Fire so let's honor the Earth as dominant by talking a little bit about that. What are some qualities that you would expect from someone with dominant Earth and what are some important issues that would come up?

Audience: Practical. Get things done. Sensuality. Uses time well. Organized. Material security being an important issue. The body and issues of the body.

Richard: Yes. Anything else?

Audience: Concerned with form, with structure, the world of reality, the world of things, of objects.

Richard: Fine. So, on the face of this, in our first broad sketch, we'd say here is a person who ought to naturally function easily in this dominant function and we'll leave it open to decide.

Now, the second dominant function is Fire. It's often interesting to take it a step further and say, "What's in the Fire?" You can look at that and see Uranus in Aries, Sun in Leo, and Mercury in

Leo, so three planets equaling four points, and that's the Fire. What does dominant Fire mean, what kind of person does this potentially give us? What are some words?

Audience: Inspired. Self expressive. Impulsive. Ambitious. Confident. Lots of energy and vitality. Optimistic. Action-impassioned. Spirituality, a big important issue. Creativity.

Richard: Good, you obviously know your astrology, don't you? All right, so we would expect that to be a dominant issue in his life.

Now, however, there are co-inferior functions going on here. Let's look at the two points in Air first, then we have a singleton and we can take that next. What are the two points in Air? Mars and Saturn which are in wide trine. (We don't have to comment on the orb at the moment, just note it.) What would we think about somebody with an inferior function in Air? What are the issues going to be? What may shadow issues be for this person? We have no way of knowing by looking at the chart how developed the inferior function is. What if it's denied? What if he's compensating for it? What are your ideas?

Audience: Reacting negatively to a new idea.

Richard: Exactly! If one is repressing or denying or projecting it, it could be new ideas or new ways of thinking, yes. Or it might be the opposite. He could be highly susceptible to new ideas because he may not be able to clearly discriminate on that level.

Audience: He could feel insecure about his intellect.

Richard: Good. It may make him overcompensate. Very good.

Audience: Works hard at communicating. Problems with objectivity.

Richard: Yes, problems with distance, too close or too far apart, seeing things clearly, thinking you see things clearly that are not clear. Absolutely. Good.

Audience: Threatened by new ideas. Problems with time and space.

Richard: Certainly could be, absolutely. Yes, time and space could both be airy situations, sure.

Audience: A tendency to rationalize.

Richard: Ah, now be careful. Don't take the next step yet, but you're right, that's a good interpretation.

Now, let's go on to the singleton. The true inferior function here is going to be Water, in which there is a singleton, and who shows up here again? Mr. Pluto. So let's for the time being never mind that it's Pluto, and talk about what would happen with an inferior function in Water.

Audience: Overwhelmed by feelings?

Richard: Yes, or *fear* of being overwhelmed by feelings.

Audience: A tendency to be cold or detached.

Richard: Yes, out of a fear of feelings or the denial of feelings.

Audience: Fear of close relationships.

Richard: Yes, why? The fear of dissolving and losing oneself into the other.

Audience: Feelings may be inappropriate and he may make inappropriate feeling choices. Fear of pain.

Richard: Sure. Or, contrary-wise, obsession with.

Audience: Rejecting feelings.

Richard: Yes. So what kinds of feelings are these that might be unacceptable? Now we can enlarge this situation because we have a singleton staring us in the face. Now we have an actual archetype crystallizing for us and who is it? It's Pluto in Cancer, and never mind what house he's in for the moment, let's leave him alone there. So all this watery quality is Plutonian in its nature, now derive that.

Audience: Expressing feelings is a sign of weakness.

Richard: And that may be the reason they are unacceptable and must be denied. "My feelings are so passionate and explosive and dangerous and so much coming from the underworld that I must hold them down."

Audience: He may use feelings in service of his power drive.

Richard: Very good.

Audience: Fear of his own dependency and neediness?

Richard: Yes. Pluto as a singleton. "If I become dependent and needy, I'll be devoured, I'll be eaten up by my neediness." Also, my feelings are dangerous because they may be annihilating, so if I touch into my feelings at all, I'm automatically bringing in the sulphur and brimstone of the dragon. Therefore, in order not to do that, maybe I have to deny all feelings, or project them.

Audience: Wouldn't he control and manipulate the feelings of others?

Richard: Yes, excellent, because that's where my power comes from.

Audience: Could it be a complex about home and mother?

Richard: Yes, and all the archetypes that cluster around Cancer like home, mother, homeland, family, woman, nurturing. Yes, all of these things are loaded with underworld stuff.

Audience: He fears the power of other people's emotions?

Richard: Yes. So other people's emotions must be controlled and we bring in now the projection going on.

Audience: Could it also be to protect people from other people's power?

Richard: Yes, I'm protecting you from other people's Plutonian energies and here's a classical projection. I mean, who is Pluto anyway? Of course, Pluto is *me*, but unless I can acknowledge that Pluto, it can't be me. Therefore, I must deny it, or repress it, or project it and make it you. So there are devils around, but where are they? In what do they lodge, is the question.

Audience: A fear of transformative experiences.

Richard: Like death and sex, yes. Okay, now that singleton Pluto is stationed in the 9th house so we might as well add that in, too. What quality does that add into our rough draft? In other words, what arena in life? Never mind profession for now, just in what *setting* will this be dramatized out on for this man?

Audience: In his belief systems, pursuit of God, group beliefs and ethics.

Richard: Laws, ethics and systems, all these Sagittarian, 9th-house kinds of things. That which we believe in, that which is grace, that which is divinity. Yes, of course.

Now, whether or not we know about archetypal Pluto—the dark, the dragon, the fear, eros, power from the underworld, images of things like Hades raping Persephone—we know Pluto is the rapist, the seducer in one way or another. And whether it's the seducer to knowledge or the seducer to light, because Lucifer means The Light Bearer, there's always something that is seductive and snake-like, serpent-like in Pluto. We tend to think of that as dark, but not all people have denied the serpent. The Egyptian initiate always wore the erect Cobra in the band around the head, showing the Plutonian energy coming out of the third eye, so not everybody has seen the serpent as a form of evil.

Here's another thought about Pluto in the 9th house. The higher mind would in some way need to incorporate this dark principle. How he would incorporate? We don't know. It's the whole Eleusinian Mysteries of the triad of Demeter, Persephone, and Hades-Pluto. Originally Demeter and Core were one and the same, two faces of the same archetype. Hecate is also in there, but we can't say the metaphor is the myth and the myth is the planet and the planet is the person. We have to say it is *like* this, or it *smells* like.

Audience: I think I smell Demeter in this.

Richard: Maybe you do and you're right because on one level Cancer is the great, binding mother, and any time you touch on Cancer you bring in mother, so I would certainly say great mother issues are already implied here.

All right, enough about that, let's go on to orientation. We see Personal = 5, Social = 7, Universal = 1. Let's take a look at the dominance in Social signs and see what might be some of his characteristics. He likes people around him, in his immediate vicinity, and that's one of the differences between Social and Universal. Social wants them around close enough to get your aura on them and Universal says, "The whole world is my bailiwick." The idea of validation from society is important and the question we talked about before, that social signs are *moral* signs. Not necessarily that the morals are good, but that morals, morality and taboos always become an issue. How do people get along with interrelations with each other? On some level or another that's going to be important.

Now, the inferior function here is in Universal signs, so we have Saturn. This time let's look at Saturn first and then Universality. What issues come up if Saturn is a singleton? If it's a singleton, remember, the likelihood is of it becoming an inferior function. So what do we expect to come up archetypally when we invoke Saturn?

Audience: Rigidity. A sense of inadequacy and inferiority. Crushing repressiveness. Fear. Depression.

Richard: Authority and authority figures are all involved in the archetype in a Jungian sense, so we're invoking Cronus and Cronus has two faces. The loving, wise father in his benefic face, the all-protecting one who enforces the laws to protect them. The other is the devourer of his young who protects his position and power by destroying all competitors.

Audience: That would be disciplined and there would be wisdom, structure, boundaries and guilt.

Richard: Yes, and I heard one of you say you're getting an overwhelming sense of the idea of sin and the overwhelming need to contain it, put boundaries around it, structure it. Yes, and what you are saying is you're starting to get a "nose" for something, but you could be dead wrong if you then automatically say this is a philosopher, or a teacher, or a psychotherapist, or whatever. The minute you do that you stop the creative process, because you just stuck the pin through the butterfly. Let the butterfly fly, and stay away from *who* this is and concentrate on *what* are his qualities. What I want to do is just focus on the little teeth at the moment, then we'll put it together.

Now, this is a singleton in Universal signs, so what does that mean? In some way he projects this on to the collective, or the collective is making him do this. "I am doing all these things, but it's only in the service of the collective and the greater good, or of God, or of things outside myself." And perhaps, I am identified with that. The archetype then becomes inflated to being, "It isn't me, it is this destiny." As so many of the white lighters I know would like to say,

"I am a channel for the forces of the higher above, it isn't me that is doing it, I am simply in the service of something higher than myself." So what is implied is, whatever I do, I'm doing it because *who* told me to do it? The great Cronus up there, or the great Pluto (the devil made me do it), or God has spoken to me and said thus it shall be. Would that necessarily be conscious? No.

Let's look at Personal, Social, and Universal houses. This is the realm where he will act out these things. I didn't mark it here, but it's interesting that Saturn is twice a singleton in the chart. Every time a planet is a singleton, and it might be three or four times a singleton in the chart, that further stresses the tension. Archetypal Saturn now is bearing two powers here—singleton in Universality and singleton in Personal houses. So it's carrying a dual thing, in which case it can be very interesting to confuse the two. We've already talked about Saturn, but now it's operating in a different realm. Saturn is the only planet in the first four houses, the arena in which he is to get in touch with who he is, what his needs are, what his early life and environment is, his security needs and so on. Saturn carries the weight for the whole thing. What does that say to you? It's an inferior function, so he could have suppressed it or repressed a lot of that personal stuff. Why? He doesn't feel good enough or entitled to it, afraid of it or guilty. It might be an overpowering father, so that may be a theme we want to investigate and develop later. The father or a parent, the authority figure at least, in some way becomes an overpowering figure.

Audience: Might he universalize his need for control?

Richard: Good. So my fear of getting out of control may make it necessary for me to universalize this function in Aquarius and control everybody else. That's a projection.

Audience: Could be a great deal of difficulty with communications.

Richard: Yes, but on the contrary, if it's a *compensatory* reaction, it might be, "I am the mouthpiece of God." He may be an overcompensating communicator who might personalize responsibility for the world so, in the 3rd house, "It speaks through me, through my communication mechanism." Remember that the dominant function is in Universal houses, everything is up here in 9, 10 and 11, so that's the arena where all of this stuff is operating. What does that mean? Where does he feel at home? Out there among the masses, the group, the collective.

Audience: What if you have planets in personal signs but in collective houses. Do you use the collective to satisfy the personal needs?

Richard: Yes, the motivations are personal but the arena that it is acted out on is universal, so there is a tendency to confuse myself and the universal world.

You get the same reflection down here in the 3rd house. You have a planet (Saturn) that is naturally connected with the 10th house (Capricorn), in the natural sign of the 11th (Aquarius), down here in the 3rd house and that is a personal house. There can be a tendency to confuse *my* needs and the will of the universe. They are very much the same. It's like you turn the dial and all of the numbers turn directly. He might try to take personal responsibility for collective issues and that is often the confusion between the universal and the personal.

Audience: Could he do it through an artistic pursuit?

Richard: Certainly. Now let's look at the major configurations. We have a T-cross in Cardinal signs. We have Mars opposed to Uranus and Moon, both forming a T-cross to Pluto in Cancer in the 9th house. So, now we have the singleton Pluto the focal point of the T-cross and the planet focalizes in the 9th house with a tension between Mars and Uranus. Let's talk about that tension first of all. What goes on with Mars and Uranus anyway? A lot of erratic energy, lots of anger, a tendency toward spontaneous combustion isn't it? Reckless. Impulsive.

Audience: There also is a suggestion that the personal Yang energy of Mars has exploded for some sort of collective cause, so it could be revolutionary.

Richard: Yes, there is a bit of a revolutionary right there. One of the things that happens when Mars gets tightly hooked into the outer planets, Uranus, Neptune, and Pluto, is one tends to transfigure anger and it becomes "righteous anger"—we call it *outrage.* "I'm not angry, it isn't me, I speak for the collective." And with Mars in Libra, " Angry? Who, me? No, I'm smiling and charming." So if I'm angry, who is it that makes me angry? It's others. It's you.

Audience: Because we need that, you know the world needs that, too, it just needs to be balanced. We need people to be angry about what's happening to the world or the world isn't going to survive very much longer. Also, I believe he's inventive, a lot of creativity.

Richard: Sure, *inventive* use of anger, but what there is here is polarity, so what happens is you get this black/white. There is one thing or the other, Mars *or* Uranus.

First of all, what happens in the Libra-Aries opposition? It's me and others, self and others, so that's the issue that comes up. I-want-what-I-want-when-I-want, versus you. Now Mars and Uranus are both naturally Yang planets, and Mars and Uranus like each other. But what kind of energy comes out when they like each other, what's their romance all about? Truth-seeking, excitement, risk-taking, that kind of thing. Ah, somebody brought up the word sexual. That's interesting. Why? Mars is fundamental libido energy. Mars is phallic, thrusting, outward energy. What does Uranus have to do with all that? Unusual, spontaneous, eccentric. It's like either/or. I either go Mars or Uranus. What happens? They end up in polarity with each other. I don't like the word opposition anyway, I prefer to call it a complementation. It becomes an opposition only when it's either/or. So I become my Mars, angry at Uranus, and what things then become projected on Uranus? Uranus can become shadow. What are those things that my Mars in Libra gets angry at?

Independence, deviation, individuality. A possible place for shadow is the opposition, one place or the other can go into shadow. Why? Because we can't live with the duality. So if one is going with the Mars, then the Uranus falls into shadow. Mars becomes angry at the eccentricity, the abnormal, the unusual, the different, that which doesn't conform. Or, Uranus becomes angry at Mars, "I want to explode and transform and change all anger, assertion, libido energy, sexuality, tribal stuff, competition and so on." Do we know which way it's going to go? No. We don't know which is going to be in shadow and whether it's integrated or not.

Now, what intervenes in the middle of this? What carries the brunt of this powerful, fiery, passionate, Yang-masculine energy in the Mars-Uranus? The singleton Pluto, and now we have the potentials of a complex shown by the singleton Pluto in Cancer in the 9th, triggered off by the Mars-Uranus opposition. Now I'm starting to smell brimstone, at least potentially. The stuff is getting darker. The potential is for Pluto getting rabid because of the Yang energy of the ruler of the Ascendant (Pluto) in the 9th house squaring the Yang planets Mars and Uranus. It's likely to be explosive, not quiet or repressed. It is very unlikely, with the pressure from this Mars-Uranus, that the Pluto is going to be repressed very much. It might go into denial, but at great cost. The Mars-Uranus is going to force that Pluto out into action in the outer world and I smell the barking of the three-headed dog Cerberus who guards the gates of the underworld. And what is he barking about? Well, here he is stationed in the 9th house. The Pluto can't retire, Mars and Uranus won't let it, it's not in the nature of the square and it's not in the nature of Mars or Uranus to let it alone. So now we have the irresistible force and the immoveable object—the hammer and the anvil. The image that comes up for me on a psychic level, is a blacksmith hitting this hammer over and over again. What images come for you?

Audience: I see the repressed rage on a personal level projected onto government figures or systems. A hanging-judge.

Richard: Very good. So now it's okay to begin to paint in broader images, and there's a difference between an image and a judgment. Here are examples of images for me. I like "A rending, tearing, rabid rhinoceros." "A swarm of red-hot mosquitos." Those are images that are useful to me but that's not what I'm going to sit down and tell somebody in his or her chart. These images now build up—visualizations, colors, sounds, tastes are important. "Tapioca pudding that after one bite turns out to be loaded with red pepper." Images that work for you, metaphors, characters out of drama, are useful in building this up—it's part of the artistry.

Audience: It seems that the usefulness of all this preliminary work that you're doing is exposing yourself to the greatest, horrific potential that could be there, which you won't get when you meet the person because all this is shadow. At first it seemed like, why look for all this, and now I'm really starting to appreciate the value of it.

Richard: Yes, and that's why this is a *Magic Thread*. We're unwinding the thread for what purpose? To go down into the heart of the labyrinth and find that Minotaur. And what I'm looking at is what's possible and I'm not making a judgment on it. I'm still totally open. Of course, I know who this person is, so it's hard for me to be objective and subjective at the same time. But if it's a chart of somebody I don't know, by doing this system and keeping away from results like this is going to be a doctor, a lawyer, an Indian chief, or value judgments like this is an evil or bad person, this person is disturbed or sick—by staying away from those things, then I can be open to process. What I'm trying to show you is the value of moving step by step through the structure and I realize it puts a few hobbles on you by saying, "Wait, hold back, take it one step at a time, don't put too much together yet because we will get tangled up in the ball of yarn."

Now, the outlet of the Pluto T-cross falls in the Capricorn 3rd house, again emphasizing that the missing leg is Capricorn and the 3rd house. We've already seen the singleton Saturn in the 3rd house, which is saying more or less the same thing. What's missing? The tension is experienced up here in the 9th house and is resolved down through the 3rd house, now how will it be resolved? Through authoritarian ways of communicating the rigid mind set of some kind. The thing that prevents all this from running amuck and out of control is to get into this Capricornian opposite shadow, so somehow I need to psychically put a cork in this T-cross. And what corks it up? Well, Capricorn rigid control, structure, becoming an authority.

Next, I am uncomfortable with the Moon-Uranus conjunction here. Moon-Uranus is often the symbol of the abandoned child, the child who inwardly feels abandoned and it's also the child who feels special, unusual. Moon is a nurturing figure and Uranus is the wanderer. I think people with strong Moon-Uranus contacts in their chart innately have to live through the myth of abandonment. "Someone is going to leave me." It almost invariably means problems with the mother, or with the maternal and nurturing thing. Uranus doesn't like Moon. Cancer and Aquarius are in quincunx. They have an awfully hard time because they want opposite things. Cancer wants holding and wombs and umbilical cords and nurturing and closeness. Aquarius says, "Give me space, I can't breathe. I have to go away from you in order to find myself." So Moon-Uranus at best is an uncomfortable situation.

Audience: Couldn't it be mothering in an impersonal way?

Richard: Well, it would have to mother in an impersonal way, but the baby needs mothering in a *personal* way and surely, that may be how it was experienced, as impersonal mothering.

Also, you may have a child who comes into the world and rejects closeness, who has a difficulty with it. There's a duality. Moon in Taurus certainly wants touching and closeness, yet with Uranus in Aries, some part of it says, "Leave me alone, back off, get away from me." I have people with Moon in Capricorn opposed Pluto who come in for counseling and they'll say, "I was never picked up, my mother was so cold and withdrawn I never got any nurturing." That's the myth. Then you meet the mother who says, "Every time I picked you up you would scream and cry and hit me with your little fists. You'd let your daddy pick you up but I couldn't touch you." Do you see what I'm saying? *We invoke certain responses from people by what we innately are ourselves.*

That's why I'm asking, how does the man mythologize this? I don't know, but certainly there is a conflict in the need for physical closeness, emotional nurturing and touching, and the desire for freedom and pull-back. Did he set up his mother to withdraw from him? Was there an erratic closeness and back and forth between mother and child—sometimes very there for him, sometimes totally involved in something else? Did he erratically signal to his mother, sometimes "Touch me, pick me up," sometimes "Leave me alone," so maybe mother withdrew?

Audience: Is there implied mind-body split with Moon-Uranus?

Richard: Yes, it very well could be and specifically, because of a Taurus-Aries conjunction here. That's a particularly tricky conjunction because Aries does not like body, Aries likes energy. Aries ignores its body. Aries without Taurus will burn itself out like a flaming comet. That's why Taurus in the scheme of things must follow Aries because Aries is pure, primeval energy. Taurus reacts to that by binding and holding in, anchoring and securing. So there's an uncomfortable conflict that goes on in here.

Audience: Would there be an attempt to objectify instincts or an attempt to transcend them?

Richard: That's often what happens with Uranus, Neptune, and Pluto when they are in contact with very primitive, personal planets like Moon, or Venus, or Mars. It is unacceptable to let this function on the mundane level so, "I must transcend this and elevate it in some way. This stuff is filthy or base or unworthy," so there is a devaluation of the primitive function and it must somehow be raised.

Audience: Might this also mean that he was put in foster homes or adopted?

Richard: It could be, but that's a *result* and, although it might indeed have happened, I don't want to say that at this point because it stops my creative function.

Audience: Perhaps the mother may have been Uranian and working on her own process of transformation.

Richard: Yes, I get mother was indeed Uranian to some extent because I see Aquarius on the 4th. The atmosphere in the nurturing home was a Uranian-Aquarian thing.

Also I'm interested in this 29th degree Node in the 4th house, for whatever that is worth. It says something to me about the whole early home environment and the background. Aquarius, in one sense of the word, can become quite detached from the people and things. Aquarius is not a "kind" connection for baby nurturing; it's not a good nursery sign at all. It gives a type of nurturing in terms of freedom, which is very valuable for the child at a certain point. For instance, Cancer gives very good nurturing at the early childhood part of babyhood. You see someone with Moon-Cancer in the 4th house and you say, "Isn't that wonderful, the perfect, nurturing mother." Yes, maybe when the child was an infant, but when the child gets to the terrible 2s or at adolescence when he or she needs to begin to separate, that's when the problems may begin. Uranus and Aquarius in the 4th house may not give an awful lot of early nurturing, the inner baby may not be getting much stuff, but the nurturing becomes just right for the person at the point of adolescent rebellion. So there's a lot more to nurturing than just babyhood.

Audience: The spiritual and the physical seem to be at odds in the chart with the T-cross.

Richard: Yes and it's shown over and over again in this chart. I would say that he has picked up and internalized the split in his mother, who herself was of the flesh and wanting to in some way escape and elevate from that. I would say this comes from the root, the family myth, the stuff of the home environment that he came from. Was it literally mother? I can't say, but I suspect it.

We're hunting down shadows right now, and I am hoping that this is a very developed, conscious, integrated individual. But if he was, I probably wouldn't have him up here because it's more fun to work with people who have shadow rampant all over the place, as you can see by my choices. When we get to work on the chart of the homework I've given you, you'll see here is somebody who is working on her stuff. So there is another way to go, but I want to show you first what happens with people who apparently don't. And how do you judge someone? Well, by his or her work. So I can't say whether this person is integrated or not. You'll have to look at that yourself.

Audience: It seems to me this man's personal emotions could be sublimated to wild movements or revolutionary causes which he might act out in a very aggressive way.

Richard: I agree with you, yes.

Audience: Might he have a rare or unusual illness and through that come to know the elements of his unconscious qualities and be able to heal or treat because of that illness?

Richard: You're getting that from the 6th house quality? All right, the 6th house for me is an area which I call the repair-and-maintenance-department on a psychological level. It's how we deal with things that break, and not just physically in the outer world, but things inside like how do we problem-solve? But it's also easy to project—who's problem are we solving? Is it mine, or is it out there? That can become the confusion. So there is somewhere that sense of illness, something that is wrong or broken and needs to be fixed. Is it in me? Can I internalize it and acknowledge it, or do I suppress that and project it out to become a fixer of the world? I'm glad you brought that up.

I want to touch on one other item. I'm interested in this clump up here in Virgo in the 10th house and it's an interesting contrast to the Leo Midheaven. The 10th house mask (what's given out to the world), is this Leo with the Sun in Leo in the 9th house conjunct the Midheaven. What does that sound like to you? Warm and royal, shining, glowing, king-like, charming, generous, Apollo "the bearer of the light," heady and bright—nothing dark, nothing dirty, nothing unclean. One of the archetypes of the Sun in Leo is the Hero, the divine (as opposed to Mars which becomes the Warrior). It is Percival in search of the golden Grail who was all bathed in golden light.

But *inside* the 10th is all this Virgo stuff. Here is this dark underworld, potentially *Yin*, in-turning function that may indeed have resolved the tension between this Mars and Uranus by squelching both of them. And Pluto has the capacity to do that. In unconscious and unindividuated people, if there is any kind of contest, Pluto always wins. Even the Greeks said that in the last analysis, Hades carries all, because we always end up going down into the underworld and from there we have come and to there we return. Round and round, the snake eats its own tail—we begin out of that and we return to that matter again. So Pluto does do that, this big shadow figure. Just looking at these things in Virgo—Jupiter, Venus, and Neptune are odd planets to be in Virgo. I'm not quite sure how comfortable they are there, because Virgo seems to nit-pick and sort and analyze. Of the many fine qualities of archetypal Virgo, generosity or expansiveness (Jupiter) is not one. Reaching out toward others either in an aesthetic or sensual way (Venus) is not natural. Falling apart into chaos and surrendering (Neptune) is not natural. What Virgo wants to do is sort and structure and pick through. So what do you get from that particular little clump up there?

Audience: Jupiter is in its detriment, Neptune is in its detriment and Venus is in its fall.

Richard: I don't necessarily go along with those fundamentals of traditional astrology about detriments and falls, but nevertheless, planets are more or less comfortable in certain situations. That doesn't necessarily mean any bad, qualitative things for the planet. It forces the planet back on itself and you may get a strong compensatory reaction.

Here the Leo seems to shine on the surface, Sun in Leo conjunct the Midheaven, while Neptune, Venus, and Jupiter are not conjunct the Midheaven, they're sort of hidden beneath. So Sun in Leo conjunct Midheaven is the opening of the door, but once you get inside there is Neptune, Venus, and Jupiter in Virgo. The wrapping on the package is Leo, but inside the package you have something quite different (and we also should point out the Sun-Saturn opposition that's a polarity between the adult and the parent). Virgo is very much concerned with dirt. Virgo always has a broom in hand. It's different from Scorpio who has an enema bag. Scorpio is concerned with filth, and that's different from dirt. Virgo is psychically dusting all the time.

So one of the fundamental things I see in this chart is the major conflict between an extroverted, outgoing, positive, warm, generous thing and something in behind it that wants to check that all the time and doesn't trust those impulses. Pluto wants to take the Mars and Uranus down into the underworld where neither one of them are particularly comfortable. Remember we talked about Hades dragging 300 foot, brawny Aries down into the underworld, transforming him and sending him up? Here's where you get the fanatic. When Pluto can do that to Mars; Mars comes out now a killer with a mind. Mars himself is totally un-shrewd, but add Pluto to it and he learns a deviousness. Instead of being pure, archetypal Aries, which Mars normally wants to be, he's also attracted to the Scorpionic functions. When he is in any way in touch with Pluto he is dragged from his normal Aries function over to Scorpio and can function quite well there. He is much more dangerous in his Scorpio function than he is in his Aries function, because Scorpio is clever and Aries isn't. Aries is very smart, but that's not the same thing. Scorpio is deep and scheming.

So I see an enormous dichotomy, an enormous tear or rending in this personality. He might get other people to do the "dirty" work, or he might project the "dirtiness" on other people. How do I live with the dichotomy between everything here that is light, golden, outgoing, warm and generous and the other part that is concerned with the yuck in the underworld? Do I identify with one, deny the shadow and project it out on other people?

Audience: Might not there be anger at women with the Moon involved here?

Richard: That's a very interesting point here, anger at women, and whether it's his own inner mother, or his literal mother, or his own anima, or projections of the feminine onto women, yes. Maybe, with his Moon in Taurus, it's the idea of classical Eve. Maybe it is Eve and woman and things that are feminine that are "the work of the devil" and keep me from my Uranian ability to rise—it's woman who binds and holds you down. Could very well be.

Now it's time to tell you who this chart belongs to. It is one of your local Lynchburg, Virginia residents, Jerry Falwell,[8] the famous upholder of traditional morality.

8. Jerry Falwell, 1933 – . Baptist minister and TV evangelist, founded political action group *Moral Majority* in 1979; strongly condemns homosexuality, pornography, abortion, and favors prayer in public schools. Born August 11, 1933, Lynchburg, VA, 79W08, 37N24, around 12:00 P.M. EST. Koch houses. Source: From twin brother to friend of astrologer; time is uncertain.

CHAPTER FIVE

⚘

PERSONAL IDENTIFICATION: DEATH AND POLARITIES

Richard: Before we begin something new, are there any questions about material we have covered so far?

Audience: What is the difference between a singleton and an inferior function?

Richard: The singleton *focuses* the inferior function, the missing function does not focus it. The singleton anchors it in to one particular area, it highlights the planet involved, it highlights the house that's involved, it draws the energy into that particular area. The missing function has no place to attach itself to. It floats. It's loose. And I think, at this point, rather than more definitions, you have to experience more and more of it before it really begins to sink in. There's only so far one can go with definitions and then you have to begin to experience it.

Audience: How can one work with a missing function?

Richard: Well, just because there's nothing there, it's still archetypal and there is something within us that hungers for completion, awareness, and consciousness. You can trust that either the will of the Gods, or the Fates, or the desire for completion within will pull us toward that completion. And we do find it don't we? That's why you find Mark Spitz[1] ending up as a swimmer; Goethe[2] and Schiller[3] ending up as writers; Byron and Keats with their missing Fire ending up writing romantic poetry. So trust that there is something innately desiring completion within us that will find it.

Here's where insight can lead to change. If the insight of looking at your chart, instead of terrifying you, says "Aha! Well, I have missing Water in my chart, what am I going to do about that? Maybe I ought to go into some depth psychotherapy. Maybe I ought to go into music. Maybe I should check myself out to see if I'm being clean and complete about my feelings." Someone may say, "I have a missing function in Earth, where am I manifesting that?" Rather than being terrified and simply saying, "Oh, my God, there's something wrong there, I'm going to do without forever. There's something wrong with me. I'm a mess!" say instead, "How am I manifesting this missing function in Earth? How am I dealing with it? Am I over-eating? Am I addicted to drugs and alcohol? Am I obsessed with making money?" Do you see what I'm saying? You'll always do *something* with it, but there's a proper sacrifice to be made to each archetype.

Let's say you have no planets in Fire in your chart, you lack energy and vitality, but you're married to Mr. Fire. You're doing *something* with it, but is that the best and the most you can do? Or, you're missing Earth and you're making up for it by eating. Well, you're doing *something* with it and maybe you have to eat until you become 450 pounds before you say, "Hey! Maybe it's time for me to do something else with it." So we're doing stuff with it all the time, perhaps psychological defense mechanisms, but it doesn't just stop and cease to function.

Audience: So what's the proper sacrifice for the proper God at the proper time and in the proper place?

---

1. American swimmer who won record seven gold medals at the 1972 Olympic Games.
2. Johann Wolfgang von Goethe (1749-1832): Generally recognized as one of the greatest and most versatile European writers and thinkers of modern times. Best known for his dramatic poem *Faust*.
3. Johann Christoph Friedrich von Schiller (1759-1805): German poet, dramatist, philosopher and historian, with liberty and dignity for all as the overriding theme in all his works.

Richard: That's called the mystery of existence, but it's an important question, too. That is hopefully what our knowledge of astrology and our examination of our own astrological chart can tell us. That is what we should be looking at in the chart, not to terrify us, but to say, "With Pluto in Leo in the 9th house, what is the sacrifice?" Pluto always requires a going down into the underworld, a death and rebirth. The Leo requires what? The awakening of the heart. The awakening of creativity. To become one's own Hero. And, if you understand the archetypes of the signs, you'll pull it out.

At the seminar in Orvieto, Italy, we spent a whole week going over the archetypal promise and metaphor behind the twelve signs. Listen to the tapes of that conference, *The Hero's Journey*,[4] if you haven't already done so. Each thing requires its own sacrifice. You don't sacrifice the Venus in the same way you do the Sun. The house tells you the arena in your life in which you must sacrifice that. If you have a planet in the 10th house, you cannot sacrifice to it by marrying someone to do it for you, although that may originally be what you attempt to do. Ultimately you probably will not find that satisfying.

So if you know what the planet *means*, you know what the planet *wants*. Neptune wants you to dissolve. You must dissolve in order to open yourself up to the psychic, intuitive realm. If you're hard and closed and tight and rigid (that's why scientists have such a hard time with metaphysics), if your belief system has declared for Mercury above all else, the rational mind above all else, then Neptune is seen as a threat. The point of the fact is, if you look back on your life to see the sacrifices that were *forced* from you, you will see the area in which you need sacrificing. That's because the god doesn't sit there mildly waiting for you to say, "Okay, here's your bowl of cosmic oatmeal!" No. The Gods, the archetypes, are out there all the time and you choose the sacrifice. Remember what I said a few days ago, in order to sacrifice something, you have to acknowledge it first. So you're not sacrificing anger by never getting angry. You have to *own* it first and if you are not in touch with or asserting your anger and living with it, you cannot sacrifice it.

I think what happens so often among astrologers is we look at the chart and all we see is a chamber of horrors. "I don't want Pluto under any circumstances," is really what people are saying. "Please

4. *The Hero's Journey*, 16 tapes. Available from Pegasus Tapes, P. O. Box 419, Santa Ysabel, CA, 92070.

take me out and let me have a Pluto-ectomy!" or Saturn, or Neptune or Mars, or whatever it is. The bottom line is, "I don't want it, thank you very much!" But, that's not an option. So how do you make your peace with it? How do you learn to live with it? You see, that's what we should be looking at the astrological chart to determine, not terrifying ourselves into immobility, and I have to agree that it's exhausting. Life is exhausting. *The Magic Thread* unwinding down to the heart of the labyrinth is not for the purpose of getting a peanut and jelly sandwich. It is a Hero's Journey, and at the bottom is a Minotaur waiting for you.

What is the difference between the Hero and all the rest? Why is the Hero a particular archetype? The Hero is the one who girds his or her sword by their side and goes out and says, "I challenge my life." We move from Aries to Taurus to Gemini to Cancer to Leo to Virgo and on through the cycle. The twelve signs of the zodiac are a *process of unfolding* in life. We go from the divinity of the awareness of one's existence in Aries to the focus on the material world of safety and security in Taurus, which then again we must leave in order to go into the world of Gemini where mind is awakened. There we learn to walk and talk, and we now separate ourselves from this magical Eden. Then Cancer is the parting with the mother, the breaking of the umbilical cord, and as we go from babyhood to childhood to adolescence to adulthood, something must be sacrificed along the way.

In order to go from babyhood to childhood, what has to be sacrificed? Helpless dependence. In order to go from childhood to adolescence what has to happen? A wider awareness of "the other" and in a way, innocence must be sacrificed. When we go from adolescence to adulthood, what must be sacrificed? To some extent, the dependency upon peer-approval in order to achieve individuality. Do you see what I'm saying? But what we want is, we want it both ways. We want to have it without having to give anything up for it. We want to drag intact through our life our infantile dependency needs, our childhood innocence, and our desire to say, "Somebody out there has all the answers, not me." That's our romantic desire, which I call the Venus stage, that is very normally connected with adolescence. "Somebody out there, some magical person, is going to come into my life and transform me and we'll go off into the sunset and live happily ever after." That's an archetype. It's very much connected with the ideals of Venus and in developmental themes, it is particularly connected with adolescence. We want to keep that dream intact and take it into our lives. I was working with a woman very recently who is 80 years old and has been a Yoga teacher for many years. She is very enlightened and has degrees from European universities. She wanted me to look at her chart and tell her when she was going to find the wonderful man in her life that she has been waiting for all this time!

So, you see, the point I'm making is that everything is appropriate to a certain time and place in our lives, and part of the sacrifice is saying, "If I am evolving, then I must in some way give something up in order to become something else." The word evolving comes from two Latin words out of Greek, *volare* and *evolvere*. *Volare* means ascending up, and *evolvere* means unfolding, like the petals of the lotus. You can't be the flower and the bud at the same time. *If you're going to be a flower, you must give up your bud-ness, and once the flower goes to seed, you must be prepared to sacrifice your flower-ness.* Life is full of sacrifices that are demanded of us. If you're a mother, you must give up certain things within your life, freedom for example, and the desire to be the infant yourself. Youth and beauty and health are all taken away from us one after another.

Scott Peck says it very beautifully in his book, *The Road Less Traveled*.[5] He says, that we must sacrifice the innocence of our childhood, the dreams of adolescence, the pride of adulthood, the opportunity to win, and that every relationship, no matter how dear or wonderful, must some day be taken away from us. Your children, if they're normal and healthy and happy, will eventually have to leave home. That's a sacrifice on the part of the mother and the father as well as on the child. But what about the person who is not prepared to do that? "Yes, I let you go, but I don't want to let you go. I want it both ways." The gods don't like that and that's where the gods come in and intervene. And we say, "Look at these terrible events that are happening to me," but it's the gods saying, "Well, you naughty person, you want your cake and eat it too!"

---

5. M. Scott Peck, *The Road Less Traveled* (London: Hutchinson, 1978; New York: Simon & Schuster, 1988).

So, if you were to find the most perfect mate, the idealized-other in your life, if that kind of gift should ever come to you, what you have to be aware of is that some day you'll have to leave each other. So it is a fact that we as human beings, as mortals, are capable of dying and that gives us the capacity for evolving. The gods do not evolve and they're jealous of us for that. They are fixed, they are immortal, they are archetypal and none of them ever change. *So the gift of evolution is at the price of our mortality,* and what happens is that we want to become as the immortals, we want it all. And we want it all right now. And we want opposites at the same time without giving up the other. That's why we have so much trouble with oppositions in our society, because oppositions imply either/or and we say, "Well, if I can't have this and I can't have that, you know what I'm going to do? I'm not going to have either one. I'll show you, I'm going to sit here and sulk until I can have them both." Never mind that I could do this first and then do that, or this in this part of my lifetime and that in that part of my lifetime. Or, how can I take this opposition and paradox it and turn it into something like the Orientals will do: "Do you want the black one or the white one?" and I'll say, "Thank you, yes."

So that's what I'm referring to when I talk about sacrifices. It's interesting that the Latin roots of the word sacrifice means "to make holy," and that's what our chart should show us. However, I think what happens to us is that we want to use astrology to figure out how we can have all pleasure and avoid all pain. That's what we do. "If I could just get on top of these transits and these progressions a little better, a little deeper, I can prevent some awfulness from happening to me." It's amazing to watch beginning astrologers (and unfortunately even some who are intermediate or advanced and should know better), running around in perpetual terror of their own chart. We want to look at that astrological chart and say, "Okay, I'm in master astrology and I've got it, this is it, this is the answer." It isn't *it*, because the deeper you become, the wider your perception, and the deeper and wider your chart becomes. As you know, if you've studied astrology for years and years, your chart is changing all the time isn't it? But it isn't your chart that is changing, it's your *perceptions* that are changing. There is no given answer. You can't say, "Richard, look at my Saturn in Cancer in the 2nd house and tell me how to sacrifice to that," as if there is a formula. That's the attraction of going to the typical astrology reading. Somebody says, "Give me all the answers. Look at this piece of paper, look at my life and put me all together." And it probably takes them at least two hours to do that!

Audience: But in a counseling session shouldn't we tell people what their central themes are in life?

Richard: Actually, we all already know our central themes, but we don't know that we know them. All of you know what's going on in your life. Get into your process and see what's happening with you— where are your aches and pains?

As an astrologer-counselor, I'm concerned with what is called the *presenting problem*. When somebody comes into a consultation I say, "Why are you here?" And hopefully within ten minutes I'll know what's going on, what the ache is. And the presenting problem is not always the fundamental life-issue, but we must deal with what is here and present right now. What's happening to you now? Are you having trouble in a relationship? Do you see a pattern in that? Is it a health problem? Are you lost and concerned about your life direction? I promise you that it's not a great mystery going from the inside out. Going from the outside in, look at the chart. Where is the singleton? What is the missing function? Is there a conflict based around a major configuration? Check out the focal point of the T-cross. What sign and house is it in? And is there a formula for how to deal with that? No there isn't.

As astrologers, one of the things we must sacrifice is that there is "good" and "bad" in the chart. There isn't. It is so hard for all of us. I learned astrology from the Max Heindel school of astrology, where if you have Mars square Saturn you were nibbled to death by rabid wombats in the public square at Full Moon. So many of us have learned that stuff—that Saturn is a major malefic—and once you've taken that in with your basic study of astrology, can you ever then contemplate a transit of Saturn or a Saturn return without terror? And that is the main sacrifice you have to give up. You have to have your Saturn because if you didn't, you wouldn't have any backbone or skin and you'd fall to the floor in a puddle of goo.

That's the problem. We're saying, "Oh, I've got a bad transit coming up,"—a debilitated something or that horrible word "affliction"—"I have an afflicted Moon in my chart." Well, every time you say that, *you're* the one who is afflicting your Moon. Each time you say that, you're establishing that Moon as being afflicted. Now, sacrifice giving up the word "affliction." Why do people like things like malefics and afflictions and bad houses and everything? It's a good excuse. "Well naturally I can't remember anything; how could anyone with retrograde Mercury in Pisces opposing Neptune in the 12th?" That's that, and I'm sorry. "Naturally I have a bad temper, with Mars conjunct Uranus in Aries, wouldn't you?" So I call this the metaphysical cop-out and a lot of us love our astrology for that reason. I know people who have been studying astrology for twenty-five or thirty years who still do that. "How are you?" I'll say to a friend astrologer I haven't seen in many years. "Well, Saturn is on my Ascendant," and I'm supposed to understand that that means "awful," right? Or, "My progressed Moon just conjuncted Uranus," and I'm supposed to say, "Oh, pity you, you poor, poor thing."

Audience: You said we all know our themes, and I'm not sure we do, because our themes lie in our unconscious, and that's such a subjective part of us that it's difficult to objectify.

Richard: But you don't ever *know* your theme. All you can know is what you know now. And so the point is, how best can you know what it is you know now?

There are techniques for doing it. Psychotherapy is one. How many of you have been in on-going, depth psychotherapy? If you have I believe you're intuiting a little bit of what I'm talking about. How do you find these things out? The student of Zen once said to the Master, "You're a man of great wisdom. What is the path that I should follow?" and the Master replied, "My child, follow the path that has *heart* for you, because all paths lead to the same place anyway." So, if you pursue your dream, pursue your passion, that itself will lead you to unfolding. Is it music? Is it dance? Is it drama? Is it astrology? Is it understanding the world? Is it botany? It doesn't matter. Whatever charges you with passion will lead you down the labyrinth. That's what makes the Hero and Heroine of us all. The only thing that gets us to break the umbilical cord and go out in search of the Holy Grail is the desire to say, "There's something out there that I need and want and I wish to pursue." If we sit back, still enfolded in a kind of psychic fetal position, we're not going to find it, or we're going to have a great deal of trouble finding it. So, there are techniques. Dream work is a wonderful technique. Record your dreams. Your dreams will tell you, over a period of time, what is going on in the unconscious.

See if you can shift your examination of what events mean to a different level. In other words, instead of seeing events as things out there that happen to me—the *cause* is out there and happening to *me*, (the effect)—turn it around and say, "What is this event symbolizing to me in my process of on-going self-discovery, awareness and consciousness?" One of the things we astrologers do is separate ourselves from the event. "Uranus came to my 7th house and divorced me." You see, that's how we tend to think of it. Rather than, "What does Uranus signify archetypally? What does the 7th house mean? What does the event that happened mean to my own process?" Or, in other words, "Why have I happened to this event?" We talk about things as happening to us rather than we happened to it, or we were open to it. We see relationships as accidents that happen by fate. They aren't. You know, the Greeks had a saying: "Man be wary as you walk down the road. Around the bend you may meet the Goddess herself." So the gods and goddesses come to us archetypally in the forms of the relationships in our lives. What does it *mean*? Peel the onion. Life is a perpetual process of onion-peeling. You think you have it down, then you have another layer and you get closer to the heart. And what happens when you peel an onion? You cry. It isn't easy.

Audience: The basic astrology textbooks that many of us have read and learned are so terribly negative.

Richard: Yes, I agree, but that's changing. I read the same books that everybody else did, I was brought up on that, too. Then, after about a year of terror, I said to myself, "No, wait a minute. There has to be something else other than that." So it's not enough just to say I got bad food. Make the food better. Now you have books by wonderful people like Stephen Arroyo, Liz Greene and so on, so now you have something else. Here is the sacrifice. Can you give up what you first learned? That's not easy and I don't kid around when I call myself a born-again astrologer. I went through one crisis when I first got into astrology and I said, "By God, it works!" Then after several years, I had another catastrophic experience and said, "But, wait a minute, it doesn't work this way."

In addition to the astrological cop-out, we also have the psychological cop-out. "Ah, my parents did it to me." It's very easy to do that. Again, cause is out there and effect is me. You know, in the days when Freudian theory was popular you said, "I had a negative mother and I was never breastfed and father was away from home and there were all these Oedipal things going on and then little sister came along and got all the attention and she was the pretty one— well, no wonder I'm damaged!" Isn't that nice? You can go the rest of your life like that. First of all you find a therapist who agrees with that. "Yes you are a poor damaged person because you got these bad parents. And we also agree that probably you'll remain wounded the rest of your life, but we'll do what we can. I'll see you next Thursday for your fifty-five minute hour." So there's a danger in that kind of trap, too.

Many astrologers also will say, "You had better come in for your six–month checkup because transiting Uranus is coming on to your Midheaven." So do we make our money by fear and terrorizing people, or do we free them? *Agape* is the love of the gods that says, "I love you by freeing you," and the gods have given us the gift of astrology, not to bind us and terrify us, but to free us. If you are still of the Max Heindel school of astrology where things are terrible and there are malefics, where trines are good and squares are bad and the 12th house is evil, and you are still intent upon living in this kind of psychic dark night of the jungle, then you're probably having a real hard time here this week. The kinds of things I'm teaching are based upon the assumptions that you know what I mean when I talk about archetypes, and process, and evolution, so if you're literalizing this stuff, you're going to terrify yourself. When I talk about Mengele's Pluto in the 12th house, someone grabs a notebook and starts looking through the family, "Oh my god, Junior has that!" Or I say, here's somebody with a Moon, Mars, Uranus in the chart and talk about the damage coming from the mother, and somebody says, "My god, my child has that! What have I done to my child?"

We should be at the stage in astrology now when we can think in terms of *principles*. I had a professor in pre-med when I was going to be a doctor and he was talking about diseases. He said, "This is the first day of the class and we're going to be talking about pathology all during this semester. What I would like all of you to do is within the first two weeks, please choose for yourself one or two appropriate horrors and stay with them all semester. Please don't have *everything* we talk about. If it's going to be the Bubonic Plague stay with it, don't shift into Diphtheria, it's too confusing and it's hard on me." It's the same thing in a beginning psychology class. Everything you hear you say, "Yep, that's it, I know that's me. That's what I've got, I know it!" I remember when I first had an abnormal psychology class, I was ready to kill myself. "That's it, I know that's me. Yep, schizogenic mother, that's right. Tendency toward addiction, melancholia, yep, that's it, I know it's all me." But there's a time and a place for that. In the beginning you learn by personalizing, you learn by saying, "What does that have to do with me?" And then, by golly, give it up! Let go of it, grow up, let go, break the cord, become whole. If you've studied astrology for more than two years and you're not doing it, you had better really rethink it.

I want to get into some of these issues and then I want to get into the chart of Lynnie Ozer, because I think it's important also that you see there is triumph in the world. That a person who has suffered very greatly can, through the suffering, arrive at a new awareness and awakening. And I hope you haven't read her story and come to the conclusion that she has achieved enlightenment and now all her troubles are done. Because, if you have seen that, you've misread it. It doesn't work that way. But right now I want to talk about another particular problem and that's the idea that if something is wrong, someone must be to blame. It's either Lucifer's fault, the snake's fault for coming in and tempting me with the apple, or it's Eve's fault for having tasted the apple, and it's Eve's fault for having tempted Adam, and it's Adam's fault for being weak and taking it. Ultimately, it's God's fault for setting up the whole paradox in the first place. So, part of us really believes that if there is pain or hurt in the world, there's a wrongness around that rather than a rightness. But pain is a natural part of the process. That's why we have three Water signs in the zodiac—Water signs constellate the quality of pain.

Remember we mentioned before that in the archetypal scheme of things there is a borderline between Cancer and Leo? That's where

we fall between the Personal and Social. There's a borderline between Scorpio and Sagittarius and another one between Pisces and
Aries. We do Fire-Earth-Air-Water in a particular orientation and
then we must shift. A transformative experience must happen, a
kind of umbilical cord must be broken in order to go on to the next
level. And that's the sacrifice and pain inherent in the Water signs.
Cancer says, "If you're going to move out from Personal to Social,
you must break your psychic umbilical cords to your family and
your past." That's not easy to do, it's painful and how many people
do it? Not a lot. Maybe, even in this room, not a lot. Scorpio says, "If
I'm going to move on from the realm of the Social to the Universal,
something must die in me. I must die to the world and face the
dragons, release myself so I can be born again on to the Universal
level." That's not easy, not many people make that. Why? What's the
opposite of Scorpio? Taurus. And Taurus says, "Thank you very much
but I'll sit here under the Yum-Yum tree and eat a banana!" It's so
much more comfortable. The same thing happens when we move
from Pisces to Aries. We have to sacrifice chaos. This is what Jesus
was talking about in his parables, if you just listen. He says, "He
who is last shall be first." You must surrender everything in order to
be born again. That's what he meant. You have to accept the sacrifice in Pisces before there is a rebirth into Aries.

So we can't hang on and give it up at the same time. You know,
Buddhists have done the Buddha and Christians have done the
Christ. Something I read recently put it very nicely, "Buddhists have
forgotten the Buddha's sorrow and Christians have forgotten Christ's
joy." We tend to think in that simple black and white. The world is
not just a veil of tears. Christ took his suffering on the cross gladly.
It's called a *passion*. That didn't mean he was hot for being up on
the cross, that's not what passion means. It means he gave of himself totally and caringly. If you're a Christian, that's what you should
understand from that beautiful act of communion. By taking in the
symbolic blood and body of Christ, you're sharing in his sacrifice
and redemption. What a beautiful, powerful thing that is if you believe that.

Now, for you who have begun to guilt yourselves by looking at
the Moon in your children's charts and thinking, "Oh my God, what
have I done to my child!" let me say this. Things do not begin with

parents. You came from someplace, too. If you take a look at charts generationally, you'll see patterns of how things descend through families until finally someone stands up and says, "No more!" Now that person is often rejected by the family because he or she is breaking the family myth, whatever it is. It may be that women are weak and helpless and vulnerable and should not be powerful and educated. Then along comes one woman in that chain, it may take ten generations to do it, and she says, "I am the one that's going to be the exception." Well, she's got a struggle ahead of her.

So remember that we have family myths. I don't like to think in terms of victims and victimizers. You haven't done anything to your child. All you can bring to a child is what you, yourself, are at a given moment. It's not your fault that you are where you are in your process, you're on-going, too. And another thing to realize is that we know enough about astrology to see that there is something in human nature that is innate, you're born with that given chart. I mean, I don't think there's a little bureaucracy up in heaven that's saying, "Here's someone who is going to be born into this chart—Moon conjunct Mars, Pluto, Saturn in the 4th house—let's look at our files and find a terrible mother." And it's your child and you look and say, "They chose me, I was a terrible mother." So remember, there is something innate in the astrological chart that says that a given child is going to mythologize events and the relationships in life, whatever they may be, in a certain way. That's why I don't do the astrological charts of newborn babies. There's nothing you can say to the parent that doesn't horrify them. Nothing. "Your child will be rich and famous." "Oh my God, it will have no privacy!" "Your child will be sensitive." "Oh, the poor thing will be wounded." "Your child will be a great intellect." "Oh, oh, he'll be standing out from the crowd, he'll be abnormal, the kids will poke fun at him." There's nothing you can say about a newborn child, because all of the parent's hopes and projections dump upon it.

So remember, as I said before, what is the basic ground of the experience we live in, what is our mythology? It's based partly on the idea of the collective archetype and I don't care how much you love your child, you can't make it not die. That child is going to die someday because death is archetypal. And that's the basic fear of the parent, "I want to protect my child from all this *awfulness*." I don't mean just physically dying, I mean the emotional dying that is constantly part of life. If you can't accept it in your own life, you can't have that gift to give to your child. If you're still trying to hang on to Eden and live in that kind of magical world, then that's one gift you don't have for your child. Protecting your child from pain and suffering is not the gift it appears to be. Naturally, you don't want the child to go out in the street and get run over by a car. Naturally it hurts you to see your child come home with a black eye and say the other little children have been cruel to me. It hurts you, you want to protect the child, but you don't do the child any favor by believing, "My inadequacy is apparent and has caused this hurt in this child." And you don't do the child any favor by saying, "Here, my dear child, come back in Eden with mother where everything is safe and I'll protect you from this." That's no help.

I know a lot of stuff is being evoked in you this week and the on-going process of dying and rebirth is not easy, but Sagittarius follows Scorpio and you don't get truth until you slay the dragon. You don't get the act of grace and redemption without the crisis and catharsis, the dying and rebirth that comes with Scorpio. So, all I can say is, it's archetypal that we all must die, it's archetypal that we all know it and it's archetypal that we all don't *want* to know about it. So the way most of us deal with it is to stay in Taurus and not become aware. We stay innocent, refuse to bite the apple or take any risks in life because it smells like the pit, like the underworld, in which case we do not develop or evolve. And that's what the myth of Eden and the apple is all about. It's the myth of dying—you die to your innocence, are expelled from Eden and reborn. Cherubim and Seraphim with flaming swords guard the way and you can never go back. Well, not everybody elects to bite the apple; we would rather live in our unconsciousness. If you choose to live in your unconscious, okay, that's your choice, but then you wouldn't be sitting here, right? And, although it isn't easy, remember that it is the capacity for being mortal that gives you a soul—the gods are soulless. It is the capacity for dying that makes you able to love. You can love your man, you can love your woman, you can love your child—the gods have no capacity for love, they only lust. It gives you the capacity for artistic creativity—the gods do not do that in and of themselves. They sponsor it, but they do not create it. I hear a lot of people saying, "I want the rose without the thorn, tell me how to do it. I want the rose without the root, I want the rose to stay forever blooming and not to drop its seeds." Or, "I accept that it has to happen and I want you to tell me how to accept it." I can't do that because there is no formula for that. It's what life is all about— teaching us for our fifty or sixty or seventy or eighty years, how to do that. First of all, it is accepting that it *is* and then the rest of your life is, "How do I now cope with it and live with it?"

Now what if you're a dominant Earth function and your husband is a dominant Water function? Both of you have inferior functions in Air and along comes this dominant Air function child. Whose fault is it that there is difficulty in the relationship? Is it your fault because you have dominant Earth and inferior Air? No. Now, is it your job to try and work on increasing your airy function? Well, maybe in one sense that's why you were given a child with a dominant Air function, to help you become aware of that. Maybe that child rejects you on first look. You know, I believe the chart extends itself beyond the paper—it's a living thing and there's an aura. The child feels, "I'm a dominant airy type and you're earthy, I don't like your energy—stand back from me." Parents intuit that children reject parents, it isn't just the other way around.

I think there's another problem in our society and that is that the arts should be helping us to cope with these questions and these crises. And, just like the church has let us down at this point, arts have let us down. As Aristotle said very clearly, "The purpose of drama or music is the idea of catharsis." Drama, by the way, began as a religious ritual—a religious ritual in worship of Dionysus, He of the multiple personality and He of the demonic and He who gets torn apart into pieces and hopefully is resurrected again. The Dionysian rituals gave birth originally to theater, but what is the point? What is theater supposed to do? It enacts archetypes. And, according to Aristotle, the shared pity and terror is a catharsis for the group. For example, Medea is so enraged at being betrayed by her lover that she slaughters both her children. The community, by being able to join together to watch this horrible action, experiences a catharsis and cleansing. In other words, she gets to do that for me. I don't have to do that—she symbolically acts that out for me. And the reason that it works as a catharsis or a cleansing is that two elements must be combined. Not just the terror and the horror of this woman who has killed these children, but *pity*. You pity her even in the horrible thing that she has done. That's what good drama is all about.

Now, what's happened to us in our day is, unfortunately, we've forgotten the pity, so in order to increase the effect, we keep escalating the terror. I mean, there's terror enough in this world without turning it to our entertainment media, but the moguls and the powers that be look around and say, "Well, that's what the people want, more violence, more bloodshed." You know you see the typical kind of violence on TV and in films today and you don't get the cathartic experience. Why? Take *The Godfather* as an example, or *The Shining*, or *Jaws*, or whatever, there's no catharsis. You walk out of that kind of experience saying, "Yuck! The human condition is lousy. People are lousy. I feel sullied, I feel dirty having exposed myself to this and I don't care if they all die." That's no catharsis.

So, we are in a period now of great transformation. The old things have not worked and many of the new ones are not yet formed. The things that the church is supposed to give us, the ritual of cleansing and renewal, whether it's Yom Kippur among Jews or the Easter resurrection among Christians, we've lost a lot of that. And I'm not saying we should go back and find it again, but we haven't gotten to what the next thing is yet, so it's awfully hard. We're cut adrift. Frankly, I think part of our process and evolution is that we've cut our moorings from the old stuff that has worked for us in the past and there are no new answers for us. This is forcing us inward on ourselves toward a greater process of individuation, and people are hurting now. And I'd rather not think of it as a win/lose situation, because that gets us stuck in that dichotomy. Possibly, our collective unconscious needs to learn pity, or to remember it.

Now I want to talk about some polarities. The basic seven planets, and particularly the basic five—Moon, Mercury, Venus, Sun, and Mars—are the planets of our day to day living experience. These are the normal things that get us through our life. Planets of survival. Day to day living. It's the three outer planets I want to focus on for a moment and what their transpersonal effect means. These are the planets that link us to the collective, to the archetypal. Most traditional text books do not have many nice things to say about them, because when Uranus, or Neptune, or Pluto come into our life they are always upsetting. That is their very nature. And, of course, in typical fashion, when they began to be discovered, astrologers decided all three were malefics. If you don't understand it, make it a malefic. Other people try to say, "Well, they're so far out they don't really affect you on a personal level, they're only collective or transpersonal. Therefore, if you're going to have an aspect between them, it has to be 2° or they don't really work." Well, they do very much work! These planets are the link between the personal and the collective, and they come as a gift from the gods, from the Universe, to help us in our transformation.

Moon through Saturn: Moon says, "Here is the beginning and the origin and everything is safely tucked into the womb," and part of us wants that. Saturn says, "Here is the limit of the real world, here are the boundaries of the real world, according to what a particular society at a given time says it is." What is reality? Reality is relative. Saturn defines the reality of the group at a particular time and place. In the 17th century, if you didn't believe in witches, you were considered crazy or one yourself. Today, if you *do* believe in witches, you're considered crazy. So below the Saturn world, reality shifts. For instance, take the Victorian times when dress codes were very strictly organized. My grandmother had a terrible reputation in Chicago because when she got off the trolley she would lift her skirts high enough that the boys who gathered around could see her ankles. She, in her own day, was a Uranian figure and a scandal to her community. So the labels that we put on these things are relative.

Above the Saturn world, reality does *not* shift because here we are dealing on the archetypal level and that is forever. We may *perceive* things differently, but they themselves are not. So it's Uranus, Neptune, and Pluto who help us. They are our good friends, our counselors who help us break through these structures. What is it that young pilot said about flying? "To break the surly bonds of earth and touch the face of God." Saturn is "the surly bonds of earth," and it's Uranus, Neptune, and Pluto who help us break that bond. But the earthy part of us that wants to remain in Eden doesn't like it. That's the part of us that is a cry-baby and says, "Leave me alone," or, "Let me levitate and go up to the sky and up to the clouds, but let me do it without having to pay a price and not hurt too much, please." So the gift of Uranus, Neptune, and Pluto is always a double-edged sword.

Let me explain individually with each one what they do. The function of Uranus is to shatter ego—Sun (Leo) and Uranus (Aquarius) are natural opposites. At some point in our development it is extremely necessary and critical that we establish who we are. Just looking at the symbol of the Sun, I think, shows us that. It's a circle with a dot in the middle. To me it looks a little like an egg with a yolk in the center and I like that as an image. It's like there's a hard little shell around here and when we're young that shell is very soft, like a young egg is, then gradually as we begin to develop and grow, that shell hardens and hardens. What is that other planet that is opposite the Sun? Saturn. So, this shell around you protects this soft, developing soul or self or greater person. If there were no protective shell here you'd get the *boundary-less* person. Here's where you get into things like severe psychopathology, the borderline kind of personality, or ultimately even going into psychosis. So we need that shell around this growing spot that might be the core of ourself. But what happens is that Saturn tends to harden and harden until finally there's no more room for growing inside.

Along about that time we summon Uranus in—Uranus the shatterer, the awakener, the trickster who yanks the rug out from underneath. Humpty Dumpty falls off the wall and all the king's horses and all the king's men can never put him back together again, but it might make a good omelet! So what happens with Uranus is archetypal and it doesn't matter whether or not Uranus is in aspect to the Sun in the chart. It is a shattering of ego and the ego rebuilds and forms itself again. Then along comes Uranus and shatters it again, but if it doesn't do that, instead of being motile or in process, we become rigid and stuck. There are a lot of people who do that and say, "No great disasters ever happen to me, isn't my life wonderful?" "I am the same person I've always thought of myself all my life, nothing has really happened to shift and change." And maybe some of us see that and think it would be the most desirable thing in the world, if only that could be me! So that's why the Greeks said, "The gods love best those they try the most," or they say, "The gods will not give you anything you cannot handle."

Audience: You call Uranus the trickster, doesn't that mean playing a joke or prank?

Richard: No, not to me. I differentiate the trickster from the prankster and it's my own derivation, it's not Jungian. The prankster is the one who is only playful or mischievous, but the trickster uses a quick and artful way of getting a result—he makes you see the light. The trickster in Shakespeare's *King Lear* is the Fool, and interestingly enough, that's why in the royal court we always constellate the King and the Fool. The Fool always wears this sort of funny crown. He satirizes everything that happens. He gets away with everything in the court. He lifts up the Queen's skirts and all taboos are broken for the Fool. It's also interesting that some of us are even caught into that archetype where we play that we are the fool, the awakener, the trickster, with our jingling bells and the skull on the stick. We bang the king on the head and like the fool in *Lear* who says, "Prithee master, I think *I* am truly the King and *thou* art the Fool." And the King says, "Truly, Fool, I think thou art right!"

So it is the king within us that is shattered by our archetypal fool, and that is the trickster that comes along and says, "Hey, get off your throne, your high place here and come tumbling down off the wall and shatter a little and reform. It's okay, it will all come back together again." That's where fate is so important. It's helpful to have parents who say, "I know you're suffering, my child. I can't take away the suffering but I'm here for you, I understand and I'll help to the limits of my experience. I can't make it better, it's not my fault, it's not the fault of the Universe, it is just that way. Now, what are you going to do about it?" Uranus is a gift, but it's a gift with a double-edged sword. It's not a pleasant thing to have happen and it's not easy. I remember a Uranian experience that I had when I was first exposed to astrology. It shattered my whole world concept, and of course, my conception of who I was. I was a science major in school, I considered myself a very rational person and I knew astrology was nonsense. Yet I started reading books and I had my chart done and then I knew it wasn't nonsense. What happened? Crack went the egg! And it doesn't feel good when it's happening, but if you can see it *in process* you see the gift.

A sudden break in a relationship is painful for you. It shatters your illusion of who you are. What if you're married and you've taken your whole ego-identity from your relationship and you've gone unconscious? You haven't seen what's going on in the relationship, because for you it's a kind of Eden. Suddenly your husband comes home one day and says, "Well, kid, I'm marrying my secretary." And you say, "I didn't even know anything was wrong!" Well, you constellated the trickster. It's not his fault you didn't know anything was wrong. Do you see what I'm saying? Uranus comes as what seems to be *the unexpected event*. The only reason it's unexpected is because the limitations on our ego prevent us from seeing what is going to happen next. Our ego says, "No, no, no, I don't want to look at that." Like somebody brought up before, we know we have to die but how do we face that? I don't know. That's a mystery, I don't know. The way most of us face it is by not facing it, so when it comes (Pluto), it comes as such an overwhelming thing. And again, a part of that is cultural. We live in a culture that does not honor death, doesn't face it, doesn't look at it, we don't like pain. We think that if we buy enough things and eat enough things and own enough things that we will in some way be like the pharaohs who spent millions and millions on building pyramids and taking all their treasures to incur an afterlife. Well, we do the same thing, but where the pharaohs built treasures in their next life, we try to do it in this one.

Let's take Mercury and Neptune. Here you get another shattering. Mercury says, "Hey kids, this is how it is." Mercury is our capacity to put into cognition and logical structure the sensual world around us. Mercury is our way of labeling and valuing the things we see, smell, touch, hear, taste. After Adam and Eve were in the Garden of Eden, the first thing they went about doing was giving everything names. Because to give it a name, the name has a meaning. All names come from meanings, there's etymologies in words and the word is the value. "In the beginning was the word." And among the ancient Jews, in fact all ancient peoples, the word, the name, the God, is so important that it cannot even be said, because to say it is to touch in on that numinous kind of power.

So Mercury, on a more psychological level, is our rational, cognitive mind and all the things we've learned, also all the things we've heard. It is through Mercury, as well as the Moon, that we take in our family values, our family myths. How do we do that? We sit around the fire and Grandma tells us, or Father or Mother in their admonitions to us, tell us the family tales. They tell us our epic. Just like the Greeks heard about their origins sitting around the fire and hearing the bard sing of the heroes who went to fight at Ilium.[6] So we all get that as part of our family tradition—the prejudices, the ideas of what reality ought to be—on the level of Mercury. Mercury is a far more important planet in the chart than we often give it credit for being. I mean, it's many other things besides, but it is at least that. Now what Neptune does, the gift of Neptune, is it sabotages all that. Neptune says, "No, that's not right." Neptune is the illusive illusion maker, the one who blows fog and mist that covers up what appears to be the truth. It is the deceiver, the illusionist, the mesmerizer, the magician that pulls the rabbit out of the hat. "Wait a minute, I don't think I saw what I just saw!" "Well, maybe you did and maybe you didn't," says Neptune. And does it matter? Yes, it matters, because the Mercury part of us deeply wants to hang on to what we know to be true. This is our cognitive place that keeps us anchored in reality.

How many of you have ever had a psychedelic drug experience? Well, if you have, you know that Neptune goes right for that Mercury, doesn't it? Suddenly, that's not a wall, it's a pulsating bowl of jello! Many of us in the 60s and the 70s wanted to play around with that for many reasons, but we were trying in some way to bring in our Neptune. And of course, as often happens with these transpersonal planets, to touch them is always a danger, and many people burned themselves out on acid trips. (I had a good friend who flew out of a fourteenth story window because he thought he was a bird.) So, when Neptune comes along with its dissolution, we fight it with everything we have. And things are seldom what they seem. Things are different. Things shift and change and Mercury doesn't like that. So one of the things that we hang onto in the Sun is our ego, our self-concept, and a second thing we hang onto in Mercury is our cognitive, human thinking mind that says, "This is how the world is. This is how I am and these are the values that I put on it." I mean, here we are in the South and, up until the 50s, in their mother's milk southern children learned that black people may

6. Ilium or Ilion; name of Troy, meaning city of Ilius, the founder of Troy.

be okay, but they're not part of our world, they're separate. There is almost three hundred years of Mercury information, legend, myth, and fairy tale made in the South. Even religion was dragged into it when it was said that the bible shows that there should be slavery.

So, you don't suddenly wake up one day and say, "Oh, that's been clearly wrong!" In order to get out of that stuck-ness, the transpersonal planets come in. Neptune must, like an acid dripping on something, eventually dissolve Mercury. "Wait a minute, maybe that's not true." A famous scientist once said that a new scientific idea never prevails by convincing anybody. It's when a new generation grows up who has learned that idea from the very beginning that it becomes part of their system. So if you think that scientists are suddenly going to turn around and say, "Isn't astrology a wonderful thing?" forget it! A whole generation of people have to die out. Why? Because our Mercury resists its dissolution by Neptune and the shifting face of reality.

In academia, the astrologer's Neptune is playing to Mercury and academicians resist it. When I first began to present a psychological approach in astrology, do you think I was met with open arms? No, there were insults, books thrown, people got up and walked out of the room. "Who does he think he is with all these negative epithets around Uranus, Neptune, and Pluto." Well, that's part of the change. We do this personally as well as collectively. Societies do the same thing. Societies, in a sense, get their own ego, their own way of thinking, and as soon as we get solidified along comes a collective upheaval—collective Uranus, or Neptune, or Pluto jolts us out of that—and it's painful. It's painful when we have war and revolution and cataclysm in the world, but that's also part of the natural cycle of the universe.

Pluto does the same thing. Venus is Aphrodite, the giver of life and security, she's earth-mother. She's the archetypal ruler of Taurus who says, "Here is the womb and safety and warmth and touching and a nice quiet garden with plenty to eat." Pluto is the rapist that comes in and rips Eve and Adam out of Eden, which should not be described as the *fall* of man, but rather, the *awakening* of man and woman. In leaving Eden, Adam and Eve found their humanity, but it was painful and at a price. Unfortunately, that wonderful story has been misinterpreted. Pluto is the one who rips away the unnatural relationship of mother and daughter—Demeter and Core—and he's the one who always comes like a thief in the night. Pluto is the one who comes and rapes and seduces us and tears us away from this very safe Eden. Well, naturally, we don't like that. The Venusian part of us, the Taurean part of us, (and it's in Venus-Taurus that our basic ground is established), resists with all its might the functions of this Pluto. And that's fine, because if it didn't resist, Pluto wouldn't be interested! That is the dance between Taurus and Scorpio. Pluto goes for the virgin, he doesn't go for the hetaera.[7] Why? Because she already knows. This stuff is attracted to innocence, it's Eden that he wants, it's Eve that he's after, it's Core, the maiden, that he's interested in.

So there is archetypally with it, not only in the collective but within us individually, this Plutonian seducer that seduces us into the underworld to free us from this trap that the earthy parts give us. Is it right and proper that we resist? Darn right! Dylan Thomas,[8] a double Scorpio who ought to know, says, "Do not go gentle into that good night." He's talking about the death of his father and when his father was dying he wrote this poem for him. He doesn't say do not go. He says, "Do not go *gentle* into that good night. Rage, rage against the dying of the light." So that's the difference. Yes, rage against the Pluto coming in and the Neptune and the Mercury. Do not go gently, but *go!* Now, can it be made easier? Well, yes and no. On one level these things are so archetypal and primordial and universal that it can't be made easier. And on another level, it can be made easier. What are the things you do to enrich your life? How can you touch in on these transpersonal levels? Well, *honor* the suffering, *accept* the resistance to the suffering and *accept* the suffering. Follow your heart, live your life, try to become a warrior.

This is what Carlos Castenada is saying. The essential message in all of his Don Juan books is to live the life of a warrior. Be ready, because death is at your hand at every moment. You'll never know

7. In ancient Greece, a professional courtesan or concubine.
8. Dylan Marlais Thomas (10/27/1914—11/9/1953): one of the best-known British poets of the mid-20th Century. Dylan Thomas, "Do Not Go Gentle into That Good Night," from *The Poems of Dylan Thomas* (New York: New Directions Publishing, 1971), lines 1,3.

when he is going to strike and by knowing that, you're free. What he means by being a warrior is not being Yang or Martian, he means being *aware*. Isn't that what they teach you in martial arts? They are not teaching you how to be aggressive, they're teaching you aware-ness. They're teaching you to *see* and there is a part of us that doesn't want to see. That's natural, so don't beat yourself up about that. I mean we do need to protect our ego, we do need to protect our thinking, we do need to protect our basic security system. Of course! That's why these planets are in a constant, dynamic battle. And that's why in a way we do face Uranus, Neptune, and Pluto by transit with a little fear and trembling. Yes, but meet the god halfway.

That's what I'm talking about with "sacrifice" and that's what astrology theoretically ought to be able to give us. Remember what I have said, that clarity does not necessarily lead to change, but know-ing this, can we then prepare ourselves for it? If we know we have dragons to fight, wouldn't it be useful to try and lift the sword a few times first? Toughen up the arm? Develop a little muscle? But as long as we stay regressed into infancy, when we think we don't have to look at all these things by remaining unconscious, they come anyway and then we're not prepared to meet them. Are you follow-ing what I'm saying? So these three wonderful planets are gifts, they're great, great gifts. And they're not nice gifts all the time, in fact, usually they're not. They are shattering experiences. Are they always negative? Well, ultimately, no.

Falling in love is an experience of Uranus, Neptune, or Pluto: we fall passionately, unexpectedly, deeply in love. It shatters our ego, it boggles our way of thinking, and very often it's the completely wrong person you ever thought it would possibly be for you. Re-member the song "Bill" from *Showboat?* "He's not the guy at all" that I had imagined, he's not tall and so on. He's short and dumpy and funny looking and I don't know what it is, but "he's just my Bill." Well, that's what often happens. So along it comes and it shat-ters our way of thinking. Every time we fall passionately, erotically in love, and I don't necessarily mean with a person (you can fall passionately in love with the clay that you're sculpting or the music that you're writing), but every time you do that it shatters you. The person who lives the creative life is on the edge constantly. You see this so clearly in great works of art. You see that caldron churning in there. Listen to the music of Beethoven or Bach and you'll hear it. Look at the works of Michelangelo or Van Gogh and you'll see it. It is the stuff that gives us the gift of this transcendent creativity in our life. Birth and death and all these archetypal things bring it in to us. Is it right that we resist? Yes.

So remember the point. It's not the *not* going into the night, because we all go into the night, it's the not going *gentle* into the night that's important. We honor the resistance and we honor the change. They are both true. If we do not honor the resistance, then we feel guilty, as probably a lot of you are doing now. You may be thinking, "Why am I so stubborn, why am I not getting along with it, I should be totally evolved by now!" Or you may be saying, "God, I've had ten years of psychotherapy and I've still got problems," or, "I've studied astrology for ten years and I'm not enlightened, even though I took a weekend of EST as well!" But you have to honor that part, too—that there is resistance, that change moves slowly, that we grow, that there is a dynamic between what I need to keep myself intact and the things that are going to shatter me apart.

In a natal chart when these three outer planets, Uranus, Neptune, and Pluto, are strongly configured with the personal planets, (Moon, Mercury, Venus, Sun and Mars) you can guarantee that some of these issues are going to be fundamental for you in your life. And I say to you, you are among the blessed, because you are the person who is chosen for greater possibility and enlightenment and the price you pay for that is greater pain and struggle. So each of these planets are not kind to these poor little babies, Moon and Mercury and Venus and Sun and Mars, who just want to go along their own little innocent way. Little Goldilocks is going through the woods and Little Red Riding Hood is thinking she's going to grandmother, not expecting any wolves at all. Then along come these three fellows and wham! So it is painful. In the natal chart, every time one of these three planets makes an aspect to these four inner planets, actually five including Jupiter, but especially the first four, we realize we have a life in which on-going cycles of important shatterings, psychic cataclysms, and transformations will be happening. And one way to sacrifice to the gods, because you've been asking how, is don't resist and don't resist the resistance. Therein lies the paradox and I can't help you out of that. I'm saying what Dylan Thomas said in another way and it's a paradox, it's a quincunx. "Do not go gentle into that good night." You have to go, but don't go gently.

I can tell you one thing you should do, I know you want advice and I will give you advice from my heart. Be as the Zen master said to be, "Follow the path that has heart for you," and that will lead you, willy-nilly, into all of this. What is that path, "follow your heart"? I can't say what your heart must tell you, but don't go to an astrologer and say, "Please look at my chart and tell me what the path of my heart is." Your duty and your destiny is to find your heart and you know where your heart is. You may not *know* that you know, but you know. And the creative experience is so rich and important. It is so important to have something that passionately involves you, I mean *passionately* involves your whole being. Music or art or dance or theater, you don't have to be a professional, just so that it touches your soul, that it does something to you. Not saying, "astrology is my hobby." The minute somebody says "hobby" I immediately know that they've pushed away all the demonic part of it. The Greeks said, "Those who are lucky in life are possessed by their daemon."[9] The daemon of creativity takes you over. The Greeks thought a person who was in love was mad. They would say he's possessed by the daemon Eros or Aphrodite. That person is possessed and has gone temporarily crazy. So we don't really expect rational behavior from this person. The god is with him now.

Audience: What you're saying seems to differ from traditional psychotherapy that tries to help people *adjust*, while what you're saying is to deal with it, but go beyond.

Richard: Exactly. And this is where Jungian and archetypal psychology, and transpersonal psychology, begin to deal with and honor that part. Even psychoanalysis. What are we saying? Analyze the psyche. That's a paradox in and of itself. What we're trying to do is make Mercury and Neptune come together. I'm not saying it can't be done, but it is a paradox.

So it is the transpersonal movement in psychology, the archetypal movements that are able to acquaint us with this wider world outside of ourselves. We don't even have a language to talk about

9. In ancient Greek religion, a supernatural being of secondary rank; also a guardian spirit; genius; also called daimon.

these things—we have to use myths and symbols because we haven't developed that area of our consciousness so we can communicate. And in our desire for doing that we import from the East, but we don't import it all. First of all, what Hinduism or Buddhism or Islam is in the East now is not what it was meant originally, so we're taking the transformed philosophy that already has been transformed in the East and trying to import it West and understand it. We throw around words like Karma and Dharma and Kundalini and Prana and Yoga and we study these arts. I'm not saying we shouldn't do it, it's right that we should do it, but we think, "Aha! that's the truth and that's the answer and that's the way for us."

I'd rather see myself as an *educator* than an advisor. The root of the word educate is *educare*, to bring up, and *educere*, to lead out, and that's all we can do as therapists and astrologers and counselors. We can't *give* anybody truth or enlightenment. All we can do is *educere*—lead out, bring out. That's why I say your job is to follow the path of your heart, and it's not for me to say how to do that. We live in a society oriented toward success, and you don't paint or draw or write poetry unless you're going to be brilliant at it and make money. Whereas in other cultures, that isn't a requirement, so people participate. Here in the South, you'll see men whittling on sticks, and they don't have to send their work to the Museum of Modern Art to feel gratified. But we who are too civilized get hung up in the expectations of our culture. I've talked to so many people who say, "I've always wanted to dance, but it's too late to be a dancer." I say, "Why don't you just dance for the joy of it?" "Oh no, no." Or, "I would love to write poetry, but I would know in the beginning my poetry would not be very good." I say, "Isn't that okay?" "Well, I would be ashamed to show it to a publisher." "Why can't you just write poetry for yourself and your friends?" If you want to create Eros, try communication. Eros loves the committed, Eros loves passion and that's the other face of Pluto. Pluto is Eros. Pluto is the original love-force god of the universe. He's not just depth, dark Hades, he's also Eros, the god of love. And when Eros comes to you, he seduces you and loves you totally, and shatters you by doing that. Michelangelo surrendered to his Eros in his sculpture and said, "My passion is to release the form hidden within the stone." To release, to lead out the form hidden within the stone, that is his passion.

Audience: I wonder why before you said the gods don't love, because it seems that love is a basic principle of the universe.

Richard: They do love, but not in the sense that we mean it. The love of the gods is *agape*. The god says, "I love you enough to leave you alone, I love you even by shattering and destroying you." It's an impersonal love, yes I love you, but it's not Eros, it's not Scorpio, it's not love of the heart. The universe, the world of archetypes loves you impersonally, not personally.

Think of our phrase, *falling in love*. Falling. Where do we fall to? It's falling down the well, and you fall either into the bottom of Neptune's sea, or you fall into the pit where Hades the seducer lives. And there are many myths about what happens to Core-Persephone after she goes down into the underworld. In some stories she becomes the mother of Dionysus, he of the divine madness. In other myths she gives birth to Chaos, but those are later myths I do believe.

Persephone does not really come into her own until she eats the three seeds of the pomegranate, a very important Plutonian symbol, and whenever she is portrayed in statuary she always has in her hand the broken pomegranate. Remember, she returned from the underworld because the gods forced her to come back to her mother when Demeter was grieving and not allowing the crops to grow. They made a compromise and Persephone was allowed to return to her mother part-time. However before she left, Pluto tempted her with the pomegranate and here we get Lucifer doing exactly the same thing with his apple. And you must eat of the apple. Why eat? You have to take it in you. (By the way, the apple in Eden was no apple. They don't grow apples there, at least they didn't then. It was a pomegranate.) Now, why the pomegranate? What does a pomegranate do when you break it open? It bleeds. So the symbol of the breaking open of the pomegranate is the breaking of the maidenhead and we say she has *lost* her virginity. What a terrible thing to say! Why don't we say when a woman has the broken maidenhead, that she has *gained* her womanhood, not lost something.

So Persephone, by breaking the pomegranate and eating it, has not been deflowered physically since she's already been raped, but has psychically gained her womanhood and become whole. She goes from Core, which means maiden, to Persephone, Queen of the Night and shares the underworld now with her husband. A student of mine, a male student as a matter of fact, who had many planets in Taurus, once described the sign as "voluptuousness demanding to be violated," and I can't put it any better than that. Aphrodite is voluptuousness demanding violation. It's no accident that Core goes tripping away to find this narcissus and, by the way, who put the narcissus out there to attract her? Aphrodite again. Aphrodite understood the Plutonian.

The collective consciousness is more aware of Pluto now than before, since Pluto has not only come home to Scorpio, but is now very close to its perihelion, where it's closest to the Sun, and to its perigee, when it's closest to the Earth. Pluto is now inside the orbit of Neptune so it is coming close to us and we feel it around us collectively, don't we? Atomic bomb explosions, new psychotherapies, horrible diseases that may now lead us to great breakthroughs in great cures, nuclear devices that get out of control, the destruction of the environment and the ecology. So there's a lot of terror out there that we have to face on a day to day basis, and yet, that is the passage of renewal. The Chinese used to have a curse that said, "May you be born in interesting times," but the Greeks looked at it another way and said, "The Gods choose the best of all mortals to be born in times of trouble." So, which is right?

Audience: I've read another version of the Persephone myth that she was not raped and dragged into the underworld by Pluto, but went willingly to help those who were in terror there.

Richard: I have never heard that one, and I believe it may be a result of the feminist movement not being comfortable with the idea of rape. The process that's going on is a rape, but we don't need to literalize that, it's a metaphor. It's a seduction, and that is the nature of Pluto, and there is the divine tension between that. Yes, to some extent we can be more ready, but again, "Do not go gentle into that good night." Core wants to hang onto her maidenhood and yet there's a part in her that says, "I know I must be empowered," so it isn't just the narcissus that leads her away. There is something in her that hungers for completion, that leads her away toward that flower, toward that experience. What is it in Psyche that makes her light that lamp and look at sleeping Eros? Something in her demands more, she demands to come out of this safe, protected world in spite of the pain that she knows. So, yes, that's a kind of consent.

CHAPTER SIX

THE CASE OF LYNNIE OZER

This is the chart of a woman named Lynnie Ozer, (see Chart 5 on page 168), and an article she wrote[1] expressing her feelings and experiences, which she said she's happy to share with other people who are learning. After you read it and study her chart, we will discuss it together.

HIDDEN DISABILITY

by Lynnie Ozer

This is a special evening for reflection and gratitude. Tomorrow I will be graduated from New York University with a doctorate in German literature—the culmination of eight years of dedication. A momentous occasion in anyone's life, it is a miracle in mine because I was born retarded.

When I was sixteen months old, I was diagnosed by a team of endocrinologists at Duke University as a cretin dwarf, or a child born without a functioning thyroid gland. Desiccated thyroid was orally administered, and after one month I was transformed from a

---

1. *Hidden Disability.* Reprinted with permission of Lynnie Ozer and *The Journal of Rehabilitation.*

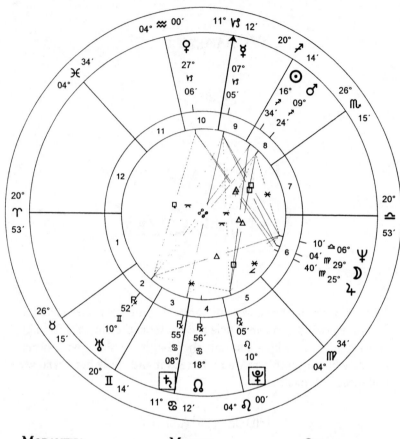

MODALITIES
Cardinal 4
Fixed 1 (♀)
Mutable 8

ELEMENTS
Fire 5
Air 2
Water 1 (♄)
Earth 5

Yang 7
Yin 6

MISSING
FUNCTIONS
N/A

STELLIA
N/A

SINGLETONS
♀ Fixed
♄ Water

ORIENTATION
(Houses)
Personal 2
Social 9
Universal 2

ORIENTATION
(Signs)
Personal 2
Social 5
Universal 6

Chart 5. Lynnie Ozer.

Born December 8, 1944, Montclair, NJ. 74W12'34, 40N49'33 2:36 P.M. EWT,
Placidus houses. Source: birth certificate.

jaundiced, bloated blob with a protruding tongue to a normal looking infant. One of the doctors told my mother that I would most
likely be physically normal, but due to the lateness of the diagnosis,
permanent mental retardation was highly probable and ultimately
would rest in the hands of the mother and God.

My parents brought me back home to New York and began their
determined battle for my normalcy. They became my therapists,
making me walk when I crawled, reading to me day and evening
until a spark was ignited in my dim awareness. At the age of 4 I
began to read and devoured every book I found. The mental retardation was completely gone! It was fortunate that I had books and
the companionship of my parents because the neighborhood children would have nothing to do with me. Despite the doctor's prog-
nosis, my physical development was severely retarded. I could not
walk without falling and was still incontinent at 5 years old. Fairytale
figures became my friends, and I erected a fortress of fantasy to ease
the loneliness. Moreover, my parents gave me the autobiography of
Helen Keller, which strengthened my own determination to be able
to function independently. I fought to learn to ride a bicycle even
though I fell off it constantly. My mother sent me to dancing school
to develop my coordination. I was never exempted from standards
set for my peers. High grades and good manners were expected and
my parents were strict with me regarding all infractions.

When I was 9 my father took a position as a rabbi in a small
Long Island town. I was the "new girl" at school and that in itself
posed difficulty. During physical education classes the competitive
upper-middle-class girls discovered my inability to perform at their
level. I became, as a result, the outcast and scapegoat for my class-
mates who would follow me out of the locker room screaming
"creep" and "freak" at me. After school they would walk beside me
as I headed for home, imitating my awkward gait. To avoid the
taunts, I would hide behind trees until the children were gone. Sum-
mers were worse. My parents sent me to camp, believing that the
fresh air and sports would be beneficial to me. That should have
been the case, but the girls at camp could not comprehend why an
ostensibly normal child could not pitch a ball straight or swim a lap
as they could. I wasn't even able to run to first base in a ball game
without falling. After the games, the little girls would wait until no

adult was present in our cabin and then pounce upon me, hitting, scratching and biting. "You told us you never had polio," they screamed, "then why can't you be like us, you freak?" How could I have explained cretinism to them when I myself didn't understand my condition? I only knew that I had to take my pills every day of my life. My mother constantly emphasized the urgency of this. It is important to mention that I tried my best to be good at the sports at camp and at school because I never felt that I had the right not to do my best. My upbringing ensured that sense of duty in me. No matter how I tried, the children saw the results and not the efforts. Because there were no crutches to excuse my lack of ability, my peers perceived my failure as laziness or spite. I grew to hate the children who tormented me, however, I hated myself even more, certain that I was repulsive and inferior. I never fought back or retaliated verbally. Instead, I sat in my room and prayed that harm would befall my persecutors. Corroded with resentment, I was on the way to becoming mentally as well as physically ill.

My parents had no idea of what was happening to me. I was so ashamed of the constant rejections that I kept silent. It was only when the drama teacher at camp told my mother how the girls were abusing me that the truth began to come out. I was never sent back to summer camp. Then, a fifth grade teacher called my mother in to tell her that I was severely disturbed. At this point my mother sought the advice of a psychiatrist who told her to let me express verbally all my rage against the children who humiliated me. Otherwise, he warned, I might become psychotic. She took his suggestion seriously. I will never forget the night after a dance recital, when my cousin told me I had moved like a cripple and ruined the show. On the way home I was hanging halfway out of the car window, screaming at the top of my lungs, "I hate Judy! God, make her a cripple too!" My father blanched, but my mother whispered, "Charlie, let her get it out of her system, this may save her."

When I was about 11 years old, my mother explained my condition to me and stressed that the constant rejection I suffered at the hands of my peers was not my fault. Both my parents increased their efforts to be companions to me. When it was discovered that I could sing very well, I was promptly given voice and piano lessons. By the time I was in my early teens, I had some status at school because of the leading roles I was given in the musicals. I began to dream of being a great star. My mother, with her usual realism, saw the obstacles that my still faulty coordination would present on a stage and discouraged my ambition. My father, however, nurtured my dreams, constantly telling me how beautiful and gifted I was. This compensated somewhat for the brutalization my self-esteem had undergone at school and at camp.

My father deserves a great deal of credit for my survival during the childhood and teen years. If my mother gave me grit, he healed the wounds dealt me by the other children. My mother set me on the firm ground of reality, which prepared me for life's hardships later on. My father gave me the wings of fantasy I can don at all times. The anchor in reality and the ability to dream thus complement each other. Rather than preach at me, my father lived the decency he expected of me. For example, he found a wallet on the street and promptly brought it to the police station. Although he suffered severe depressions periodically, he never yielded to them and became dysfunctional. My father, and my mother as well, were always motivated by a strong sense of obligation to others. A breakdown would have meant, for my father, reneging on his obligations. He willed himself to weather the storms when they struck. A week before I entered college my father died of leukemia. During the last year of his life I had an example before me of courage and simple dignity. He promised me he would always be with me, and he was and is. To this day I draw from the wellspring of his legacy. On his gravestone the epitaph stands: "Noble spirit sweet and strong. Wild heart full of dreams." My mother wrote it and expressed therewith the very essence of the man she had loved for twenty-five years. When life seemed least worth living for me, my father would say, "Darling, it takes a realist to believe in miracles." I often use that phrase to encourage myself and others. There is no doubt that I am indebted for whatever I have achieved and surmounted to my valiant, loving parents.

Before I turn to an account of my adult years, I feel it is vital to try to objectify the cruelty I experienced from my peers. That cruelty was not leveled at me personally, I have come to understand. The girl next door to me had epilepsy. After a seizure she was kicked by a child in our neighborhood until she bled. The treatment accorded to me and the epileptic girl must be viewed against the background of the times. Those years were the 1950s, a decade of rigid conformity. Any manifestations of differentness, whether physical or mental, were viewed with distrust and hostility. My condition falls into the category of hidden-disability. Diabetics, epileptics and others with illnesses that are not immediately apparent, are expected to be like everybody else. When our illness reveals itself, it is usually uncomprehended and hence condemned. Children in my generation were not taught compassion for abnormality. We who had hidden disabilities did not fit into the world of the able-bodied and were not really a part of the world of the visibly disabled. Thus, we straddled both worlds, trying to maintain our balance. The marches of the 1960s, the Women's Movement and the Gay Liberation movement all paved the way for a new consciousness for the disabled. Now we like to refer to ourselves as physically or mentally challenged. The media have done a great deal to change the image of those who suffer from any form of disability. Beginning with the play and the ensuing film "The Elephant Man," there have been such films as "Mask" and countless television documentaries, as well as episodes in popular series depicting the handicaps created by society for the disabled person. The television series "Highway To Heaven" recently showed a story in which a paraplegic lawyer defends a young man with a misshapen face against the charge of assaulting a blind girl. An episode like this one and many other television movies act in the service of enlightenment, changing the disabled person's self-image and also societal attitudes toward disability.

To return to my own story, adulthood has been far better than childhood or adolescence. When I entered the university I found caring friends who knew nothing of my past and I was careful to hide the fact of my illness from everybody. Since I did not have to engage in sports, there was no problem. However, despite my happiness at college, the depressions which had plagued my father began to attack me. They occurred from the time I was 19 and usually lasted a few weeks or even months. Now, with maturity, I find the depressions becoming easier to control. When they come—these tidal waves washing over me—I fight them, refusing to be overwhelmed. Like my father, I have never allowed myself to reach the point of dysfunctionality. In the musical "The Fantastiks,"[2] the narrator says:

> Who understands why spring is born
> out of winter's laboring pain
> or why we must all die a bit
> before we grow again?

After these bouts, I emerge from the tunnel of the mind stronger each time.

When I had completed my undergraduate work in singing and drama with high honors, I spent seven years abroad teaching, translating and singing concerts. Although my performing career was only part-time, it brought me an enormous sense of worth. Admiration healed, and still heals, the wounds as nothing else can. Out of a sense of obligation toward the medical profession which had made it possible for me to lead a productive life, I took a graduate degree in medical translation and worked during my sojourn in Munich as a translator for a psychiatric research institute. When I returned to New York I found there were no jobs to utilize my talents as a teacher or translator. Thus, I took a job as a bilingual administrative assistant in a music publishing company where I sank into a massive depression because office work did not strengthen my ego. Again, I pulled myself out of the despondency and worked fanatically until I was promoted to the level of assistant director of the rights clearance department and German Language Specialist. Still, I was unfulfilled creatively.

One evening my mother came to my apartment and told me that she had the solution to my problem. She would pay my tuition toward a doctorate in German literature. She believed that the involvement in reaching such a goal would be more therapeutic than lying on a psychiatrist's couch. When I said that I felt like nobody because I had failed to attain the recognition I had envisioned for myself, my mother took a crumpled piece of paper from her purse and quietly told me, "You have not had the success you wanted and certainly even deserved. That is true. But you have achieved something rarer than most successful people. Don't ever underestimate

2. Tom Jones, *The Fantastiks*, from *Best American Plays: Sixth Series, 1963-1967*, edited by John Gassner & Clive Barnes (New York: Crown, 1971), p. 223.

your accomplishment in overcoming your illness and all the problems in your childhood. You were privileged to triumph." Then she read me the poem that was on the piece of paper. The last verse of "Flowerings" by Olivia Hale is:

> The way of all fulfillment goes
> through darkness to achieve the light.
> The root whose daughter is the rose
> was nourished in the utter night.

Thus, my path toward the goal of a doctorate began.

During the years in which I attended classes I distinguished myself and earned the respect of my colleagues and professors. Again, being admired soothed the hurt that always lurks beneath the surface. Then, in the spring of 1982 classes ended and I had to prepare for the oral examination required in order to be permitted to begin the dissertation. I noticed I had difficulty absorbing what I read. A sudden weight gain convinced me I needed more medication. My doctor refused to consider this because she thought I would go into a state of thyroid toxicity resulting from an overdose of medication and leading to high blood pressure and even stroke. At night I would try to study and think that if my dosage was indeed correct, as the doctor maintained, the medication was no longer working and I would become retarded again. I would drink myself to sleep, sobbing in terror, and soon I could not sleep without a bottle of wine. Then it became a pint of vodka. Finally, my mother saw my state and demanded that I increase my medication, which I did. I got slimmer and able to absorb the literature again. However, the drinking continued. I passed the orals with distinction and then faced the problem of my alcohol dependency. When I saw that I could not stop at one glass of wine, I stopped cold and have never had another drink since. Strangely enough, living with my thyroid condition made it easy to face my drinking problem. I think the reason for recidivism among alcoholics is that they usually have not been acquainted with the limitations imposed by a disability other than alcoholism, and alcoholism is a form of disability. I had the advantage in this case because I already knew how to cope with the restrictions of illness and the feeling of being different.

During the next three years I worked on my doctoral dissertation and continued at my job where I enjoyed the support of both colleagues and superiors. In addition, I began to sing at night clubs from time to time. My mother found a new doctor for me and he discovered that I had indeed been under-dosed. I go for blood tests regularly now to avoid the consequences of incorrect dosage. The experience with my former thyroid specialist was an object lesson. We disabled people cannot blindly trust anyone simply by virtue of his or her position as a specialist. The patient can often sense something wrong before it shows up on tests. I know I have to look out for sudden weight gain or weight loss, lassitude or excessive energy, inability to absorb information or steel-trap apprehension. Above all, I must have my blood tested every few months even though I find the experience unpleasant. In the course of the last two years I have also found a voice to express my situation as a woman with a hidden disability. Writing about it transforms the pain from a prison into poetry.

It is already eleven o'clock. I have written steadily for two hours. Yes, I've come a long way, but there is still a great deal to change. Even if I don't live in the past, it lives in me. A humiliation or rejection opens up the scars and leaves the wounds exposed. But I cannot indulge myself in such vulnerability any longer. I am happier than I have ever been and I am loved by many people. My vindictiveness does me more harm than those whom I wish ill. I resent the past and fear the future rather than cherishing the present. Many people suffer far more from their disabilities than I do—in their adulthood as well as in their childhood. The gratitude I should feel at all times is not always there. Like a fearful horse, I stand before the hurdle of the past, wading in the quagmire of old injuries. Will I be able to rise above this, too? Will I be able to transcend it and make it meaningful instead of destructive? I look at my father's picture and recall how he loved to sing with me the freedom song, *We Shall Overcome.* He would want me to try—at least to try.

Tomorrow I will have my Ph.D.! The road was long and sometimes rough, but I did it! I ask myself sleepily, would I want to have been spared my disability? No, I wouldn't change anything. My mother's words come back to me, "You were privileged to triumph."

The End

Richard: Now, how did you feel about reading this story? I would be interested in hearing some subjective opinions.

Audience's various comments: I am suspicious of the way she seems to idealize her parents....I was touched....I work with disabled kids so I, too, was very deeply touched....I was inspired....I was puzzled about where to find the disability in the chart....I don't know what's wrong with me, but I heard all these negative feelings running around and felt she wasn't getting any better....I was amazed at how cruel people can be toward someone who is disabled....I was impressed by the kind of support she got from her parents and the importance of that in being able to overcome that kind of trauma....I don't know if I should admit it, but it made me cry.

Richard: Well, I'll admit it, it made me cry, and I find that I agree with everything that everybody says, the negative and the positive.

I think what we have here is an example of the Hero's Journey. In this case we have a heroine and her journey. You find a soul struggling, fighting, full of flaws and she has not ultimately triumphed. I think she makes that quite clear. She's had battle after battle, and I think we can certainly see some negative things within this personality. She reveals herself I think quite clearly to the eye. She's not all wonderful; she's not a person without dark stuff and shadows, naturally not. She has paid a price. The things that have happened to her, or the way she's mythologized them, have scarred her. She is wounded in ways where some of these wounds will never be healed. I think she's as honest as she can be and there's a great deal to be said for that. I say, *as she can be.* Maybe not as honest as we would have her, but is anybody, including ourselves? So you can only be where you are at a given moment. I think she was generous to share this story.

Is there a face of narcissism in all this, as has been pointed out by some people? Is there an enormous amount of self-involvement? Well, I can see an argument for that and yet that does not in any way deprecate what she's gone through and who she is and what she's become. I think it's amazing to see somebody fighting against odds and, in a sense, winning or triumphing. And even at the end of it doesn't she say, "Am I done with this, am I healed, is everything all right? I've worked my way through from being a diagnosed cretin dwarf, who is supposed to be retarded all her life, to winning a doctorate in German from a university." And that's not the end of her story by any means.

Let's take a look at the chart from the point of view of some of the things we're saying. Examine it also from the point of view of the transpersonal planets, and also the things we've learned about our weight-scale in looking at the chart. Let's go the other way around this time, because now we have some subjective information. Let's look at some of the statements she has made about herself and see the correlations we can find in the chart. You can go about this any way that you want; but first, let me point out some of the highlights that show up for me. You can choose what you like of this.

I'm impressed by this singleton Pluto in Fixed signs—that singleton Pluto in Leo in the 5th house and ruler of the 8th. I'm not going to comment on it right now, I'm just pointing it out. We've seen an awful lot of the negative uses of singleton Plutos over the last couple of days. It's nice to see Pluto when it's being used in another way. Has she been down to the depths and the bottom? I think so. Over and over again. Okay, next we have dominant Mutable in the natal chart with eight points. In terms of elements, Fire and Earth are rather equally divided. Air is an inferior function here, with only two points, and let's not be unaware of that, specifically because what are the planets that occupy the Air signs? Uranus and Neptune. So I think we must pay close attention to that inferior Air function, specifically because we know a lot about her and what her issues are. Then finally, we have a singleton planet in Water, and here Saturn shows up again. That's another character we're familiar with from some of the charts we've looked at. This is Saturn in Cancer in the 3rd, right on the cusp of the 4th house, and it's her 10th house ruler. Personal signs are certainly an inferior function as are Personal houses and, of those planets, only Uranus and Saturn are found in the first four houses and in the first four signs, too. That should say something. Yet, her dominant house placement is Social houses. And isn't that interesting, especially with some of the issues around socializing that she's had: how critically important it is, how powerful the wounding has been for her in that area?

There's a very powerful yod to Mercury, and this is almost a classic example. Mercury has an awful lot to do with intelligence, coordination, communication, and the functioning of the mind, and the yod to Mercury in the 9th house in Capricorn comes from Pluto and Uranus. From the singleton Pluto on one side and the Uranus on the other, this is a very powerful configuration. What we have is a *completed* yod, because Mercury is opposite Saturn. This is a special kind of major configuration in which there's a cork in the hole, and so Saturn takes on special significance. Saturn on the cusp of the 4th house, ruler of the 10th and we'll see what that Saturn does for her, or how she experiences it.

Another thing is the T-cross between Saturn, Mercury, and Neptune. Neptune is the focal point of the T-cross in the 6th house, ruler of the 12th, with Saturn and Mercury opposite, so here again is this emphasis on the Mercury. Mercury is the planet linking two major configurations together. Focal point of the T-cross is Libra in the 6th house and it out-lets into Aries in the 12th house. So, just with that, we're loaded with information, aren't we? And one other thing that I'm particularly interested in is the 29th degree Moon conjunct Neptune and Jupiter.

Audience: Mercury rules the thyroid.

Richard: That's one of the rulers. I have heard Venus and I don't know for sure, but my guess is that it could have to do with Venus because Venus does connect with the throat. There's a wide range of opinion on Astro-Endocrinology and it seems logical that Venus is the thyroid. I'm really reluctant to go far out on a limb; maybe Mercury has something to do with it too; I don't know. I connect Venus and Jupiter with metabolism, too, but I would say that Mercury may have something to do with it. This is an area wide open for research. I would love to find an endocrinologist who would become interested in astrology, it's a vastly important area.

Audience: I know medical astrologers who have done a lot of work on it and feel that it's Venus.

Richard: Okay, let's let it go for now. I'm much more interested in the psychological impact on her than what really rules what gland, aren't you?

I think a very important thing to begin looking at in her journey is the influence of the parents in her life. Over and over again she talks about their support, their structure, their insistence on normalcy, their not letting her get away with being an invalid, with being weak or helpless, their instilling and inspiring her with courage, their general applause, their pushing and nudging. From the tone of the way she expresses, she idealizes these parents. I'm not entirely sure there are no negative connotations to all that—I should not say negative, I should say a price to be paid for that. She doesn't really describe any price that she might pay for that in her story, but there is one line, "There is no doubt that I am indebted for whatever I have achieved and surmounted to my valiant, loving parents." That's a wonderful thing to say and I'm not denying the truth of the subjective experience, but I'm a little uncomfortable with some of that. She makes no mention of a relationship in her life. What is her personal relationship life like? She doesn't ever talk about that, so I think that in some way there is a connection going on here. I wonder if there was an oblivion to her emotional needs on the part of the parents and just a desire to push her forward.

It seems, at least from her description, that more of the nurturing comes from the father than the mother. And more of the authority, you know, the kind of "Buckle up your bootstraps baby, get out there without whining and complaining," comes from the mother. And looking at the chart, with the ruler of the 10th house coming to the 4th, is that the nurturing comes from the archetypal authority figure—the reversal of the parental role. Plus the Moon, the 4th house ruler, is in the 29th degree of Virgo, and I get a very Virgonian feeling from this mother. The kind of nurturing one gets from Virgo is not the same as one gets from Pisces or Cancer. And first of all, Venus is in the 10th house, which is a kind of love affair with Daddy, and then the ruler is in nurturing Cancer. Although Saturn as a planet is not particularly comfortable there, nevertheless it is in Cancer and it is the only planet she has in Water. So there is more to this than meets the eye.

Audience: It reminds me of the myth of Hephaestus, Vulcan from Olympus, who was crippled, deformed, and thrown out of heaven by his parents. I'm wondering if there's something to the parents' pushing this girl out into the world and, perhaps by making her a "cause," they don't have to work on the relationship between them.

Richard: That's an interesting point. Vulcan was kicked out of heaven both by mother and father, (Hera and Zeus), In fact, he was kicked out twice. First he was born slightly deformed, kicked out and then further damaged, so he was always in some way wounded. That is a very interesting image and I hear some interesting tones in her article. However, a lot of this may be written in thanks to the parents and there may be a hidden agenda in that, but nevertheless, the parents seem rather two-dimensionally-wonderful. But motivations are neither black nor white, pure or evil—motivations are colored, they're layered. And here we get back into our onion image. You peel the onion and you can find deeper and deeper and deeper levels of motivation. Having a subjective or apparently selfish or even narcissistic motive is not necessarily wrong either. I mean, that's part of the human condition.

Audience: I wonder how individuated she is and, if she's living out her parent's desires, what happens when they are gone?

Richard: I agree with your concern and I think there is a problem for her in this umbilical tie to these "savior" parents. Of course, the father is already dead and only the mother surviving, but I'm concerned, too, and wondering where she'll go with that next. Also, disabled children may wonder if they have inherited a bad gene and is there, on a subconscious level, a resentment toward the parents?

Since I have met her, I will give you some of my subjective impressions. She came to a lecture that I gave in New York recently. I was talking about power, powerlessness, the underworld, and the shadow, like I usually do. We got into Hitler and Nazi Germany and the holocaust, and she was particularly moved about that, having studied in Munich. She spoke up and said she was diagnosed retarded and shared some of her experience of what the sense of powerlessness meant for her.

Physically she's quite attractive, she's striking and more than unusually good looking, at least in my subjective opinion. Yet there was something around her that was impenetrable. The minute she spoke, her woundedness showed, her vulnerability, her openness and willingness to share. A crackling intellectuality, I mean absolutely articulate. She got a round of applause after she spoke, just from the floor, and she spoke very impassionedly about Germany and the Jewish situation, which was the structure of what she was saying, but she brought her subjective experience into it. And, all I have to say is subjectively I was impressed. When this article arrived in the mail I didn't connect it with this woman because I never did ask her name. So after I read it I telephoned her and then put the two things together. That's the limit of my experience with her except, as I mentioned before, in our conversation she said she was happy to share this with other people who are learning.

Back to the chart, I think we need to focus on the lack of Water, also the question of anger and how she may have dealt with it, which I think is a very critical one. First of all, talking about the inherited disability of some sort or another, I am interested in the ruler of the 4th house (which I see as genetic inheritance from the past or the family), in that critical 29th degree. I find in my experience, that Moon in 29th degree is not an easy placement. Of all planets, the Moon in that shaky 29th degree says to me that on some level an early life experience, something connected with the nurturing, with the feeding, with the basic security system, is awry. Remember we said that the 29th degree has a rather Neptunian cast to it anyway. There's a shakiness. I suspect something of damage potentially in the 29th degree, not necessarily irreparable, but when it is the Moon, and especially the Moon from the 4th house, I'm wondering if it indicates something inherited from the past. I don't want to get into issues of Karma or destiny because I think that's a little presumptuous to assume. But, whatever it may be, this 29th degree Moon as ruler of the 4th house does indicate something inherited from the past.

Also, notice the Nodes in the 4th-10th house axis, for those of you who are particularly fond of looking at them. That also seems to point up the same thing in Cancer and Capricorn. The 29th degree Moon is also conjunct Neptune, which is a 12th house Neptune (ruler of the 12th). So what did we say about a Moon-Neptune contact? A lack of differentiation between child and mother, a tendency to merge, remember we talked about that. In this case the mother becomes archetypal. When Neptune has to do with mother she becomes perhaps the *mater-dolorosa*, the sorrowing mother, she becomes this mother who is the savior. Or, she becomes the other— the devouring, chaotic, underworld mother who seduces me into chaos, the mother who gives double messages. So Moon-Neptune I think automatically, in and of itself, gives indications of trouble in differentiating from the mother, from the motherland, from the clan, from the family. I see strong problems of umbilical-cord-breaking with Neptune, just as I do with Moon-Pluto for different reasons. So the mother, then, does not become quite real. I'm uncomfortable whenever there is a nurturing planet, like Moon, connected with the 12th house ruler, or the ruler of the 4th in the 12th, or the ruler of the 12th in the 4th, or the ruler of the 4th conjunct the ruler of the 12th, which is what we have here. It makes me uneasy because the 12th house is where we want to retire from the pain of the world.

Many people with Sun or Moon in the 12th house, for instance, withdraw from the pressures of the world. We talk about it as being withdrawn or institutionalized, the monastery, the nunnery. I connect the 12th house with collective unconscious and also repressed personal material, so I am wondering whether this does not give further ammunition to the fact that this idealized- mother or savior-mother may have created a problem in which the daughter is going to have great difficulty differentiating. And her mother, above and beyond the call of duty, dedicated herself and devoted herself to establishing independence of the daughter.

Isn't it interesting that Lynnie wrote that the doctor told her mother that the child's future condition was "ultimately in the hands of mother and God"? Now, I wonder where Lynnie got that information? I wonder if that was what the mother told her, and if so, mother and God are lumped together and there's another twist in this little story. Mother equals God and mother is your savior and look what I have done for you. That's another face of that Neptune, "Look what I have sacrificed and given up for you." Here is Virgin Mary, sorrowing and suffering at the bottom of the cross. So I think that's true, I think there was the sacrificing, saving mother. But everything has its price, so nothing is either good or bad on the face of it, and indeed, I wouldn't be surprised if, without the dedication of this mother, she may have remained retarded. So here we have, literally, a savior-mother and yet, what are the implications behind that?

Often a person who has a great deal of damage in the early part of life, especially in the critical socialization period, tends to grow late. They are stunted emotionally, and it takes a very long time, many years if ever, in order to catch up in the socialization process.

So what comes with an early handicap or disability is a deprivation of the magical, Eden-like world of the child that pays off later, with certain kinds of strengths, but also with a certain kind of fragility and weakness. Whatever the reason for her rejection by her peers and the loneliness and suffering that she endured at the hands of other children (I'm not so sure that part of it didn't have to do with her and I'd like to look at that), the mythology of how she has put it together is that she is damaged in her process of socialization. I also feel that certain things that need to be experienced in their own developmental phase, were not. And if a certain amount of protection and nurturing that comes on the Lunar level is missing, it is very difficult to replace later. Some healing can be done, but it's difficult to replace it. Same thing with the socialization process. If we miss a certain kind of peer socialization that happens during early childhood with playmates and siblings (and you notice she doesn't mention a sibling), or peer group structure that happens during adolescence, I don't know how that is replaceable later. Apparently both were damaging experiences for her.

Audience: I think the father could have been separated and apart from this whole process with the Sun conjunct Mars and opposite Uranus, so I'm wondering if the daughter was really all the mother had and that's why she was so dedicated to her.

Richard: I think that's a very good analysis and you see how paradoxical is the human condition, how many-layered it is. It isn't so simple to see things in terms of a simple line across. As they say, "An enigma within a paradox in a conundrum within a riddle." Remember we were talking about the eye of the beholder, and I have not heard any of you say anything that I can't find a certain basis in logic for. These are parents who believe in pushing, nudging, forcing, never mind doing what's easy—get out there and struggle. And she, herself, subjectively seems to feel that the parents did the right thing.

Audience: Will you say something about her bouts with depression, which she seems to compare to her depressive father?

Richard: Yes, that's very interesting. Notice that she is a dominant Fire-Earth type and one of the ways I describe that type is that it's like a Sherman Tank. Here we have the inspired flame and the determination to *do*. Did she inherit this from the parents or mythologize it as an acceptable way to behave in life? Certainly it seems to be from the parents, at least from the mother. And yet, the inferior function here is Water, so at what sacrifice the ability to do and to make and to hang-in-there and stand tough—at what price on the level of the Water inferior function? And I'm wondering whether these recurrent bouts of depression are the suppressed Water finally beginning to rise to the surface. Whenever you have a Moon-Saturn contact, as I was saying before, it seems to imply this sense of early, irreparable deprivation on some level. It can be mythologized in many different ways, but it's like this inner hurt or itch that cannot be scratched.

I want to say just a little bit about Moon-Saturn. When I was first getting into astrology, I read about detriment and how debilitated the planet was when found placed in its opposite sign. I decided to check it out on my collection of charts of celebrated people and I looked at Sun and Moon signs. By far, on the curve, the highest position for the Moon by sign (I didn't do aspects), was Moon in Capricorn, which is supposed to be its detriment position. And what position do you think I found for the Sun? Aquarius, its detriment position! So that set me to wondering. Is there something in the lights being in a place where they are *put-through-it* so to speak, that often forces them—not always, obviously because everybody is not a great celebrity in the world—but forces a kind of sublimation or compensation that says, " All right, I've endured a lot. There is something here not completely right or flowing in my world, and by God, I'm not going to be held down. I'm going to do, I'm going to show them, I'm going to make it, you'll see." I get a sense of that here. First of all the Moon is widely square Saturn, it's an out of sign square wide by about 9°, but I'll include it. Saturn is disposed of by the Moon anyway, so I think that's a quality that needs to be looked at.

Audience: I think the mother is uncomfortable with the daughter's repressed or sublimated emotions, her lack of Water, and tries to direct the daughter away from exploring them in psychiatry, encouraging instead, academic studies in a doctoral program.

Richard: I find that I can support your opinion quite a bit there. I wonder what the mother's agenda is, especially since the daughter apparently so readily agreed to that. What is the mother afraid the daughter might find on the couch? Is it feelings of rage and resentment? Is this another argument for the fact that the mother really doesn't want the daughter freed? I see this Saturn in Cancer here so close to the borders of the 4th house. Did her mother have big trouble repressing feelings? I don't know whether it's a mistake, but my intuition of this is that she's going to end up on the couch sooner or later anyway. And I also suspect that when she does that, she's going to find a lot of rage and resentment toward her mother that at the present time she's idealizing. Then, and only then perhaps, will she begin to break this umbilical cord.

It's interesting she mentions nothing about adult relationships at all. I find that an interesting lack. Woundedness in childhood seems to want to armor the feelings. What happens is that very early on in life we make decisions and those decisions are often unconscious. We need those decisions in order to survive and one of them is, "I'm not going to let them hurt me any more. I cannot take this kind of pain." This is what often happens with Moon-Saturn contacts. Another thing that happens with Water inferior function is it's either all the way on, or all the way off. There is a tendency to have wild swings. I am either wallowing in the depth of my emotions or, if it is too much and overwhelms me, I turn off the switch and go on with other elements of my life—the Fire, the Earth, the enthusiasm, the drive, the doing, the accomplishing. There is a dominant Earth function and Earth says, "Solve your problems by *doing* them. Never mind wallowing in self-pity or sadness, get out there and do it."

Now here is the paradox. I'm not sure that this very thing she learned is what saved her as a child, but I'm also not sure what damage the saving did. Do you see what I'm saying? There are layers and layers of this. Sometimes one has to take surgery in order to save one's life and at great cost. The leg may have to be amputated because gangrene has set in, and yet is there a price to pay for the person who survives losing the leg? And what I'm beginning to suspect and put together here is that perhaps in her words, "I was never exempted from the standards set for my peers. High grades and good manners were expected. My parents were strict with me regarding all infractions. They made me walk when I crawled, reading to me day and evening until a spark was ignited in my dim awareness." So I think a very important thing to see in an astrological chart is that things which may be appropriate and right at a particular stage in development, have a kick-back effect later on when the parents cannot adapt their behavior to the changing needs of the child. Maybe this kind of firm, loving, guiding, pushing, optimistic hand was exactly right at the time when she was so early forming, and maybe later on in her life she needed encouragement in other things. Of course, the mother did encourage her to express her anger, but the idea of avoiding the psychiatrist's couch may not be appropriate.

I suspect this young woman lives alone. My guess is, although she never says anything about it, that she isn't married and I seriously doubt if she has ever lived with anybody in an on-going relationship. So behavior that is necessary and right at the moment may be the foundation for what neurosis is all about. The things that we learn in order to protect ourselves and to survive at a particular place and time, become inappropriate later on in life when we need to move out of that phase and on to other things. So, yes, horrible and unusual circumstances call for strong measures and she got the strong measures as a child, but was she able to move on to the next phase and when? These are the questions that puzzle me and I don't really have all the answers.

Audience: But she seems to have found fulfillment in her particular accomplishments.

Richard: Yes, she has in some way ingested the parent's values that making it, accomplishing it, getting there (wherever *there* is), somehow will solve it and, in truth, it has. As she says, "I know my troubles are not over, but my success has contributed to my healing." Her journey is nowhere near done.

She talks about doing what very often the lost child does. She has fantasy friends. She learned to love her books. She couldn't relate to her peers. Here again is the Neptune, focal point of the T-cross and the Neptune conjuncts the Moon—the fantasy mother, the fantasy world that nurtures us. Many of us who have strong or prominent Neptunes, or a damaged or hurt Moon, learn early on to encourage fantasy as a way of feeding that thing that's missing. It's not uncommon, I'm not surprised to hear that.

Now, I want to look at this Mercury for a second—Mercury as the focal point of the yod between Uranus and Pluto. Obviously Mercury has a lot to do with the mind, with cognition, with the early on impression of the danger here of being severely retarded. Remember, she must stay on her medication forever or she will slide back into retardation, as she describes when she was under-medicated. She began to blow up with weight and lose her balance and coordination and couldn't absorb what she was reading. So there's the threat, the Sword of Damocles[3] hanging over her head, that at any moment I could not only die, but at any moment I could lose my mind and slip back into that soup of retardation that I came from. And that puts Mercury in Capricorn saying, "By God, I'm going to prove it, I'm going to accomplish it, I'm going to have a Ph.D., I'm going to get up there to the top!"

Now, notice the quincunxes come from Uranus and Pluto, of all things. I mean, here we have the two devastating planets of deep transformation and what we call *the catastrophic experience*. It's like Uranus and Pluto here agree, "Let's have a catastrophic experience and Mercury is going to be the one to experience it." Mercury is in the 9th house, where Lynnie proves her triumph by getting a degree in a foreign language. Capricorn is "a degree," "in a foreign" is 9th house, "language" is Mercury. Isn't it amazing sometimes how literal the astrological chart can be? And what is so interesting is that this terribly, terribly, tender, vulnerable, hurt Mercury is filled here on the bottom by the Saturn and here's where these parents come in. It's like the parents become this "cork" in this terrible, painful situation. In other words, the yod-ness of this is blocked by Saturn and I connect Saturn with both parents here with ruler of the 10th on the cusp of the 4th. "The structure, the discipline, the repressing of my feelings is what has made me survive." And when she loses her parents, first her father is gone and I think when the mother goes, there's going to be an enormous crisis for this young woman. An enormous crisis, which I have confidence in her handling; I don't know her, but I hope or intuit that's the way it's going to be.

---

3. Sword of Damocles: Dionysus suspended a sword by a single hair over the head of Damocles, who then realized that power and wealth are dangerous possessions. Any impending disaster can be referred to as the Sword of Damocles.

Audience: With her Mercury in the 9th house opposite Saturn and square Neptune she could build up a whole inflated or fantasy notion of her identity and who she is, so why do you believe this story is true?

Richard: I don't believe that it *is* true and I don't think it is *not* true. What we're seeing is somebody's myth being acted out. And if what we're looking for is truth, we're not going to find it, that's the danger. We think we can look at an astrological chart and find truth, but we cannot. We're going to find degrees and degrees of mythology.

She's not in therapy with us—we are not able to peel the onion and really get down to the bottom level. What we have here is a subjective story, obviously full of her own many multiple motivations. Self-congratulation? Maybe yes. Narcissism? Yes. Need to evoke sympathy and pity? Maybe yes. As she admits quite frankly, she's starved for congratulations and applause, she is still vulnerable to any hint of a rejection. It is important for other people to validate this journey of hers. Is there something neurotic in it? Well, yes, I'll go along with that. We don't even know if this story is the bottom line of her own reality of how she sees herself. This is a story that she's given out, she didn't just write this for me, it was written before she came to my lecture. It's a statement about herself, an open journal which, I suppose, she felt she could, or needed, or had to share and when I told her I was going to share her story, she said she didn't mind.

As I listen to all your comments, isn't it lovely to see what's happening here? What are we all really revealing? Is it so much about Lynnie, or a lot about ourselves? That's the thing that is so interesting to my ear and that's why I'm saying, "in the eye of the beholder," what is truth? Obviously, we don't know. Whose myth are we dealing with? First her subjective myth of herself, then our myth of her and the world and relationships, and we see them through our own eyes.

Audience: With her mother so involved in pushing her to excel, perhaps she didn't get the touching, nurturing kind of care to make her feel lovable, and so the taunting of her peers only validated her feeling that she wasn't lovable.

Richard: Yes, and is it necessary for the mother to love that child by "fixing" her? That's part of the Moon in Virgo. Virgo is the repair and maintenance department, and Moon in Virgo is the mother who is constantly "fixing" you. But the interesting thing about Virgo is that the process is never done. You're never fixed and never good enough for me.

So now I am more willing to buy the argument that, in a sense, the mother's pushing of this daughter is a lot of compensation coming out of her own feelings of guilt or inadequacy. Out of love, yes, I don't deny that. But I seem to envision this middle-class Jewish family with this kind of horror thrust on them and, with the Venus on the Capricorn Midheaven, the importance of putting on the face, the mask out here in the world. Mercury up on the Midheaven also says that it's important to be smart and intelligent, to accomplish it and "make it" in the world. So I think, certainly there was love and sacrifice, but I believe the parents had their own motivations as well. I'm also wondering about this father—this "wild heart longing to be free"—who was a depressive and seemed to live a rather frustrated life. What is all that? We don't really know what the dynamics are in this parental marriage except what she has mythologized in this story and which sounds like this divine, wonderful marriage between two wonderful people, but something in me doubts it.

Audience: And it took them so long to see what the problem was, perhaps they were in denial. Then they didn't even tell her what was wrong with her until she was 11 years old!

Richard: Yes, waiting so long to tell the child what the truth is, I get a heavy defense system going here, a heavy armor and defense system. It's like, "We're not going to fall apart, we're not going to be thrown into our Pluto and get annihilated, we're not going to get into our Neptune, be devastated and fall into chaos, we're going to hang together, we're going to be tough, even if we have to deny and repress an enormous amount of material, we're going to do it and we're going to get through."

I think it's clear from the story that the mother controls the daughter very closely. The daughter decided, on the basis of what the mother said, not to go for help in psychiatry. I am extremely suspicious of the mother's motives in this. Obviously we have the mother's agenda here, and what she's saying is, "Getting into your feelings and exposing the wounds and the soreness, even at the price of healing, is not as good as making a good face in the outer world and accomplishing." I really hear the mother's value here.

Audience: But she says a fifth-grade teacher alerted her mother that she (Lynnie) was severely disturbed and her mother sought the advice of a psychiatrist, so we don't know whether she went into therapy then or not. She may have been in therapy for years and perhaps her mother found she was getting nowhere so looked for other ways to help her. And another thing, with Sun in the 8th house and Pluto in the 5th, it says that this is a woman who continually needs to regenerate, and there's a tremendous amount of courage, strength, and determination, so she really deserves a tremendous amount of credit.

Richard: I agree with that. Let's look along that theme.

First of all, the Sun and Uranus are in opposition in the chart, and we talked about that before. The egg is shattered over and over again. That ego cannot be left alone. There is a constant urge to push off and shatter and regroup. Or, is there a denial of that? Has this self-image cemented in a kind of Saturnine way and Uranus is rejected? I don't know. But one of the things about the Sun-Uranus person is he or she always feels like an odd duck! You always feel odd-man-out, "Nobody understands me, I'm unusual, I don't fit in, there is a difference about me that makes it hard for me to adapt to the world around me." And that is a given; I mean she came in with that. The other is the Sun-Pluto trine in her chart. It says that a part of my ego-conception of myself is Sun in Sagittarius, the fire-brand, the flaming sword, and conjunct Mars, "I am the fighter, the warrior." Sun-Pluto is "I am a survivor," but is it necessary for my construction of myself to constantly be like the Phoenix—to burn myself up in flames, go down to the ashes of the depths and renew over and over again? You find this very often with Sun-Pluto people. This self-annihilation happens over and over again? There is no getting *there* because life is a perpetual plunge down into the underworld where there's more renewal, and coming back up. That's why it is the Hero's Journey. This is a lifetime process for her.

One more thing I want to mention here. I want to talk for a second about this persona, why she has such trouble in the socialization process. When you read the script it sounds like the whole world is a pretty bad place, and I got dumped on, and I'm a victim, and aren't people cruel to people who are different? Well, yes, that's true. People are cruel to people who are different, and children can be very cruel. It's even true of animals in nature who tend to gang up on something that is different or deformed. So as far as that goes, I have to validate it and say it's true, but there's a big *but* for me. But, I say, wait a minute, what is she bringing into this, too, with her own attitude and feelings? First of all, remember the inferior function in Water? Does she share much of what she really feels with people? Is she so armored against wounds? Is she living in expectation of being rejected (Sun opposing Uranus)? What we give out to the world reinforces what we get back, and that reaffirms our myth, and the circle goes on.

Look at this Ascendant—Aries rising—so right away we get the warrior. Sun in Sagittarius trine Uranus and the Aries Ascendant. From this I get something rather fiery, assertive, independent. Remember it's a Uranian-Plutonian-Sun, don't forget that. So there is something unusual and strange and probably very powerful about her, but something may be very off-putting. I get the sense of a very intense, flaming, demanding kind of thing that just might put people off.

Audience: And with her Mercury of communications opposite Saturn, probably when she communicates her timing isn't right, and she gets a negative response.

Richard: Excellent, yes I agree. Mercury in Capricorn in the 9th house, the focal point of the yod, opposed to the singleton Saturn in the 3rd house, the only planet in Water, says that much of what is projecting from her gives the impetus to what she's getting back from the world.

Part of the hero's journey is the archetype of the *divine return*; having gone into the underworld and slaying your dragons, or in the process of slaying them, you come back and tell your story. You come back and part of the return is the image of the up-turned Grail. I connect the sign Aquarius with the Grail and the archetype of the divine return. It's not enough just to get to Capricorn, where you achieve a kind of person-hood or perfection, or replace the divine archetype father. There's another step. The step is Aquarius and that's why Aquarius is down on one knee. I don't think it's just humility, I think there's a burden here to carry this stuff. And part of the healing process is the renewal of the world by pouring forth the Water of the subjective thing that I have experienced and suffered. So telling the story is an important healing device for her. And when I told her that I was going to present this chart in a conference, she said, "Thank God, I can't tell you what this means to me; send those people my love because I've told this story to be shared." I think this is part of the process of the healing that's going on.

Audience: But doesn't she have to deal with her rage? It seems to me the only way she has been able to harness these energies is to feel worthy only through things that are external, and she sends her love to unknown, outside people, so where is her love? All of the stuff that she does is outside, but what about the inner part?

Richard: I think you're well reasoned, and I agree completely that she's got a problem with rage, no question about it. This is a very furious person, and justifiably so. We hear it in her words and we see it in her chart. Sun is conjunct Mars, so how do I identify myself? Her ruling planet is Mars, and this Mars is opposing Uranus, quincunx Saturn, trine Pluto, sextile Neptune. It is involved with all of the outer planets. The quincunx from Saturn, in and of itself, is enough to turn a deep, repressive rage inward. I think also that part of her catharsis and cleansing is getting rid of the rage, and here's the trine from the Pluto and the sextile from Neptune. I'm not so sure how far she is away, in consciousness, from her knowledge that she is a very angry woman, and I think she knows it. I don't think she pulls any punches. I agree with you also that she's wounded, that she has a long way to go. My feeling is that she's on the path. My feeling is that this is a noble, wounded, hurt soul with many flaws and faults, who in many ways is not individuated, much as we might like her to be. I agree she probably has a problem with relationships, but she's not walking the streets or a drug addict, dead, or a suicide, or institutionalized. As the cigarette ad goes (which I hate), "You've come a long way, baby," but she *has* come a long way.

Sure, I see the weakness, I see the whininess, I see the narcissism, I see a certain lack of differentiation, I see negative cathexis [4] of a lot of stuff with the mother, I see problems in expressing her emotions, I see all of that. And even with all of that, I say here is a person on the path. She has worked hard and she's on the road—what more can we be except that?

Audience: And isn't there a connection with Hephaestus in her need to get love from external accomplishment?

Richard: Yes, absolutely, that's an excellent point, thank you. Hephaestus never feels he is entitled to love, he has to earn it. And he has to do it by forging out of earth and fire things of usefulness and beauty for other people. Was he happy in his marriage? No way. He married Aphrodite, Venus the goddess of love, who betrayed him left and right. None of the gods ever liked him, he was a drag at a party. Hephaestus was not the guy you hung out with, he never recovered from his wounds and yet he lived. That's part of this particular journey.

And here's the trap. Jung said that to the degree that we are not individuated, we tend to think people either are like we are, or ought to be, and I think I'm hearing some of that in the room tonight. I'm hearing a lot of wisdom and very good astrology and I am also hearing a lot of projection—naturally so, because you can't be anybody else other than who you are. Everything everyone has said is true, or possibly true, and that's the incredible thing about astrology. We are not dealing here with a linear "given," we're bringing our own life material into it. Notice how you responded to other people in the room—how some people push your buttons with what they say and some people say, "Yes, yes, yes, that's right." And yet the arguments astrologically are all there—I haven't heard a person make an argument that I couldn't support astrologically. It's the *interpretation* that we sometimes quarrel with, isn't it? And on some level I think everybody has been right.

4. Cathexis: psychoanalytical term meaning concentration of psychic energy upon a person, fantasy, idea, or object. From the Greek *kathexis*; kata - thoroughly and echein - to hold.

CHAPTER SEVEN

INCEST IN THE FAMILY

I want to begin with two clients of mine, the names are pseud–
onyms, and they are sisters. I want to tell you a little bit about
their backgrounds so you can begin to look at the charts and follow
along as I tell you about them (see Charts 6 and 7 on pages 196 and
199).

I first began by seeing Joan. Joan is 40 and at the time I saw her
she was in the middle of what she characterized as a mid-life crisis.
She had a very high administrative job with the state. At the time
she couldn't sleep, she wasn't able to keep food down. She is one of
eight children and, according to her story, she ran the house from
age 11 until she left. She has never married. She is an extremely intelligent and articulate woman, as is her sister. At age 27 she had a very
important consulting job in Washington. She had that job for about
nine years and was fired in 1977. She is very vague in terms of describing what the circumstances were as to why she was fired, but she feels
that she engineered it herself because she really couldn't separate from
the family and it was an excuse to get her to come back home.

In her description, she was physically, psychically, and sexually
abused as a child—physically and sexually by the father, physically
by the mother—psychically by both, but particularly the mother.
She is terrified of intimacy with men and has had only one sexual
experience in her life. She has been tested as *borderline* and borderline

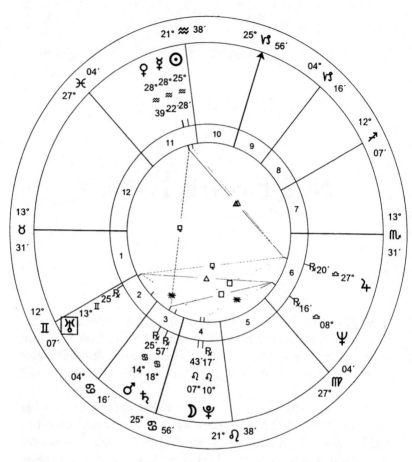

MODALITIES
Cardinal 4
Fixed 8
Mutable 1 (♅)

ELEMENTS
Fire 3
Air 8
Water 2
Earth 0

Yang 11
Yin 2

MISSING
FUNCTIONS
Earth

STELLIA
N/A

SINGLETONS
♅ Mutable

ORIENTATION
(Houses)
Personal 6
Social 2
Universal 5

ORIENTATION
(Signs)
Personal 3
Social 5
Universal 5

Chart 6. Joan.
Birth data withheld for confidentiality. Placidus houses.
Source: birth certificate.

is someone who is not psychotic but carries pre-psychotic tendencies. Some aspects of the personality can function very well in the world, but just underneath there's a pocket that can erupt into psychosis. She describes herself as bright and competent. I certainly can support the brightness, because my impression of her was that's exactly correct. She is extremely articulate and I thought she had a large dose of self-awareness. She says she is not trusting and has never trusted. She describes herself as a person who is not nurtured and is not nurturing.

She has been in and out of psychotherapy of many kinds for a long time, is now under a psychiatrist's care, and is on medication. She has been unable to work and she says all of her therapists have just "hell-fired" her. In other words, they have kicked her out of therapy one after another and, in her terms, described her as "hopeless." When I worked with that particular statement a little bit, she found that all the therapists agreed she has gone as far as she can go in terms of self-understanding and there is a deeper level that she simply will not go after. She's an extremely controlled kind of person. She said two of her therapists have said they have never seen such a great lack of connection between the inner adult and the inner child. I call that to your attention because I would like to address that issue in her chart.

Her mother is now dying of cancer. Her parents live nearby and she sees them regularly. Her description of the mother is interesting because we can compare it with her sister's description. We have a solar chart for the mother (Chart 8 on page 214), which I think will be extremely interesting to look at and, by the way, I do believe a solar chart has great importance. If you can't get a timed chart for a parent, it's a very valuable thing to have because, even though you don't have the houses or the exact position of the Moon and the aspects to it, you have so much information that it's a shame to pass it by because you can't get an exact time. In Joan's words, the mother is vituperative, insulting, and puts her down. The mother has been described as charming, warm to outside people and everybody who meets her says, "You're so lucky to have such a wonderful mother." The family is intensely Catholic. She and her sister both describe that the mother was the adored, only child of a wealthy, very religious family, and that the mother adored her father, the grandfather of these two. The mother married a man who lived in the neighborhood and vowed never to leave the neighborhood because the parents lived nearby. At the time Joan came in for the consultation, she was enormously overweight. In the family of eight (four boys and four girls) all of them weigh over 300 pounds. Two of the boys weigh over 500 pounds and all the siblings have had deep psychological or psychiatric problems. One of the sisters is institutionalized as schizophrenic and has been for fifteen years.

Now, let's look at Martha (see Chart 7 on page 199). Martha is 44, bigger than her sister, weighing about 400 pounds, and she is about six-foot-three. Martha has a doctorate in psychology and had a very high position with the state. For two years now she has been bedridden. She had what she described as "burnout" or "stress-related disability" and her description of it was that she "fell apart." She describes herself as an over-achiever. She's been hospitalized more than three times for emotional distress and she is the sole support of two sons aged 18 and 14. She was married for four years to a very violent, abusive man with a drinking problem, who, interestingly enough, was born on the same day and month as the father. (We do not have the father's chart because neither sister was sure about the year). Martha's husband drank and was abusive and she divorced him, but remarried him nine years ago because she was a Catholic. She was condemned terribly by her parents for divorcing this man. Finally she got a special dispensation and the marriage was annulled, and right after that she was terribly depressed for three years. In her description of herself, again an extremely articulate woman and obviously very intelligent, she says, "I am one-third of a person. I have the ability to *do*, but what is missing is the ability to *be* and to *have*." Her mother told her at age 2 ½ that it was the oldest daughter's duty to take care of the younger children (Martha was the oldest daughter), and from that moment on Martha says she felt that she ceased being a child. She started to be the primary nurturing person, and if anything happened to any of the children growing up, the mother would say, "Go see Martha." So taking on responsibility is the meaning of her life, as she says it. And it's shown by the enormously responsible job she has, raising her children on her own with no support from the husband, taking night classes and going on to get degree after degree until she finally got a

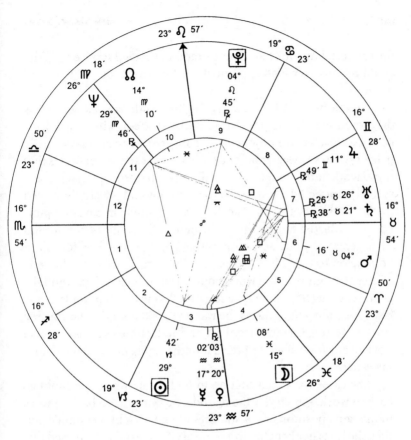

MODALITIES	MISSING	ORIENTATION
Cardinal 2 (☉)	FUNCTIONS	(Houses)
Fixed 7	N/A	Personal 6
Mutable 4		Social 4
	STELLIA	Universal 3
ELEMENTS	N/A	
Fire 2 (♀)		ORIENTATIONS
Air 3	SINGLETONS	(Signs)
Water 2 (☽)	☉ Mutable	Personal 4
Earth 6	♀ Fire	Social 3
	☽ Water	Universal 6
Yang 5		
Yin 8		

Chart 7. Martha.

Birth data withheld for confidentiality. Placidus houses.
Source: birth certificate.

doctorate, taking more and more exams in the civil service until she could get this very high appointed position that brought in a lot of money.

She crashed in 1982, experiencing tremendous anxiety. She was diagnosed with acute upper respiratory distress, which may have been asthma. She acknowledges her anger and she also says a basic belief system she was brought up with—and can't let go of—is that if you work hard enough at it, it will work. She also says that she was sexually abused by the father, and psychically and physically abused by the mother. Both parents believe very strongly in corporal punishment. Martha was teaching communications workshops for top management in business corporations on the side, in addition to holding on to this job. She collapsed in February of 1982 after one of these communication workshops, an emotional collapse, and she is presently feeling incredible fear. She has lost 200 pounds in the last fifteen months and says she was up to 550 pounds. She's feeling stuck in getting further weight off, and at the time I saw her she had not had any food at all for fifteen months, doing nothing but drinking water.

She came for a consultation to find a date when she could go back to work—*ostensibly* the reason. She wants to go back to work in the same position and if she does not go back by a certain deadline, she loses her benefits and seniority. So she has determined that she has something like sixteen months to get back at her job and she's desperately trying to clutch herself together and get herself in shape because she doesn't want to lose this position. She's been working with a psychiatrist for almost two years and she, too, is on medication. She says, "I know *why* I am, not *what* I am. I haven't trusted anyone since age 2," which, according to her, was the time when she began to be sexually abused by the father.

She describes the mother as "vituperative with a snaky tongue." She says the mother has the capacity for flaying you with her tongue by the things that she says. She says the mother is bright, intellectual, and the mother herself (are you ready for this—hang on to your hats) is a professional child-psychologist! Martha says that on a soul level, her mother didn't want children; it was a threat to her relationship with the father. And she (mother) didn't want to get married because it was a threat to her relationship with her own father. Martha has had no friends in her life that she can ever think of, is extremely isolated, as is her sister. The only one in the family she relates to at all is her sister Joan, and even they have great difficulty. So none of the siblings get along with each other. All of them live within a radius of an easy phone call from the mother who is extremely demanding and, as I said, the mother at the present time is dying of cancer.

So let's take a look at both charts from the point of view of the mother, mothering, and the early home environment. Let's begin with the Moon as a significator of mother and early nurturing circumstance and do a comparison of them in both charts. The first thing that I see is that both women have the Moon in the 4th house. Remember what they said, that to the outsider, the mother was charming, cultured, aesthetically pleasing and delightful. And when the girls were growing up, whatever friends they had said, "How lucky you are to have a mother like that," because obviously the persona that the mother was able to put out in social situations was vastly different from the person she was at home.

Looking at the aspects, Joan's Moon-Pluto captures my attention. Her experience with mother and mothering is the archetypal "dark mother" and from her story, it's easy to see it's the negative side of Pluto. If we didn't have that story, we wouldn't know that the mother's personal responsibility was so great and the situation might have been different, but since we know the family background, we can talk about that negative side of Pluto. It's especially striking that the only planets this Moon makes aspects to are Uranus, Neptune, and Pluto. So when the mother is described as this kind of archetypal force, it's really the way the daughter sees her, saying, "I'll never be able to get away from this mother." And, in spite of the fact that the mother seems to give nothing but poison, the daughter keeps coming back for more. Joan is the one that's the primary caretaker of the mother. She's constantly at her beck and call. She never can go far from the phone in case her mother needs her, and when I suggested moving away from the town she's living in to get away from this person, she said, "But how can I do that? I mean, one loves their mother, don't they?" So I find that extremely striking— this Moon relating only to Uranus, Neptune, and Pluto. Remember the description of her therapists who said they had never seen anyone who's "child" was more dissociated from their "adult"? The Moon makes no aspect to personal planets in the chart and kind of forms its own little agreement with these archetypal figures.

Although the mother is the obvious problem and there is this mythic, archetypal thing that Joan experiences as the mother, I would like to know more about who this father is because, as I read the chart, both of these women have very deep incestuous issues with the father. Therefore, the rivalry that is set up with the mother, the dependency that Joan has on her mother, may spring as much from her profound sense of guilt about being the father's lover as from the pathology behind the mother-daughter issue. It could be that it is the one thing that hasn't come up in all the psychotherapy, and the reason why these women are so monstrously overweight is because it's a way of protecting themselves from being sexually attractive. If they felt sexually attractive, it would open up the whole issue of rivalry with the mother, the desire for the father, and the fear of the mother's vengeance.

The father was described as a cold, work-oriented person who was never affectionate, never touched at all except to grope. I see Capricorn on the 10th and ruler of the 10th in the 3rd house conjunct Mars, so I get a Saturnine father.

Audience: I've noticed in a number of charts of incest victims that there were very close aspects to the ruler of the 10th house, or to the Sun with Mars, and there's sort of a narcissistic thing with a Martian father who exploits the younger child because of his own fear of potency in relationships with other adults.

Richard: Yes, and especially since the father calls the mother "Mommy," we see what kind of relationship is going on between the father and the mother. With him referring to his wife as "Mommy," where is he going to put his erotic energy? It goes off to the daughters and apparently all the daughters have been sexually abused. The mother, of course, went totally unconscious and didn't want to know a thing about it, yet at the same time she actively intervened to prevent any obvious intimacy between the father and the daughters. If there was any lap-sitting, the mother would come in and say, "That's disgusting, stop that!" But for the actual sexual stuff that went on, she claimed total unconsciousness of it and denied that it happened or that she had anything to do with it.

Let's look at the Solar aspects for the father in Joan's chart. We see that the Sun is conjunct Venus and trine Jupiter. He is the one who looks beautiful to her, the mother is the one who is the dragon. Her emotional state may be a 3-year-old Oedipus state, and it's probably that issue that needs to come out, but she's so busy mother-bashing that she can't get at it. It is significant that both sisters have agreed that the mother is a monster and I couldn't get either one of them to talk in any great detail about the father. They acknowledge what he's done and what kind of a person he was, but that's it. They actually brought in a picture of the father and he was a very handsome, Saturnine looking fellow.

Audience: Did the mother not like sex, shut out the father and unconsciously push the daughters onto the father?

Richard: Yes, this is a very complicated incest case. Since we know some of the background of the mother, remember how she was fixated on her own father—a strong Oedipal thing was going on with her own father, whom she adored until the day he died, and she never moved farther than ten miles away from where he lived. And in cases of incest there is not just one betrayal, there's two and sometimes three. The first is the betrayal by the father who is misappropriating the filial parent-child relationship and shifting it on to the erotic level. The second is the betrayal of the mother because often the mother colludes and, even when the mother is not actively colluding, the feeling of the child is mother is my protecting influence and she should know. Indeed, on some psychic level, it seems very unlikely that mother wouldn't know. I think there is inevitably an unconscious collusion from the mother and in many ways, the daughter's wound is greater around the mother than it is around the father. Here, Joan is having to carry the mother's sexual shadow. Incest is always a family business—it's never just a rotten father who takes advantage of his daughter. And, increasingly, family therapy is beginning to recognize this and is working with the whole family rather than just the father. The mother is always involved on some level.

Audience: Did the father ever have mistresses or did he ever go outside the marriage for sexual gratification?

Richard: That didn't come up, but since the family was described as rigidly Catholic, I would suspect probably not. You keep it inside, you hold it within the family and that way you prevent scandal because they live in a small town and a man of that class cannot be seen running around. In that kind of religiously structured family, maybe the father was trapped. Perhaps in another system where the father's sexual gratification was not limited to the primary relationship of marriage, it may not have been a problem.

Audience: How much does the father weigh? Is he overweight?

Richard: No he was not. He was extremely tall, about six-foot-six and large, but not overweight. The mother is described as small, petite and dainty.

I think another reason why these girls have swollen up so huge is that it's another thing that puts them in contrast with the mother. And on some level, "The heavier I get, the more unattractive I'm going to be (at least in our social setting) and the more armor I have. My defenses have been violated (on a Lunar level), so I have to protect that in some way. And if I can't do it psychically at least I can do it physically to keep the heart of me intact and untouched behind all these layers of flesh." Also in that context, notice the absence of Earth in Joan's chart. Missing function in Earth—the area where she is least capable of protecting herself—so it would not be surprising that body problems and body image are going to be an enormous issue for her. The inferior function coming up with the denial and repression of all of her sexual energy. As she said, she has only had one sexual experience in her life. When I asked her how the experience was for her, she said, "Well, a glass of buttermilk would have been nicer."

I will talk later in great depth about the Ascendant, but I think it is very interesting that in Joan's chart her missing Earth function is on her Ascendant (Taurus) and in Martha's chart, her inferior function is Water and it's on her Ascendant (Scorpio). I think the Ascendant has the nature of *The Quest*, to discover "Who am I in this world," and I think it is a very particular problem when the Ascendant manifests itself in a quality that is not represented internally in the chart. Archetypally for me, Taurus is the desire to return to that primordial Eden, to that safe, secure place where there is touching, safety, and security. And inside herself, when you look at the 4th house as the roots of the nest, her Eden was Plutonian and Lucifer came in very early. Maybe what she's doing by building this enormous body is trying to surround herself psychically with some kind of Eden-like state. She says, "My only gratification is food."

Audience: I wonder if the sexual abuse by her father was actual intercourse, since she said she had only one sexual experience.

Richard: I asked her that and Joan said she thinks so, but she has blocked it and can't get back to it. I was very careful in dealing with Martha because she was just out of a psychiatric hospital, living with a nurse, and her trip to see me was the first time she had gone out of the house in six months. She sat there shaking and trembling and I did not want to push any more than she was willing to go, but the implication was that it actually was intercourse. However, qualitatively I don't think that it matters.

The sons in the family were more physically abused than the daughters, and Martha was less abused physically than any of the others because she quickly learned her lesson that she was the "little mommy." She took on all the responsibilities and learned to play the game. There's her grand trine in Earth. She took on that earthy responsibility very early and, in a sense, protected herself. Notice here, Sun 29° Capricorn trine Saturn in Taurus plus Uranus and then to the Neptune at 29° Virgo. It is also very interesting that she couldn't recall her father's birthday. She couldn't separate which was her father's birthday and which was her husband's. They were apparently born very close together, maybe not the same day but within days of each other and she had them turned around in her mind, which I thought was metaphorically very symbolic because she was married to an extremely abusive man.

Both sisters have Mercury and Venus in Aquarius and both are conjunct. I think there's something there in the search for the ideal, of something Utopian, and the reluctance to part with the idea of some kind of an *Aquarian agape*—some kind of transforming, uninvolved love. And I'm wondering if both of them blamed their lack of relationships on the mother, and abuse as a child, but I'm not so sure that a lot of this is not inherent with Venus in Aquarius. Venus in Aquarius certainly likes relationships but, not only is it on an ideal level, it also requires a lot of space and distance. And I think it's easy for Venus in Aquarius to trick itself and say, "The right person has never come along."

Audience: My experience with incest victims has been that they frequently lack experience of one good, happy, touching relationship and, because they were sexually aroused in the incestuous experience, later in life they associate any erotic, touching contact with their early, unpleasant circumstance. So sometime in their life they have to come to terms with that and separate the two.

Richard: Yes, I agree, and one of the things in our mythology we don't like to look at is the fact that children are sexual. But there's not the clear-cut dichotomy between sensual and sexual as there is later on when our super-egos begin to come in and tell us what is naughty and what's nice. So the only moments of any kind of physical closeness or touching they had, they learned was bad. And of course, the father himself is carrying an enormous amount of guilt into the situation and therefore probably rejected the daughters afterward. The only time they could get any closeness with him was when they were being fondled.

Society has very little patience or understanding for children who experience incest. Often people assume the child is imagining it, or has invited it, so it has a taboo. You know the Freudians got very tangled up in this whole issue, the whole business of the Oedipal thing, and how much of it is fantasized and how much of it is actualized. I think it touches off a particular minefield that not only exists in the chart of Freud himself, his own pathology, but has been incorporated and swallowed whole into the lexicon of certain kinds of psychology and psychiatry that leaves the child with no place to go. The child is polymorphous-perverse, which is a terrible thing to saddle a child with—a many-shaped sickness is really what they're saying. So the polymorphous-perverse child is in some way inviting this from the parent out of its perversity, and on the other hand, the child is both guiltless and responsible. It's a terrible double-bind to put the child into.

In these charts, with their idealized father image (the Mercury-Venus in Aquarius trine Jupiter), I get the image of Athena springing full-grown from the head of Zeus, her father. She was his alone, no mother bore her. Indeed, when Joan walked in the door she came in like Athena, very strong featured and large, well over six-foot-five, but she carried the largeness very well. She used very broad, sweeping gestures when she talked, despite the fact that she was going through this tremendous period of anxiety, and I got the image of Athena. Also, I think that part of the image of "the father's daughter" is that the father's daughter cannot have another man. And that may mean either retreat into the mind and the intellect, or away from the body and she withdraws from physicality. Athena is rarely shown without her armor, without her shield. She's the warrior goddess.

The singleton Uranus in Mutable in the 2nd house I also find interesting. Remember what we said about inferior functions? Their tendency to erupt from the unconscious and take over either creatively or in a destructive way? I see this in the communications workshop where she fell apart in a nervous collapse, in fact she had a nervous breakdown. She said, "I went to pieces and I haven't got the pieces back together yet." I see that as the eruption of the Mutable and also, her dominant function being Fixed, her normal way of reacting or relating is "pull myself together." That's a quality of fixity. She must have done an enormous amount of holding in for a long, long time and Uranus down here percolates under the unconscious, waiting, like the trickster, to yank the rug out from under her. And, of course, transiting Uranus opposing it's own place is often the time of a mid-life crisis.

There are a number of transits and progressions, I don't have them all in there, to show what was happening at the time I saw her. The progressed Moon was 17° Capricorn, so just in the month before, the Moon was opposing the Mars-Saturn conjunction in Cancer in the 3rd. I think that Uranus opposing Uranus is, in and of itself, enough, but also she is within orb of transiting Pluto squaring the Moon-Pluto conjunction in the 4th, and transiting Neptune is within orb of the Neptune square. A very difficult period. Many of the people born around this time are getting their Neptune-Neptune square just about the same time as their Pluto-Pluto square. This is not such an easy situation to live with, it's quite annihilating, it's more than the usual mid-life crisis. Plus Uranus opposing Uranus, is when all the archetypes are really descending and dropping down into one's life. And I really think a lot of how that is

manifested depends on the level of homework or integration that's
gone on before.

Here we have a very intellectual person whose therapy did not
have anything to do with body work. No Bio-Energetics, no Reichian
stuff, no Rolfing. She has never in her life been massaged. I talked to
both sisters about body things. First of all they find their bodies
horribly ugly. One described herself as a Troll. One says she always
dresses in the dark so she doesn't have to look at this body. Both of
them are really very poisoned on the level of the whole physicality
thing. I suggested that she work with somebody who could work on
a very much deeper level with her, in terms of dreams and fantasy,
and I suggested for both of them, when they feel ready, to get into
something with body work. To get massaged, take hot baths, to have
their hair done. Both of them are physically quite dirty and un-
kempt. You know, dirty fingernails going along with this extreme
brilliance on the intellectual level. One of them very much needed a
bath. I also suggested to Joan that she work with a male therapist
and, since she is very sophisticated and familiar with psychological
jargon, I said that transference to a "good father" would be beneficial and she acknowledged that, she did agree. She had worked with
two women, and one very cold, distant and withdrawn male psychiatrist who doped her up on medicine, so she hadn't actually had
that kind of transference. I did suggest dream work and I did feel
that she was not ready for body work, but I wanted to put that out
there as an eventual area for her to go. She acknowledged that she
was very full of rage and so did her sister.

I'd like to get back to this Mars-Saturn thing. Joan's Mars-Saturn in Cancer, the only planets in Water, is a very difficult conjunction to live with. They work a little better in places like Capricorn or
Aries–Capricorn where they can sublimate some of that stuff, or Aries
where they can act it out in a very inflammatory way. Cancer, Pisces,
Scorpio, or square Neptune, has a suppressive effect on that particular
combination, so she is just beginning to acknowledge her rage. Martha
is much more in touch with it, because Mars is the focal point of her T-
cross and she has come a long way into accepting that anger.

Another thing I find particularly interesting is what I call erotic
significators closely aspecting nurturing or parental significators.
Mars-Saturn is one. Saturn is the Senex; it is at least partly the

father as role of protector, authority figure and wise old man—one who is my channel into the outer world—and Mars is, of course, a very libidinous planet. I often find incestuous situations, I'm not talking about physical, but psychic incestuous relations with the father, or parent, or authority figure, with Mars-Saturn. It gives a kind of double message, mixing nurturing significators with parental ones, and you see that a number of times in these charts.

Moon-Pluto, in and of itself, is a particularly psychically incestuous configuration. For me, Moon-Pluto more constellates the mother as the drama and Mars-Saturn seems to tie in with the father, although it isn't always necessarily that way. And we see it again in Martha's chart. Here's Mars in Taurus, focal point of the T-cross, and let's not forget Pluto on one end of it with the Sun on the other end, which is also the 10th house ruler in Capricorn, the archetypal 10th house sign, so I get another image of the father. Again we have the Sun-Mars and the Pluto-Mars working in potentially psychically incestuous ways. So I think there is something that ought to be born in mind about that. Just like there's a particular problem when transpersonal planets interact with personal planets, there's another particular set of issues that come up when erotic significators become involved with the parental or nurturing significators.

Martha is the one that on the face of it seems to be more severely disturbed. I mean she has been diagnosed and she's been in and out of hospitals a number of times. Martha is larger than her sister, as I said. This is the one with a doctorate in psychology, which I find interesting, since her mother was a child psychologist. And here we find they both have a similar problem. Joan is overweight with lack of Earth and also Water is low in her chart, and Martha has a low function in Water and a strong Earth function. Martha has the grand trine in Earth signs, which I think seems to point a lot to that early acceptance of responsibility. And here is the trap of that grand trine we've been talking about over and over again. There is no struggle against it, it's like, "This is my fate and I not only willingly accept it, I *pursue* it and I can't see myself in any other way except to follow this pattern," having had responsibility thrust on her by her mother, so she says, when she was 2 ½ years old.

By the way, classically with this Capricornian stuff, you have "the little old person." And another thing I often find with people who get cheated out of their childhood, specifically those who are cheated out of their infancy, is that the recoil comes later on in life, often around mid-life, when the submerged helpless infant comes bubbling up to the top and takes everything over. I want to point out that with Joan you have this very suppressed Moon conjunct Pluto, and with Uranus and Neptune it's enough to lock that away for a good forty years. With Martha, we have this Moon singleton, the only planet in Water, and Pluto is also a singleton in Fire. So I think there is a ricochet or recoil effect that happens. People who either miss out very early on in life in the Lunar nurturing, or a little later on in life when the Venusian peer energy begins to happen (the socialization process), eventually a kind of "stunting" emerges at some point.

The Catholicism thing seems powerful in Martha's chart with the chart ruler, Pluto, in the 9th house. There is an innately religious element in her that aspires to serve God and, as part of her grand trine in Earth, it has something to do with her responsibility issue. Also, the father gets mixed up with God. If serving God gets mixed up with serving the father, and if the religious teaching gets distorted, and is expressed in a destructive way—"Do what I say, not what I do"—it really screws her up. So that 9th house Pluto, which is a singleton, is very interesting, because it's an issue with Martha which is not the case with Joan. When the religious issue came up in my discussion with Joan, she said, "The family is Catholic but I left that stuff a long time ago." She dismissed it a little too breezily for me. In my dialogue with Martha she talked about religion a great deal. Remember she was the one who couldn't leave the abusive husband because they were Catholic. She divorced him, then remarried him and finally had the marriage annulled, but she said, "In my soul I'm still married to this man." Also, I think certain Moon positions are much more attracted to certain religions than others, and Moon in Pisces surely moves in that direction. Here's the *mater dolorosa*, the sorrowing mother, and she did, indeed, become the sorrowing mother at 2 ½ years old to all the siblings. But I think Moon in Pisces likes that and can easily be persuaded in that direction, so there's a certain given.

I'd like to point out a couple of things that we've talked about. Sun, Moon, and Pluto are singletons in Martha's chart. Both of the

Lights are singletons, Moon is singleton in Water, and the Sun in Cardinal. Her chart is far more dramatic than Joan's. You have the T-cross with the focal point Mars; you have the three singletons: Sun, Moon, and Pluto; you have the grand trine in Earth and, by the way, a stationary Saturn in the 7th house in Taurus, and a stationary Venus in Aquarius in the 3rd house. So, while on the face of it, Martha's chart seems to be more difficult than Joan's, here is the paradox, I have more hope for Martha's recovery than I do for Joan's. I think Martha has gone down to the pit and Joan is so together that she never will quite. Martha has experienced annihilation, she truly has fallen into madness and Joan is still on the brink saying, "No, no, no!" to it, and Joan may get physically sick if she does nothing about this.

Audience: Does the fact that the planets in her 6th house of health are retrograde add to that possibility?

Richard: I think that if personal planets are retrograde, it introverts the energy, but I would be hesitant to assign pathological meaning to retrograde outer planets in the natal chart. When a planet by progression changes direction it's an important significating thing. Her Saturn by progression has gone stationary and I think it brings up issues around that particular archetype when by progression it shifts direction. I notice that within a few years, in both charts, a planet will switch direction, going on its station, going from retrograde to direct, or from direct to retrograde, and that often seems to trigger a crisis in the life.

The thing I'm looking at is Moon-Pluto in Joan's chart and Sun-Pluto in Martha's chart, and I think there is an interesting paradox about the idea of food. When Core goes down into the underworld and becomes Persephone, she locks the situation in by eating the three seeds of the pomegranate. Eve and Adam are expelled from Eden for eating—the thing that they have taken in. I think there is something about binding oneself to this underworld through food, through the ingestion of something. And I think what's happening is that Martha is starting to vomit it up. She hasn't eaten in fifteen months, and you see, for her in some way food is tainted with this underworld stuff. And interestingly enough, Joan says she can't keep food down, she's throwing up everything she eats. Martha is not eating for fifteen months and Joan is throwing up everything she eats.

And isn't it interesting that the mother is dying now? That is fascinating. As if somehow it means the release of the food. It's like a fairytale where they've been under the spell of the wicked witch. In fact, I call this a classic case of *Snow White and the Seven Dwarfs* with the poisoned apple. On a psychic level, the food is poison, and what happens when that occurs very early in life is one gets an appetite for poisoned apples. But now, with the transpersonal planets coming along by transit to trigger that natal stuff, there's movement and things are shifting. And although the results of this may have pathological overtones, I see it from Martha's point of view as healing.

The paradox with Joan is she's full of trines and sextiles, in fact she hasn't one opposition to her name. There are some squares between Mars-Saturn and Neptune, but that's all. And the trap of the so-called "easy chart" is to adjust too easily. Martha, on the other hand, cannot adjust, she's thrust into the flame all the time. Although, on the face of it, right now she seems to be more pathologically involved, there's more dynamic struggle going on. Even with all her disturbance, and dosed up on thorazine when she came to see me, this was a far more feisty, intense, passionate person than Joan. I think they're both in the process of psychically killing the mother while she is physically dying of cancer, and they are racing with time to try and kill that mother before she kills herself. The mother's spell is lessening and they can begin to vent their anger and hate.

I also want to point out that transiting Pluto is now making a grand cross out of Martha's natal T-cross and triggering all this response. She is beginning to literally emerge, where for six months she hasn't ventured out. She told me she sat in her car for an hour, shaking, before she could get herself to drive, so she's coming out of the darkness. You know, I've often wondered what was the dialogue when Persephone came back by the insistence of Zeus, and isn't it interesting that it is Zeus who triggers Persephone to come back? It's the archetypal male sky-god who says, "We have to return this child to her mother." It's Aphrodite who doesn't like the imbalance and lures her down below and it's Zeus who brings her back. At some time I would love to invent a dialogue between Persephone and her mother when she returns.

Audience: I wonder what level of awareness the mother has, and are the sisters living with her?

Richard: No, neither of the daughters are living with the mother, they both live separately. Martha has been diagnosed as schizophrenic and has been at home under a nurse's care for the last six months.

Now, let's look at the mother's chart (see Chart 8 on page 214). Remember, we don't have the mother's birth time so this is a Solar Chart and exact planetary positions are speculative, as are all the houses. Nevertheless, do not pass by using a Solar Chart just because you don't have houses and exact Moon positions because there's plenty of information there anyway.

I want to point out Sun is a singleton in Fixed and again the Saturn shows up, this archetypal Saturn, a singleton in Fire. Of course I left out the houses because we can't know what they are. Several configurations impress me: Mars conjunct Pluto, Moon conjunct Uranus, and Saturn in Aries square the Moon-Uranus. Moon-Uranus-Saturn. Even if the Moon shifts for an exact birthtime, it's still going to be within orb of the square to Saturn-Uranus, and here's the combination we were talking about before—Mars, Pluto, Uranus, Moon. Where did we see that? In Josef Mengele, the cutter-up-into-pieces for some kind of a greater cause. There is something very fierce in that kind of combination, and the Moon seems to be on the receiving end of that, the Moon being the inner-child and the capacity for mothering as well. So the mother also appears to have felt rejected as a child, lacking the nurturing she so desperately needed, which she passed along to the daughters. And you can see how these things do not just spontaneously emerge, like Aphrodite from the sea. It's a series of links and loops from generation to generation, which often helps to relieve us from this business of constant blame. I mean, every parent is somebody's child, and that child is the child of another parent, who was the child of another parent, and so on. By widening our orientation, we can visualize these things in a very different way.

I am particularly impressed by this Sun-Neptune sextile, it being the only real aspect to the Sun anyway. Of course, there's a wide

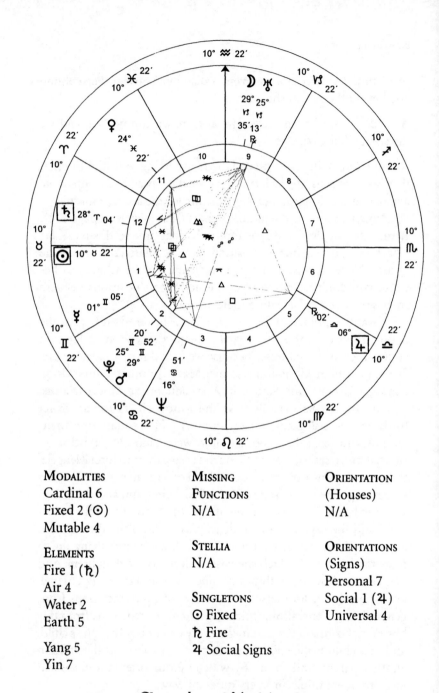

MODALITIES
Cardinal 6
Fixed 2 (☉)
Mutable 4

ELEMENTS
Fire 1 (♄)
Air 4
Water 2
Earth 5

Yang 5
Yin 7

MISSING
FUNCTIONS
N/A

STELLIA
N/A

SINGLETONS
☉ Fixed
♄ Fire
♃ Social Signs

ORIENTATION
(Houses)
N/A

ORIENTATIONS
(Signs)
Personal 7
Social 1 (♃)
Universal 4

Chart 8. Joan and Martha's mother.
This is a solar chart with Sun degree used as the ascendant.

quincunx to Jupiter, but the only way she can get to this Sun is through this idealizing Neptune. Here is this only child, adoring her father, and did she on some subconscious level set up her daughters to actually physically experience what she was psychically experiencing with her own father? I don't know. What I get from the Moon conjunct Uranus square Saturn is the mother apparently had the same set-up with her own mother, and felt extremely unwanted. I think there is jealousy in her nature because Saturn in Aries wants to be first, and Venus square Pluto is very possessive. Often, a mother who has not been given what she needs, resents it if her own daughters get something she didn't get.

This same dynamic often constellates between a father and a son. A father who is fixated on his mother, and has never been able to psychically separate and break the umbilical cord, turns in resentment on his son because the son becomes a competitor for the second mother, who is his wife. The very same thing happens in reverse here between mother and daughter, and it's a very important dynamic. This woman apparently could not separate from the desire for a kind of divine union with her mystically ideal father. Yes, indeed, she got married and had children, but in order to mother these children she would have had to give up her own infancy or adolescence, which implies, "I can't merge with this ideal (my father) if I grow up, become an adult and a mother, because I'll lose that ideal forever." That's why she had to become the mother of her husband, not the lover of her husband.

There's a silent dialogue that goes back and forth between mother and daughter. The mother is saying unconsciously to the daughter, "Well I won't destroy you. I may give you a little bit of love provided you don't try to compete with me sexually." And I see that very often configured in Moon-Venus-Pluto relationships in the chart. It's the archetype of the Wicked Queen in Snow White, "Who is the fairest of them all?" Moon and Venus together already constellates with, "Am I woman as mother, or woman as lover?" Bringing in the Pluto is, "Can I stand for my own child to replace me as either the Lunar figure that means nurturing, or as the Venusian figure, the fairest of them all?" The wicked Queen in the story wasn't so wicked until her mirror told her that she was no longer the fairest in the land.

This particular configuration starts to constellate pretty powerfully at adolescence and, for a mother, when her *daughters* hit adolescence and in the mother's chart, there is a reluctance to change. The grand trine of Moon, Jupiter, and Mercury is a closed system—a closed system in which everything is all right. It's even more difficult than a grand cross, which is a closed system in which everything is *wrong*. That is at least more dynamic with more opportunity for growth. The mother's grand trine does describe the child psychologist, however. The very intelligent Mercury in Gemini, with modern informative insights, shown by trine Uranus, trine Moon, trine Jupiter. And with her cartload of enlightened ideas filling her mind, she doesn't notice anything else. She can hide in it because she's so positive in her mental outlook, and it can be her defense against that Moon-Uranus-Saturn, which hurts so much inside her. It makes me wonder, in her choice of profession, *what* child she really felt a necessity to heal.

I find it interesting that a little petite woman picks a man six foot four or five, or whatever he was, and I think that's no accident either. Maybe this is the larger-than-life physical replacement for the God-like figure that her father was. Remember we talked about when the personal and transpersonal planets are involved? Notice the Venus is not only disposed of by Neptune, but trine Neptune, sextile Uranus, and square Pluto, and that's the seeking for the transpersonal within the interpersonal. "I want to create this archetypal divine *other* in my life, I will settle for nothing less, and father is safe to do that with because I cannot actually consummate that. Maybe my children can act out that part of it for me, so I find another man who, of course, is bound to end up disappointing me."

This afternoon we'll shift gears and get into another topic.

❦

CHAPTER EIGHT

THE ASCENDANT AS MASK

Here are the charts of Ernest Hemingway[1] and Hart Crane[2], which we'll be looking at now (see Charts 9 and 10 on pages 218 and 219). Ernest Hemingway, I assume all of you are familiar with, Hart Crane you may not know, but he was a very famous poet who died very young. As you will see, the charts are practically reverses of each other. They were born on the same day, the same year and just about twelve hours apart.

I want to talk about the Ascendant as mask and also the concept that we were referring to before, the tendency for things to become their opposites. Jung said we have a tendency to be drawn toward that which remains shadow or inferior function. There is an attraction in that opposite and until we can embrace the projected "other," the opposite comes at us in various ways—through relationships with other people, through events, through symbolic things, as in dreams.

Yesterday we were talking about the opposite of the King and the Fool—Leo and Aquarius archetypally. Our Israeli friend pointed

---

1. Ernest Miller Hemingway (1899 – 1961): American novelist, journalist, writer, considered one of the most influential authors of the first half of the 20th century. Awarded the Nobel Prize for literature in 1954.
2. Hart Crane (1899 – 1932): American poet best known for *The Bridge*, an epic poem encompassing American visions and myths, which won the annual Poetry Award in 1930.

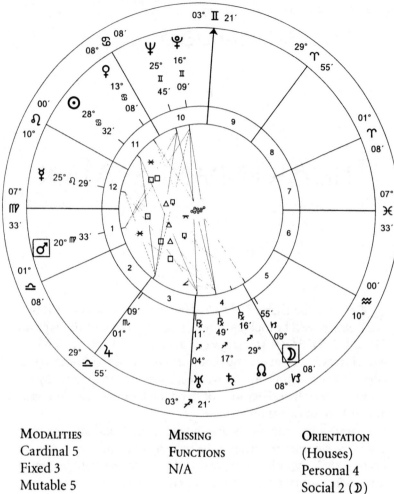

MODALITIES	MISSING	ORIENTATION
Cardinal 5	FUNCTIONS	(Houses)
Fixed 3	N/A	Personal 4
Mutable 5		Social 2 (☽)
	STELLIA	Universal 7
ELEMENTS	N/A	
Fire 4		ORIENTATION
Air 2 (Ψ♇)		(Signs)
Water 4	SINGLETONS	Personal 5
Earth 3 (♂)	♂ Earth	Social 4
	☽ Social Houses	Universal 4
Yang 6		
Yin 7		

Chart 9. Ernest Hemingway.

Born July 21, 1899, Oak Park, IL, 41N41, 87W48, 8:00 A.M. CST.
Placidus houses.

Source: Mother's diary quoted in Carlos Baker's *Ernest Hemingway: A Life Story*
(New York: Macmillan, 1976), cited in Lois Rodden: *Astro-Data II*
(Tempe, AZ: American Federation of Astrologers, 1980).

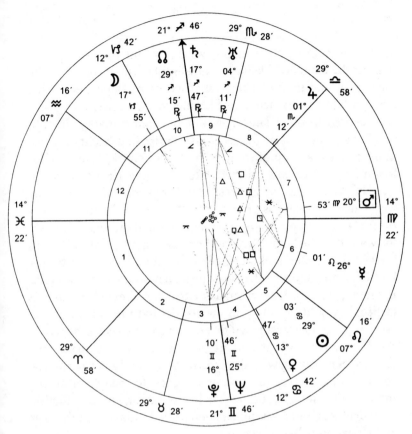

MODALITIES	MISSING FUNCTIONS	ORIENTATION (Houses)
Cardinal 5	N/A	Personal 3
Fixed 2		Social 6
Mutable 6		Universal 4

ELEMENTS
Fire 3
Air 3 (ΨΨ)
Water 4
Earth 3 (♂)

STELLIA
N/A

ORIENTATION (Signs)
Personal 6
Social 3
Universal 4

SINGLETONS
♂ Earth

Yang 6
Yin 7

Chart 10. Hart Crane.

Born July 21, 1899, Garretsville, OH, 81W06, 41N17 8:50 P.M. CST.
Placidus houses.
Source: LeGros in *American Astrology* (4/50), time uncertain
("C" data, according to Lois Rodden, in *Astrodata IV*
(Tempe, AZ: American Federation of Astrologers, 1990).

out to me that in Hebrew many *words* show the opposite quality right in the language. Nemak is King and Lemak is Fool, and she was saying that in the Hebrew language, many opposites are the same with just the switch of one letter. A very intelligent language. You see that in other languages, too, but unfortunately English, which is a wonderful language because it's rich in its ability to communicate, is made up of so many roots, like Greek, Latin, Anglo-Saxon, French, and so on, that we've lost that very neat use of words.

The Ascendant, for me, relates to Jung's idea of a mask. The word "mask" in latin is *persona* and the idea of the mask comes from a latin word *personare,* meaning "to sound through." This was the word that the Latins gave for the ancient masks that the Greeks used in the theater, and the Greek mask did a number of things. First of all, the actors work in very great arenas, and if you ever go to Epidoras in Greece, it's a remarkable experience. Literally thousands of people would be sitting in the stands, and the point was that everybody could hear, and it didn't matter so much what they could see. These giant masks that the actors wore showed that the character they were playing was an archetype, it wasn't really a person. So you had an archetype of a god or a goddess for people in various moods and emotions, such as fear, horror, terror, joy, love, foolishness, madness, and it was understood from the masks that this is an archetypal thing being acted out.

The masks had another purpose, too. They acted as a megaphone to channel the sound out into this enormous arena. That's why the Latins called it *personare,* "to sound through," from which Jung took the word *persona,* and of course, we have the word *personality.* So, the Ascendant is like one of these sounding-through masks. It is the face that we put out toward the world in our interaction with people. It is the mask that we put on, and it's made up of many things. It's made of what we might call personality, although that's such a vague word we don't really know what that means. It has to do with style, posture, the way we come across, our body stance.

There are obviously twelve archetypal personas based on the twelve signs rising, so you can talk about a Pisces-rising *type,* but remember there's more to that than meets the eye isn't there? It's going to be vastly different depending on what sign and house Neptune is in, because the position of the Ascendant ruler by sign and by house modifies the archetypal principle of the sign on the Ascendant. Furthermore, planets that aspect the Ascendant ruler will further modify that persona. Also planets making an aspect to the Ascendant will further modify the persona. So you see, it starts out fairly simple, with a sign rising, but it gets more and more complicated as you add to it.

I believe there is a certain misunderstanding about masks. First of all, people may think it's a thing that you ought to overcome, and that really isn't so. It's a part of us, just as the skin and our clothes are a part of us, and we apparently learn how to use the persona very early on in life. Those of you who are parents began to notice the effect of your children's rising sign very early on. So the first thing I want to look at is what is this mask all about, what is it masking, what's the purpose of it? Well, the mask serves very much like our clothes—it protects us from the elements. Somebody might say it's unnatural. We weren't born with clothes, and in the wild, people don't wear clothes, so maybe we should overcome clothes. It has a defensive property, does the mask. It protects us from the elements like our clothes. It protects us from too much attention, or approach from other people, and it also has another quality. There's an assertive quality about the persona; in other words, it makes a statement about ourselves. I often call this our *advertising*; this is how we are advertising ourselves.

It is no accident that people dress the way they do, especially in a society like ours. We're not tribal. We're not in ancient Greece where everybody wears a uniform, and we are not like the European countries of the Middle Ages where a person's class was told by the kind of clothes he or she wore. Now our individuality is shown through a statement by the clothes we wear. How do you wear your hair? What kind of makeup do you use if you're a woman? The question of weight, being over- or underweight has an awful lot to do with the Ascendant, because that's part of the body-mask, it's part of our armor. Not only that, then there's body-language that has a great deal to do with what kind of statement we're making out there in the world.

I'll give you a case in point. A client came to me for a consultation who had a grand trine in Fire signs—Moon, Sun, Jupiter—and she said, "I don't know why I have such difficulty making friends. Everybody tells me that I'm cold and withdrawn and hard to get to know." She had Saturn exactly conjunct the Ascendant. Her body language, when she came in for the consultation, was kind of crouched over, and she sat there kind of pulled-in. Saturn does that. Saturn is a defensive planet normally and there's a sense of withdrawal. Yet her Sun, Moon, and Jupiter in Fire signs convinced her that this is not the way she is at all. So many people have a great deal of difficulty. What's the poem by Robert Burns—"O wad some Pow'r the giftee gie us To see oursels as others see us!"[3] And it's often a very uncomfortable thing, the first time we get in touch with this archetypal mask, and some people never really do. But astrology gives us a great deal of insight into seeing how this works. It's often a shock when you first get in touch with your persona.

Here are a couple of examples. A friend of mine with Libra rising used to complain that people always said to him, "You're so together, what a happy-go-lucky person you are!" Of course, if you look at the inside of his chart, you'd see there is a vastly different thing there. That is just the wrapping on the package. He said, "I never get any sympathy, compassion or tender-loving-care, what is it that I'm doing?" Well, one time he was feeling terrible, having a very bad day and didn't want to see anybody. He was walking down the street in New York by one of those giant glass buildings, and as he approached a corner, he saw someone coming from the other way whom he knew very well. He couldn't see clearly enough through the glass to tell exactly who it was, but he knew it was a familiar figure. So, by the time he got to the corner, there he was with this big Jack-O-Lantern smile on his face and looking at the reflection of himself. Suddenly it clicked for him what it was that he did—he went right into his mask.

We don't often get a chance to see that mirrored back at us. One of the best ways to see our mask can be photographs or movies taken of ourselves, which is why it's so uncomfortable. And isn't it interesting which ones you tear up? You say, "That does not look like me," but what you're really saying is, "That does not look like the me I would like me to look like." Now, what is the reason? It is no accident that this mask forms, so I think we ought to look at the 7th and 12th houses to understand more clearly where the persona

3. Robert Burns, "To a Louse," line 33.

comes from. As I see it, the 7th house, the house of the *archetypal other*, the house of the archetypal not-self, is in a way how we visualize the world out there. In the 7th house is contained a lot of our projections in general. "What is this world that is not me?" And to the extent that we are projecting, and of course all of us do project, we begin to see this world outside of ourselves as archetypal. There are angels and monsters and devils and ogres and beautiful maidens there, to the degree that we are still not integrating the 7th house.

So the projections that we place into the 7th house are often personalized into the ideal-other, the ideal marriage partner. You see, houses are *not* people, but we personalize houses into *being* people. For instance, I don't think it is necessarily right to say the 10th house *is* the father and the 4th house *is* the mother and the 5th house *is* the lover and the 7th house *is* the wife or husband. We're personalizing something that is essentially an arena of events in which we act things out. But, of course, since we are always projecting, naturally we do project these arenas onto the proper person to inhabit that stage set. Do you see what I'm saying? If, for instance, the set is a throne room, then naturally what we're looking for is a King or a Queen.

Audience: You say we see the world as the 7th house, do you mean the cusp?

Richard: You see it in point of view of planets in the 7th, the sign on the cusp of the 7th, aspects to planets in the 7th, and so forth, just like we interpret the Ascendant. It's the exact mirror. Just as *we* are the Ascendant, and its ruler, and the aspects to it, and any planets in the 1st house, the same thing happens with the 7th. Another thing is that it's very easy to simply project across from 1st to 7th. Any material in the 1st house we don't like, we simply say, "It isn't me, it's you." Or, "Yes I do that, but it's all you people out there making me do it," and that's a projection.

Now, remember one of the interesting things we said about projections is they have two natures. We project positively and we wish to incorporate into ourselves all of these wonderful things about the "other" out there that we do not own. But when we get the package home and unwrap it, we don't like it so much anymore, because then the extremely unbalanced positive projection switches polarity and we get the extremely unbalanced negative projection. For example, a woman may be attracted to a particular type of man because he's strong and powerful (let's say she has Mars, Pluto, Saturn in Leo in the 7th house), and he's dynamic, forceful, competitive. She finds that very attractive in the beginning, but try living with it. So pretty soon she's complaining, "He's so overbearing and dominating and pompous and power driven and ego-centered and narcissistic." So what often happens is she then wants to come to a counselor and say, "Fix my husband." Where is this wonderful man I first met? He's changed." Well, *he* hasn't changed, her *perception* has changed. What she really is saying is, "My projection has fallen away and my perception of you has shifted. Shift back please to what you were when I was still projecting on you positively," and how can anybody do that? So, since he's confronted with a hobson's choice and cannot do that, she may then say, "All right, if I can't fix you and I won't fix me, then I have to get rid of you and find somebody else," and the whole process starts all over again. It's interesting how many people I talk to who think they are advertising for poets and keep getting truck drivers. They don't understand that they're advertising for truck drivers and you get what you're advertising for.

Audience: What happens when you get past the 7th house into the 8th house and into the nitty-gritty of the relationship? Do you look to the cusp of the 8th house to see what's going on in the 8th?

Richard: I never thought of it in those terms, but perhaps it's possible.

Audience: Are you saying that the 7th house is kind of like a want ad?

Richard: The *Ascendant* is the want ad because we are putting out the mask to attract the complementary opposite.

Audience: If the Ascendant is what you're advertising *you* are, saying, "This is what I have to offer," and what I need is maybe what I'm advertising *for*, which would be the 7th house.

Richard: That's right. It's like the bait you use depends on the fish you're after, and the signs work in complementary opposites.

For example, I used to teach astrology in a prison in California and Dr. Timothy Leary [4] was then a gentleman-in-residence at that institution. He would come to my Sunday classes and sit in, but he always arrived after I started and would leave before I finished. I wanted some contact with the man, so I wrote him a note asking if he would like to meet with me, and he wrote back a very nice note which said he had been looking forward to that, and did want to meet me. So I got some office space and we had a rendezvous.

He began by saying, "Ah, yes, astrology. Very, very interesting, this astrology. What do you know about I Ching?" I told him I knew a little bit about the I Ching and that I had used it. He asked, "Have you ever made a correlation with that and astrology?" I said, "Not a direct correlation, but I find that interesting." Then he asked what I thought about the Kabbalah, and I said I find the Kabbalah fascinating, especially in some of its numerological and mystical symbolisms. "How about tarot?" he asked. I said yes, obviously tarot and astrology are certainly correlated, especially horary astrology. And he said, "I have to go." We had only been together about three minutes and I was taken aback. Fortunately, however, I had seen his chart and he has Sagittarius rising, so his mask is "teacher," "guru." My role was to play the 7th house Gemini—I had to be the wide-eyed student saying, "Oh, I don't know, tell me all about everything." Suddenly that clicked in for me and I decided to make an experiment. Let's see if he asks one more question and I'll see if it works. On the way out the door he turned to me and said, "What do you know about mandalas?" I said, "Nothing. I know nothing about them and would like to know all about mandalas." "Oh," he said "I know all about mandalas." He turned back into the room and we talked for two hours, or rather I should say, *he* talked for two hours and I listened. He later described me to a third person we both know as an extremely articulate and intelligent young man!

So there is a lot of power and information in knowing about that 1st house–7th house stuff. I was guessing that he was still projecting, because he was advertising "teacher" and there were no

4. Timothy Leary: 1960's counterculture leader and founder of *The League for Spiritual Discovery*, which advocated legaliziing LSD and marijuana as religious sacraments. For a sampling of Leary's work, see his *Flashbacks: A Personal & Cultural History of an Era* (Los Angeles: J. P. Tarcher, 1990).

students available to respond to his ad. If I became the archetype of what it is he was advertising for, I would get contact with him. Now, many many people are stuck in that mask, that's how they live. Virgo-Pisces, for example, is the helper and the helpless, and there's a constant, subtle advertising for each other. Pisces needs Virgo like Virgo needs Pisces until one becomes one's own opposite. That is why I think the 7th house is the house of marriage *and* the house of the open-enemy, because when we're positively projecting, those are the qualities we want to incorporate in marriage, but when it shifts into the negative side it becomes the open-enemy. Sometimes it works the other way around. There's a marvelous line in the film *Stalag 17*, that wonderful old film with William Holden. Holden, who is playing an inmate in a concentration camp, is talking to the guy who is the head of security, and who later turns out to be a Nazi spy. They're left alone in the barracks, and the Nazi spy is supposed to be guarding Holden, whom everybody thinks is a Nazi spy. So Holden says, "Well, since we're alone together, we might as well have a bit of conversation," and the security chief says, "Look, I don't like you, I never liked you, I don't like what you stand for, I don't like who you are, you make my flesh crawl." And Holden replies, "Other people have said that and the first thing you know, they get married." So it works the other way around, too. It's interesting how that thing happens, how you're fatally drawn to something which seems so repulsively awful. Here's *Beauty and the Beast* and, maybe by embracing it, just like Beauty does the Beast, you see the other side, the positive part of it.

So part of what the Ascendant as a defense mechanism says is, "I put this mask or armor on because I see the world outside of myself in this way." The 7th house gives us some clue as to how we envision the world of *not-self* (I don't know how else to put it except to call it not-self, the world of others), which we often personalize into a projection on one idealized other that we think we want to marry. Do you take my meaning? So the mask is always the complementary opposite sign of what we are projecting onto the idealized other, it always is.

Planets can work either way. Any planet in the 1st can flop over into the 7th and be projected outward. For example, a woman with a 1st house Mars, especially a fiery Mars, may find it much more convenient in getting along in the world to simply drop it over into the 7th house. Why? Because women are socialized by our society to not be overtly Martian, so it's much easier for her to do it. Let's say a man with Venus in Pisces in the 1st might find it very easy, rather than to identify with it, to give it over to the opposite side. Can you tell by looking at a chart what someone will do? No. How do you find out? You'll find out pretty quickly after meeting the person. Body language, posture, voice, how this person comes across, makes that statement very clearly if you have the eyes to see. As astrological counselors, it's important for us to be students of body language.

What actors learn is how to get out of the trap of their mask. Why? Because otherwise they become what is called the type-cast actor and they get stuck in one role. Indeed, Hollywood in it's hey-day in the 30s and 40s kept lists of actors by their Ascendant sign. If you wanted a beautiful man with not too much fire, you'd get Robert Taylor. If you wanted a Libra rising, cool and disconnected, you get a Grace Kelly because, although everything was in Scorpio, that's what the mask was showing. If it's Taurus you want then you get Bing Crosby, or Perry Como, or Gary Cooper, or Henry Fonda— slow, easy-going. So, the movie business, which is made out of illusions, is based on a lot of masks, and people whose masks are archetypal enough can become a star without even having to be an actor. Like Marilyn Monroe with her Leo Ascendant and Neptune, of course, sitting right on the Ascendant.

Part of what the Ascendant does, then, is become a circuit that's going on with the 7th house. But there's more. Every sign is linked with the sign before it and the sign after it. Take Pisces as an example. If Pisces could be here speaking archetypally, it would say, "I am no longer Aquarius, I am not yet Aries and I complete myself through Virgo." So each sign arises out of the qualities of the sign before it—an evolutionary or developmental process takes place through the twelve signs. In other words, here is where we talk about sacrifice again, isn't it? Pisces can only *become* Pisces by no longer being Aquarius. Aries can only be Aries by no longer being Pisces. But there's a double message. "You cannot lose the Piscean-ness of it," says Aries. I'll give you another example. If we're going to evolve, you cannot become a child until you evolve out of your

infancy, and yet you don't want to lose it all either. You do not become an adolescent until you evolve out of some of the things of
your childhood, but you're not yet an adult. So we are fixed in time
and space depending upon where we're coming *from*, and where
we're going *to*. An adult is defined as a mature person, no longer an
adolescent, a child or an infant, and not yet the wise old father or
the wise old mother. So we are all in that archetypal process of movement.

The sign on the Ascendant, in a way, protects us, or *masks* us
from the consciousness of the quality of the sign on the 12th house,
which is the thing we are developing out of. That's why I call the
12th house the *cosmic closet*, because it is often material that is not
ready yet to come into consciousness, or material that threatens the
mask, the Ascendant. Indeed, you'll find what happens is that when
we fall into our 12th house, when we get an experience of this unconscious material that may be suppressed in the 12th, it shatters
the mask. Just like when we get over here into the 7th house and
truly understand our projections, we break the mask.

Audience: What if you have the same sign on the 12th house as on
the Ascendant?

Richard: Well, I have a few things to say about that. First of all, that
is a possibility that shifts with a house system. A lot of the interior
house cusp positions shift according to what house system you use,
and I don't want to get into the dogma of correct or incorrect house
systems. So I would answer that question paradoxically in two ways.

First of all I'd say, if the same sign is on the cusp of both houses
it is possible that certain qualities of the sign are repressed into the
12th and certain qualities are lived out. Some are more acceptable
than others, and it depends upon the sex and role we're playing. For
instance, a woman with Aries on the Ascendant and Aries on the
12th may find it acceptable to be outgoing and extroverted, but it
may be necessary for her to hide her competitiveness and her libido. A man with Pisces on the Ascendant and Pisces on the 12th
may find it acceptable to be moody or poetic, but not passive. What
we're looking at here is archetypes, and no matter what is on the
12th house cusp, the 12th house *sign*, the sign that is one back from
the Ascendant, is really what we're concerned with, so it doesn't
matter whether it's on the 12th or the 11th.

Audience: What happens when the Ascendant changes by progression?

Richard: Watch the mask shift. We are born with a certain natal mask, just like we are with a certain chart, but it does shift and develop. It's like a kaleidoscope. Have you ever played with a kaleidoscope? They're wonderfully funny. You have the same components, but you shake it up and it forms a different pattern. And so the progressions do change and shift; watch for particular changes when it moves from the 29th degree of one sign into zero of another.

So part of the Ascendant function, the reason we need to mask, is that we are masking from our own unconscious, at least potentially repressed, our pre-conscious material, or things from the collective archetype that we are not ready to integrate from the 12th. The mask either protects us from what we see out there in the 7th house, or it gives us the quality to go out and get what we see out there. Again, if you're fishing for salmon you put something different on the hook than if you're fishing for tiger. So the Ascendant, the planets in it and the aspects to it is the way you bait your hook and most of us are not conscious of why we wear the things we wear and why we sit the way we sit. Persona is being demonstrated all the time.

Audience: Can you say something about the ruler of the Descendant in the 1st house?

Richard: Yes, if the ruler of the Ascendant is in the 7th house, or the ruler of the 7th is in the 1st, then it's very likely to simply shift the material back and forth. Again, depending on the quality of the planet, it's saying, "Is it something acceptable for me to own?" There often can be confusion between "me" and "others." For instance, Aries on the Ascendant and Mars in the 7th, or vice versa, it doesn't much matter, might say, "Yes, I'm angry but it's because you keep irritating me," or "Of course I'm pushy because you're so indecisive." So it can be a confusion as to who is doing what. Do you ever get into arguments with people that don't ever seem to get anywhere? You're saying, "You know I'm experiencing you this way," and the other person says, "It's not me that is doing that, it's you!" Or, "I only do that because you do it to me first." It's an uncomfortable situation and the other person says, "I really pick up your hostility and I'm not hostile to you, you're just projecting your hostility to me."

Audience: How do you differentiate between 12th house planets in the sign on the Ascendant and 12th house planets in the sign previous to the Ascendant, like Aries rising and a planet in Aries in the 12th and a planet in Pisces in the 12th?

Richard: Well, I would simply look at the archetype of the planet, and, of course, the sign that it's in is the archetypal principle through which it is going to be presenting itself. Obviously, a planet in the Ascendant sign is going to be drawn forward into the Ascendant because it naturally has an affinity for it, but it might bring back into the unconscious certain qualities of the Ascendant. Let's say you have Venus in Aries in the 12th house with Aries rising. What may be suppressed into the 12th is the charming side of Venus. In this particular example, if it's a man's chart, I would say it may be possible to put the charming, sweet, more harmonious qualities that Aries has into the 12th and tuck that away. Or, let's say, a woman with Taurus rising and Mars in Taurus in the 12th: it's much easier to tuck the Mars back into the 12th house, where it's more acceptable.

Now, let's kind of hold your "what if" questions for a while and move on. Each of the twelve signs has a certain kind of tendency, a certain way of behaving. Generally speaking, the Yin signs (the six feminine signs) tend to be more introverted than extroverted. Their defensive function is more developed than their extroverted, "advertising" function, and that is very often why people with a feminine sign rising tend to seem shy or withdrawn or withheld. The six Yang (or masculine) signs rising tend to show themselves in extroverted ways, and some signs are more extroverted than others. Aries, for instance, because it's both Cardinal and outgoing in Fire, is probably the most Yang kind of quality you could have. Now, like dominant and inferior functions, we may have masks that are totally inaccessible to our experience of ourselves and to our family myths. For instance, what if you are a woman with Mars in Aries conjunct the Ascendant? That's not particularly easy, depending on which society you live in, so you may, just like the unacceptable dominant function, suppress it. When that happens, great problems can begin to occur because you have to import other qualities to try and hide what you most naturally are. Is there any way of looking at the chart and knowing that? No, but you can find it pretty well by talking with people.

Let me give you another example. A woman I know has 28° Pisces on the Ascendant and if you were to meet her, you would find her explosively energetic, loud, very dramatic, nervous, intense, fiery, passionate. She did not have her exact birthtime, or so she thought, because it was right on the hour. Anyway, she was one of these people who goes from astrologer to astrologer and all of us took one look at her and rectified her chart immediately. So everybody naturally put her into Aries rising. However, subsequently she found an exact hospital-recorded birthtime that gave her 28° Pisces rising, so it was right. But, what they failed to look at was the fact that she had Mars at 28° 51' Sagittarius on the Midheaven, and on the other side, Uranus at 29° Gemini in the 4th house, both making a square to the Ascendant! So, watch out for those instant rectifications. The power and the explosive quality came from the fact that these two very Yang planets in Yang signs are squaring the Ascendant.

Remember, the sign on the Ascendant is a kind of lens through which the planet's aspects filter. Mars squaring through a Pisces Ascendant is going to be vastly different than Mars squaring through a Taurus Ascendant and I'm not going to give you rules, like "if you've got X, then it is like Y," because we're not doing cookbooks this week. I'm sure you can begin to put some of that together for yourself. There is something of a developmental nature in the Ascendant and there is a link into *the Hero's quest*. I think it is the armor and the weapons that the hero has to face his journey. What gifts does the hero take with him in his path? I don't know whether the Ascendant is, in itself, the quest. Maybe that's ultimately the Midheaven, and the Ascendant is the armor, and the gifts we bear from the gods in order to go out there, and we don't all have the same gifts.

Here are a couple of very interesting charts, figures that in many ways are reverses of each other. The charts are exactly the same except the house cusps are reversed and the planets are mostly reversed house by house. There are a few little exceptions, but mostly the charts are mirrors of each other. Interestingly enough, you'll see that the counting system also starts to shift by house position.

Hemingway has a Moon singleton in social houses, whereas Hart Crane doesn't. The Moon has moved about 8°, so Hart Crane, born about twelve hours later, has a Moon about 8° further, which obviously shifts the Moon aspects as well.

Let me tell you a little bit about these men. Hemingway, as you know, was "Mr. Macho," a very gifted, brilliant writer, but he identified himself with the archetype of masculinity. First of all, we should mention that they both have a T-cross with Mars as the focal point. Hemingway's focal point is in the 1st house and Hart Crane's is in the 7th house. Hart Crane was a poet, a very promising young poet, and he was also homosexual. So here we have two faces of the same thing. The kind of men Hart Crane was attracted to were super macho, like stevedores and truck drivers, so what he was projecting out into the 7th, Hemingway took for himself. Now, interestingly enough, both men committed suicide. Hart Crane jumped off a ship and drowned in the Caribbean when he was in his late 20s or early 30s. He was an alcoholic and so was Hemingway. Hemingway committed suicide later on in life and, while he reportedly had cancer, supposedly the reason he committed suicide was because he had become impotent. I don't know how many of you are aware of how he committed suicide and, I hate to get grim, but metaphorically I think it's interesting. He put the muzzle of a rifle into his mouth and pulled the trigger. I leave the metaphorical implications to your imagination.

Audience: Was he also homosexual?

Richard: No, he was a card-carrying heterosexual. If you read his books you'll see that the whole emphasis is on women as objects, of man's lust and man as hunter, beast, or warrior. I don't know about you, but for me none of his women are real. His women are archetypal mirrors of the ideal of what the unbalanced man sees as woman. I find them rather annoying twits, his women, because all of the masculine qualities are gathered to him and it's quite clear that in this kind of strutting warrior pose that Hemingway had, integrating the anima or the feminine side for himself was very difficult, which is why he could not live with impotence.

Audience: I'm not sure where the macho comes in. I understand the Mars, Pluto, and Saturn, but his Mars is in Virgo.

Richard: If you're looking for true macho, don't look for Mars in Aries. It is Mars in an *uncomfortable* sign, in an *uncomfortable* situation in a man's chart that needs to prove itself. Mars in Aries has nothing to prove. He says, "This is what I am. You want warrior? Hey, baby, here I am, here's my sword." Mars in Virgo, Mars in Cancer, Mars in Pisces are much more difficult. Why? Because the Water and Earth signs tend to go inward.

My symbol of Mars in a Water or Earth sign is the Mars glyph with the arrow turning back in on itself, which is easier in our society for a woman to live with than a man. A woman's social programming says that is what she should do with her Mars anyway, but it's a very uncomfortable position for a man, and it often turns out to be the over-compensating macho swaggering bully. King Henry VIII was another Mars in Virgo in the 1st house, and you know how he dealt with his women! Also, remember that Mars is the focal point of the T-cross, and on the other ends of it are Pluto and Saturn. We've talked a good deal about that particular kind of configuration. So the pressure is on Mars to perform, and what do we know about Virgo? Virgo is the repair and maintenance sign—I call Virgo "the flour sifter"—you must continue putting it through the mill until it's refined and refined and refined and perfect. Does it ever get perfect? No, it's a Mutable sign. So there is great anxiety and unease in how one performs and I think it's very clear in his chart.

In the case of Hart Crane, it seems quite obvious that very early on he never thought that this Mars was him. It was out there, something that I complete myself through on the opposite side and yet, it comes down to the same thing exactly. So Hart Crane dies by throwing himself into the archetypal feminine, into the sea, returning back to chaos in a Yin way. Hemingway blows his head off with an archetypal phallic symbol, I'm sure you're aware that guns are phallic symbols, and he "machoed" himself to death. I also think it's interesting symbolically, that he did not take a pistol to shoot himself in the mouth. He had a big collection of guns, and a pistol would do the job, but he needed a rifle.

The two men met once briefly. As you can imagine, Hart Crane was fascinated with Hemingway, but he found him brutal, and Hemingway was extremely uncomfortable around Hart Crane, but talked about him all his life. When you polarize enough energy onto one side, you automatically constellate the opposite, and it's very interesting what happens when the two opposites meet. With Hart Crane, we begin with a sense of selflessness—Pisces, the collective sign of chaos—on the Ascendant. "I don't know who I am so I take my identity (Mars as focal point of the T-cross), by finding it in the *other*." What quality particularly in the "other"? Perfect masculinity is the ideal that I am seeking, but it all comes back to the same thing anyway, because back he goes into the sea to drown. He does not find that outside of himself. Hemingway does just the opposite kind of thing. "I am perfect order, masculinity is me. Chaos and all those soft, feminine, elusive qualities of the sea, and undoing, and the return to the collective, are out there," which he projects partly onto women and partly onto "those people" out there. He has a lot to say about cowards and weaklings—people who are soft, and people who are overly sensitive—people who don't want to go up to a rhinoceros and blow its brains out. People who are not warriors and do not go off to the war are weak and of another species entirely, yet Hemingway committed suicide because of impotence, so the thing comes back again. Virgo is a very self-protective sign on the Ascendant and Pisces is wide open.

The position of the Ascendant ruler is also important. Notice that Hart Crane's Neptune is in Gemini in the 4th and Hemingway's Mercury is in Leo in the 12th, but they're both very Neptunian qualities aren't they? What else do you see, looking at these two charts?

Audience: Moon opposing Venus is very Yin and soft, and an indicator of weak women, especially for Hemingway.

Richard: Both of the men had mother complexes; they were both very strongly tied to their mothers. Hemingway's mother was an overwhelmingly powerful woman and so was Hart Crane's, but in the reverse. One was a powerful, overt dominator and the other was a subtle, helpless dominator.

Moon and Venus, as we have said, often indicates a confusion between woman as mother and woman as lover, and that can manifest in two ways. To the overtly heterosexual temperament of Ernest Hemingway, it certainly means double messages toward his woman. He was known as "Papa" Hemingway, interestingly enough, and he never objected to that title at all. It was important for him to be

Papa. Mary Hemingway, his wife, was Mama and they called each other Papa and Mama. So there can be a double charge around women for men who have a Moon-Venus aspect in their charts. The woman is always getting double messages: "I want you to be lover, but as soon as I have you I want to turn you into mother, and then I can't have sex with you anymore because that's incestuous."

I often say that Eros is the archetype that tricks us into breeding, and once we have done that, we automatically begin to assume our family-of-origin qualities. In other words, a man may woo and marry his lover, but he ends up living with his mother. All of his un-worked-out mother stuff in projections eventually comes out and the family of origin gets reestablished again to the extent that the person is un-individuated. So a man with Moon-Venus aspects in his chart is often confused, himself, as to which he wants. One way a man may do that is to marry one woman to be his mother and then have affairs on the side for the lover, and that's what Hemingway did. He was married many times and as soon as the wife was pregnant, she became mother and no longer lover, and he began to woo other younger women. Or, as the wife starts maturing and she becomes more physically like the archetypal figure, he must go find a younger and younger woman to live out the missing Venus function, the Aphrodite. We see that phenomenon very often in men, don't we?

Notice that this is much more of an issue for Hemingway than for Crane. Why? Hemingway's Moon is a singleton in Social houses. So, when Moon becomes a singleton in a man's chart, it automatically implies a search for the ideal anima. Woman as mother is an ideal that must be pursued, so it can be a driving quest to try to complete oneself through this ideal, opposite Lunar figure. This is not true with Crane, and my guess is that Crane probably internalized the feminine in a much better way than Hemingway did. I think the problem with Crane is that he projected out his masculine with his Mars in the 7th house, plus the guilt that's induced from living in a society that condemns what he was. And, of course, notice the difference in the egos. Both the Suns are in Cancer, but Crane's Sun is at 29° Cancer, which is a critical degree, so apparently we have a much more fragile ego. In addition, the 4th–10th house axis is much more strongly developed in Hemingway's chart than in Crane's.

There's another way that Moon-Venus can be worked out in the chart of a man, and that is, "I get confusing messages from my mother about lover and mother," and, for all we know, that also may be the case with Hemingway. When that occurs, it is then very difficult to release the projection from the mother and begin to relate to other women, because the mother is giving subtle, double messages. One way to do that is to just never break the psychic umbilical cord with mother. She always is number one and I attempt to resolve that opposition by never, in a sense, leaving mother. Or, like Hemingway, I find mother and marry her and call her "Mama." Also, Hemingway only has one aspect to the Moon, so it's a very unintegrated Moon. We would have to say that, on one level, Crane has a more integrated Moon, and his feminine function is indeed more integrated than Hemingway's.

Audience: I notice they both have that very close Saturn-Pluto opposition, which makes me think they have a very strong fear of the dark powerful side of the feminine.

Richard: Yes, I think your point is very well taken. Fear of the dark power of the feminine, absolutely.

Again, we've seen so much Mars-Pluto in this conference—the charts are showing them over and over again. I did not deliberately select charts for that, but maybe that's the particular lesson of the time. Mars is forced by Saturn and Pluto into very uncomfortable, over-compensating ways. What's the reason for that? Remember we talked about Pluto wanting to drag Mars into the underworld and transform it into something else where it comes out clever and devious and sly rather than its spontaneous self? So Mars-Pluto has a tendency to repress sexuality, just like Saturn-Pluto does. Why? Mars is afraid of the demonic, of the erotic, of falling into the underworld, and it says, "If I let my libido flow and expose itself, I'll be destroyed. It will annihilate me or it will annihilate someone else." And, in a way, the penis is seen as this kind of deadly weapon, an engine of destruction. You often find this in a woman's chart, as well, and it is the fear of the phallic, "This will destroy me." One way she may integrate that is becoming phallic herself, and then you find the very animus-possessed woman—the very aggressive, powerful, dominating woman. In compensation for her fear of the external phallic, she herself becomes phallic. So you often find sexual problems with Mars–Pluto, especially in a situation like this where you have them in T-cross.

Now Saturn and Mars in a man's chart often means antler-clashing with the father, and there are also problems with impotence. Why? Because Saturn is afraid of getting out of control. Saturn is rigid and afraid of breaking down the structure. Hemingway's father was largely absent, and the mother became a father figure for him. I believe the father either disappeared or died young, and he idealized this father who never was. The father was a kind of heroic figure who died in the war or in some kind of hunting thing. On the other hand, Hart Crane had a very harsh, punitive father who was very demanding, rather conformist and religious. So Mars-Saturn in a man's chart normally indicates problems with father, and it is also a very incestuous combination. I know we always think of incestuous as running father-daughter, mother-son, but it also works mother-daughter, father-son, and here we have a double taboo on a psychic level. Not only is there incestuous stuff going on, but it's homosexual incestuous stuff, and the son in some way, or the father in some way, has mixed the libidinous energy of Mars with the nurturing protection of Saturn. It often manifests itself in the son idealizing or hero-worshiping the father, or this idealized father figure that substitutes for the father. You get the son who strives very very hard to live up to the expectations of this idealized father who may be a father-figure only in the son's imagination.

Hemingway, I think, was more crippled here because he never really did have a father, and that's what happens when you lose the parent too early. He, himself, must become this perpetually demanding father. He internalizes this father, this imaginary parent who never was, and never lets himself alone with his expectations of what it is to be a man. There is no father there to say, "You are a man, my son, I am proud of you," so he searches all his life. If you've read his novels, they are about the hunter, the bullfighter, the great fisherman, the seducer and womanizer—the archetypal male as warrior. He honors violence and "methinks the man doth protest too much." But notice that many of his male heros are destroyed or damaged in some very particular way. In *The Sun Also Rises* the hero is impotent and in *A Farewell To Arms* the masculine hero's genitals were blown off in the war. So, isn't it amazing how the chart reveals the author, and the author in his works reveals himself? A lot of Hart Crane's poetry was a kind of idealization of this loving brutal man that he did not identify within himself, but outside. Obviously they're dealing with these issues.

Audience: Isn't there an Oedipal situation here?

Richard: The Oedipal theory makes me a little nervous because it tends to be a catch-all, but I think there are Oedipal qualities going on in both charts. That myth relates to an internal desire to kill off the old man, and if I don't have a father that I can replace, then this is a problem for the son who loses his father too soon. He doesn't have this figure to topple off the wall and replace. All he's left with is an idealized, wonderful figure, a lot of which he is getting through his mother's version of him, who is either this magnificent person or this terrible ogre.

Here's something else I see in both charts. The only planets in Air are Neptune and Pluto, so even though there is no singleton, it's only these two outer transpersonal planets that are able to act through Air. Here's the desire for the voice or communication to become a channel for the collective and maybe the difficulty of articulating on a one-to-one basis is what is going on. We've already seen the artist, the passionately creative writer, with the inferior function in Air. So there is something in there that goads us on toward expressing the Neptunian chaotic, drowning qualities, and the Plutonian death and rebirth, and renewal qualities through Air.

I'm impressed by the difference in the Suns and on an ego level, the one at 29° (Crane) is a more fragile individual. Notice also, that they both have only one aspect to the Sun—an out-of-sign sextile from Jupiter. So we have very weak, undeveloped Suns, which again shows the difficulty for taking in the inner father as well as their own masculine, creative function. And yet, we have the goading toward that creative function and the goading toward trying to, in some way, "mate" with this archetypal male function.

Audience: That 29th degree of a sign might be like leaving on a trip when you've completed your preparations, but you have a feeling you may have forgotten something. And the pressure you feel to scurry around checking to be sure you've finished everything up seems negative and fragile to me.

Richard: Well, here we get stuck again in this positive–negative business. I don't think there's anything wrong with being fragile. This is the problem—when people are astrologers first and come to psychology second, they tend to see things as split between light and dark, good and bad, evolved and unevolved, and that's the difficulty we've been dealing with all week.

If we're going into a chart from a depth-psychological point of view, it's all right to talk about wounds, fragility, and "hurtness" without having to heal it right away and say, "It's okay, it's good, it's creative, it's loving, it's positive." Sure it is, everything has two faces, but the psychologist is trained to look at the *hurt* and the hurt may be the thing that brings "the bloom of the rose comes out of the darkest, deepest night." From the point of view of the psychologist, it's okay to go down to the underworld in order to come up. That's what the Phoenix is about. That's what Persephone is about. She doesn't go down there and stay there; she goes down there and comes back, she returns.

Audience: There's one thing that's bothering me and I'm questioning the interpretation of Sun at 29° of a sign, because I know people with the Sun at 29° who are so completely all-together.

Richard: Let me give you an image that I have of it. You know what happens with a star that's about ready to burn out? It becomes a super-nova. It explodes with this great radiance of light because it is in its process of self-destructing and becoming something else. So you often do see an intensely radiant, brilliant quality of the 29th degree, but there is a fragility underneath that.

Audience: In Hart Crane's chart it looks like so much of that drama is going on inside the not-self.

Richard: Yes, that's a good point, and you see a lot of that in his poetry with the pursuit of the ideal "other." With Hemingway, most of the stuff is on the east side of the chart, including the focal point of the T-cross, which further emphasizes it. The focal point of the T-cross in Crane's chart is on the side of the not-self and says, "This is what I project on and desire to complete myself with, because what I am is chaos. I desire order and structure, but of a very Yang, male sort to complete myself." Hemingway says, "Nonsense, that's what I am myself." And what is opposite that? The fear, the open enemy 7th house, the falling into the chaos, into the nothingness, into death, into dissolution.

Audience: What happens to a planet that has no aspect at all?

Richard: If it is one of the Lights, the Sun or the Moon, there is a potential for great problems. With the weakly or unaspected Sun or Moon I think two things happen. You have a desperate search for self and there is desire to somehow make a marriage between that planet and other planets. There is a sense of removal, of isolation, of separation, of some part of me being separate and cut off. In a man's chart, for instance, an unaspected Moon very well may be idealizing the entire quality of feminine and setting it aside in some place. So, the thing that gives the greatest hurt often is the motivation for the greatest search.

Audience: It seems to me in a way both of them were "lost."

Richard: Well, they both did come out of the so-called "lost generation." The world was in great transformation. This is the generation that lived through two world wars, a depression, and an enormous number of upheavals, so they did embody something of their own generation. I agree that the Sun is also one's creative self or creative purpose—the place one *enlightens*, the place of our creative source, the place that has *heart* for you. Both of them, with the out-of-sign square to Jupiter, had this conflict. There is the desire to achieve this expansion through something Scorpionic—through sex, the erotic, death, going through the underworld—and the constant forcing of a reexamination of oneself as a man and oneself as a creative man.

Audience: What about a planet with aspects to the Ascendant?

Richard: I call those aspects of *outlet,* and I differentiate them from aspects between planets, which I call mutual aspects because there is a sender and a receiver going on. Mars and Saturn are in aspect— Mars square Saturn, Saturn square Mars. If it's the Ascendant, the Ascendant is a point in space. The Ascendant, itself, is not *sending* anything, it's a filter through which things are being received, like an opening, a doorway. So Pluto *is* square the Ascendant in Crane's chart, but the Ascendant is *not* square Pluto. Pluto outlets itself through the Ascendant and filters itself through it.

Planets that aspect the Ascendant have a lot to do with the persona. I don't know much about what kind of a person Hart Crane was, but his Moon is sextile the Ascendant so something of the feminine is showing. Something of the eternal mother and something of the child. Hemingway's Moon is trining the Ascendant, so both of them, in some way, are manifesting some quality of the inner feminine. Let's take Uranus now. Hart Crane's Uranus is out of orb to aspect his Ascendant, but Hemingway's is a very close square. Hemingway's Jupiter aspects the Ascendant and Hart Crane's doesn't. Hart Crane's Saturn squares the Ascendant whereas Hemingway's doesn't. Pluto squares Hart Crane's Ascendant but Pluto is out of orb for Hemingway. Venus, another archetypal feminine planet, makes a very close trine to Crane's Ascendant and is a not so close sextile in Hemingway's chart. So you get a lot more Yin stuff flowing through Crane's Ascendant and much more Yang stuff going out through Hemingway's, besides the fact that his very powerful T-cross is angular. There is a vast difference in what is being projected out by these men, and they were true to those aspects in the way they killed themselves. Crane goes into the sea of chaos, he chooses Yin as a way of dying, and Hemingway chooses Yang. That is the myth of the return.

Audience: What in a chart can alert you to the possibility of suicide?

Richard: Nothing, there are no classic significators. Everybody is going to die, and suicide is a potential for everyone if the stress is enough, if the circumstances warrant it. The discussion of death or the manner of death is an area you should always steer away from in working with clients. I'd only get into that if the client wishes to talk about that as an issue, and only if I was working with somebody in on-going therapy would I ever approach the subject.

Audience: Doesn't the 8th house have a bearing on death?

Richard: I think 8th house is a quality of *psychic* dying. It is what we need; it is the qualities that we are constantly needing to look for in order to renew. Planets and signs connected with the 8th house have to do with our own personal descent and return, much more than actual physical death. As far as where physical death can be found, there are lots of opinions in astrology, and I don't want to get into that. Here it's more of a psychic or psychological death.

❦

CHAPTER NINE

WEAVING THE MAGIC
THREAD INTO THE TAPESTRY
OF A COUNSELING SESSION

A s we come full circle to the final day of our conference, I'd like to talk about what has happened for you during this week, and how you're going to apply all that you have learned. If you are a practicing astrologer or counselor, how do you take this material and use it with a client? I am not suggesting that I can solve counseling problems for the astrologer in one session, but at least we can talk about some of the issues. Another thing I want to discuss is, what are the things that have opened up in *you* as a result of this conference? Those of you who have attended my conferences before—"The Hero's Journey," "Through The Looking Glass," and this unwinding of "The Magic Thread" down into the labyrinth—know that it isn't just an intellectual exercise. You go on the journey and there's a lot of transformative change going on. This is not just information; in part, what's happening is therapy and it is not easy on you. So what do you do with the stuff that has come up for you on this particular journey?

Let's begin with some counseling implications and what you can do with the information—the raw material—when you come face to face with a client. How do you say things to the client; how much can you say; do you say things that may disturb the client and how? In a general way, I think astrological counselors can fall into two categories. Those who think the client is made of glass and won't say anything that may be unpleasant to hear, and those who are so impressed with their power that they purposely say unpleasant things to shock the client. In the first case, what good is psychological insight into a chart if you're not willing to share it? In the second, what benefit (and possible damage) does the client gain from being scared to death and broken into little pieces?

The counseling process is twofold. One has to do with the psychological issues of the astrologer, and the other has to do with communication skills. I feel that astrologers who are dealing with other people's problems should, ideally, have experienced some form of psychotherapy themselves, because the ability to relate to someone else with astrological material is dependent to a large extent on your relationship with your own psyche. Communication skills can be learned, so instead of talking astrologese and saying, "You have the Sun square Saturn," you could say, "Do you feel inferior much of the time?" Or, "Some people I have counseled with this dynamic seem to have a feeling of inadequacy, can you relate to that?" So communication skills can be learned, but the capacity to use those skills depends on your sensitivity.

We've talked a lot about the unconscious, and unconscious projections, and undeveloped aspects in the self and, while astrological counseling is very different from analysis, the counseling phenomenon occurs just as powerfully within the astrological session. Now, I don't think we're so powerful that we can destroy people in one session, because people are incredibly resilient. Insensitive astrologers may hurt a person, but I don't think they have the power to wreck someone's life. However, we can inflict hurt and we can waste another person's time. I think the Darth Vader side of us is likely to come creeping out only when we see ourselves as the other side of that—the white knight, the savior, the transforming one—because that again is just one half of the light against the dark. We've heard an awful lot about that during this week.

People have a hard time accepting within themselves that the dark is beautiful, the dark is okay, the underworld of the psyche is all right and not a thing that you want to overcome, not a thing that you want to transcend. The idea of the Hermes figure that guides us down into the underworld implies that we are in some way familiar with the territory we're going to. So, if we only accept the light, and the bright, and the white, and the transcendence, and the spiritual, we'll only be intellectual, which nicely puts us at a distance. It's very attractive to many of us who are in astrology because we can stand back from that chart and from that client. Many of us see a client only once, so it's easy, in a way, to stand back and pontificate. It's very different from a depth-psychological situation in which you're forced to go down into your own material in an on-going relationship with a client. It's really the difference between a casual encounter on a train where you may meet a stranger, spend an hour or two, and sometimes a lot of intimacy comes out because you'll never see that person again, but that's different from building a relationship. Different skills and different personal qualities are needed.

So, if you are only of the light, then how can you shine the light into someone else's darkness? We must be Psyche who has turned the light on, but who has paid the price for the light. And, as I've said so many times, you can't go from Libra to Sagittarius. Between an Air sign and a Fire sign comes a Water sign and you don't skip over that stuff. You don't go from cognition and communication, nicely separated and detached and objective, and leap over to the Fire. You don't have awareness and the act of grace and a reunion with the universe and a new start, without going through the Water. That is the path through it. You can't get from Gemini to Leo without going through Cancer or from Libra to Sagittarius without going through Scorpio.

I think it's very important to consider in a very deep way what defines an astrological practice. Many of you have been my students and have heard these things over and over again about the need for deep inner work and, while the inner soul is very resilient and chances are we aren't going to do irreparable damage, there's another hand to that. We must devote ourselves to developing our skills, and I think fundamental to the astrological counselor is a certain acceptance of the other person's face—to be sensitive enough to a person's repressions and denials so that you don't go like a Sherman Tank storming through the walls. Or you don't get an *idée fixe* in your head that this person has a sexual problem and, "By God, by the time he gets out of this session in an hour-and-a-half, he's going to *know* he has a sexual problem, whether he has one or not!"

I think insight must be tempered with compassion, and if you do not have compassion for yourself, you cannot have compassion for the client. But, if you have looked at your own dark side and your own wounds, and had compassion for yourself (and there's a difference between compassion and guilt and regret), you can have compassion for the client who is also struggling toward the light. Many of us come into astrology in the first place because our own lives are posing problems and challenges. Narcissistic issues are at the core, and when you gain the confidence of being yourself, the client benefits as well as you. There may be times when you should be selfish and devote time to yourself instead of listening to other people.

In your practice you also have to decide what your limits are. You will need to define what it is you do and what you don't do, and realize that because someone has paid you a fee it does not mean he or she owns you body and soul. If someone comes to you and says, "Here's your fee, now tell me when my spouse will die and give me information about my past lives," many astrologers may feel, "Well, I'm being paid for the service and this is what the client wants, so I have to provide it." I think the issue of defining your limits, making it clear ahead of time who you are, is a very important thing and there are ways of helping to define those limits. You could create a brochure that describes who you are, your background, and the way you work, so the client doesn't have a false expectation of what you do. If someone comes to me, he or she is not going to get a past life reading, but other astrologers might include that as part of their work. It helps if the client knows what to expect ahead of time.

Setting limits on time is another issue. When I first began doing astrological consultations I did six hour readings. I would be falling out of my chair and the client would be sliding under the table and then the client would look at me and say, "Do you see anything else?" Being an honest fellow, I'd say, "Oh yeah," and off we'd go for another two hours! Is there more? Sure, there's always more, so set your boundaries. Define what it is you do and don't do, set boundaries around time, set boundaries around fees, set boundaries around the kind of energy you are willing to give, and the areas in *you* that you're willing to have hooked in or involved in the

session. I think that many astrologers, many people who do astrological readings, are basically in their souls a therapist, and haven't
found it out yet. They're trying to do in an hour or hour-and-a-half
consultation what a therapist would probably do in two or three
years of therapy. Many astrologers, I think, are finding this out.

Also, set limits on your goal. I think a good question to ask
yourself is, "What is my agenda with this client and what do I hope
to accomplish?" So many of us come from wounded homes and
very early on we got into the role of "fixer" and we are perpetually
carrying around the "hungry child" that needs validating. And although that inner hungry child is often validated in reversal by being a caring parent, nevertheless the counter-transference projected
to the client—the need to be there all the time and the need to be
needed—is part of that anxious, lonely, hungry child who is seeking some kind of solace. These are the people who are willing to
answer the phone at three o'clock in the morning to rescue, and
give from an area of themselves not necessarily required in a consultation. And they may often end up feeling ripped-off, or like a
prostitute, or used. I think the child who is, in a sense, emotionally
cheated out of childhood has trouble with boundaries, and we find
that the same thing reflects itself in our personal relationships as it
does in our practice. We find that our children, our friends, or parents are also invading our space and we may have difficulty defining our limits with these people. And we say, "Well after all, it is
love, isn't it? And if one loves, doesn't one give all?"

I believe that the transpersonal planets—Uranus, Neptune, and
Pluto—are probably very powerfully placed in the chart of people
who are therapeutically inclined, and the danger in that is to confuse where the source is coming from. People who have not investi-
gated their own shadow, specifically the power-shadow and the
narcissistic part of us, get the medium and the message confused.
And just as the client is happy to project upon us that we are the
Magus,[1] that we have a hidden "in" or connection to the Akashic
Records of the powers above and the powers below, we often buy
into that and, on a deep level, believe it ourselves.

1. Magus: singular of magi, meaning priest or magician.

So, I think it's important to realize what our motivations are in being astrological counselors or therapists or readers. What's in it for you, what is your personal agenda? I always look askance when I hear a student of astrology, when asked, "Why are you studying astrology?" reply, "I'm interested in spiritual things and I just want to help people." That may be acceptable for a beginning student of astrology, but there are many people who have been practicing for twenty years and still think that. An astrologer (who will be nameless because she's not dead), who used to specialize in what she called "spiritual astrology" did, I believe, enormous on-going damage to people because her own repressed material from her unconscious constantly bubbled up and was projected into her readings. "There is nothing of the world of the dark coming out through me," she said. Well, I've had experience with this particular person and that's not true. There's a double bind here. Yes, people are resilient, yes people are tough, but people are also fragile.

Learning *therapeutic skills* gives the psychic scalpel to the hands of the surgeon, and in a sense that's what you are, because in a way, you are opening the psyche and it gives you a trained hand for doing that. I like to use the metaphor of cousin Emily who has just taken a weekend course in neurosurgery. How many of us would agree to lie down on the kitchen table so she could open up our brain? Well, probably if there were such a person as cousin Emily, she'd be psychopathic. If you were to submit yourself to such an ordeal, there would be something seriously wrong with you, too, and if not wrong with you before you started, it would be very wrong with you after the episode. And yet we, as astrologers, have all done the same thing or have seen people who have done the same thing—learning chart calculation skills on Monday and counseling by Saturday—experimenting on people. There's a certain necessity for practice, and you practice by getting feedback from a live person. So training in the skills gives you a steady hand with the scalpel, because no matter what you're doing there is a certain quality of cutting, there is a certain quality of opening. And the next thing is exploring your own unconscious material, so you know what it's like being on the other end. Then having been through that experience, you're not going to be so likely to slide into the kind of narcissism or power traps—the medium, the Magus, the healer—as you might otherwise do.

Audience: Are there getting to be so many astrologers that eventually there won't be enough work for all of us if the field gets overcrowded, like lawyers are faced with now?

Richard: If you're strongly motivated and you're dedicated and you love your work, it doesn't matter how many astrologers there are, there's going to be plenty of work for you. You'll build your own clientele because nobody can do what you as a unique individual will do in your particular way. So there's room for everybody. I believe that both with therapists and astrologers.

One astrologer once said to me, "I'd love to live in the San Francisco Bay area, it's so beautiful there, but you moved there first." And I said, "Come, there's room for all of us." Because you see, you create a climate, a climate of good work, just like the Jungians in Zurich created a kind of climate. There's room for everybody. The world has never said, "The Ark is full so tell the genius he may not get on the boat." Trust in that. A little time and patience is what's necessary, so I would encourage anybody who is motivated to get a degree, if that is important, and to get training, licensing, and build a practice. I promise it will come.

I'd like to mention a wonderful book from Spring Publications titled *Power in the Helping Professions,* by Guggenbühl-Craig.[2] It has a profound message for the counselor and therapist. I think he deals with certain latent Plutonian issues that are going on within, and driving the person toward being a counseling person. It's a wonderful little book and if you've already discovered it, take another look because it's worth a second reading. There is also Alice Miller's *Prisoners Of Childhood: The Drama of the Gifted Child,* which is about the issue of the narcissistic wound of the therapist, and also necessary reading. Also, once you discover Spring Publications you may get their catalogue and there's all kind of books that will lead you to other discoveries. They publish some marvelous books.

Audience: How do you find a good therapist for yourself, especially if there aren't any around where you live?

2. Adolf Guggenbühl-Craig, *Power in the Helping Professions* (Zurich: Spring Publications, 1976).

Richard: If I could not find the kind of therapist I wanted in the place where I lived, then I would move to a place where I could find it. I mean, it would be that important to me, and indeed, I did do that at one point in my life. I think it really depends on what you're looking for and where you're going.

I frankly am attracted to the idea that the person who wishes to be a counselor should get counseled. The person who wishes to do therapy should experience therapy. If you are interested in becoming an analyst, go through analysis yourself. What's even better is, if short-term therapy is as far as you want to go, take it one step further, yourself, and go into analysis. Maybe the therapist should be one step ahead of the kind of practice he or she is actually trying to deal with. I think it's not too hard to find somebody who is good, even in the more remote areas of the country. You may not be able to find a Jungian, or the right kind of Jungian for you, but I'm sure that there are people with good insight everywhere. And really, it's the person rather than the school that's most important.

I think the danger for the person who is attracted to astrology is to inflate or levitate and want to stay in the realms of the Air and Fire, the intellectual and spiritual. And by contrast, I think the proper kind of therapy is something that drops you down into the Earth and Water, into the body and psyche. For that reason, I think that psychosynthesis, as an example, and which in many ways is valuable, can be a very bad trap for the person who is a practicing astrologer because of its tendency to always ascend upward. When we talk about a depth-psychology we're talking about something that manages to take you down into that labyrinth where you can deal with feelings, where a certain amount of transference can take place, where there is the possibility to explore shadow issues. And certain therapies that are overly intellectualized or overly spiritualized have a tendency to *avoid* shadow. Since that is a natural tendency anyway among people who are metaphysically inclined, I think to complement that quality we need something that *invites* shadow.

I think there's another danger, too, and that is that people tend to think, "I have to wait and keep myself separate until the perfect person comes along. There's only one therapist, one Magus who is going to transform me and I might make a mistake, so therefore I will not get involved with anybody." We do the same thing with our romantic inclinations. We romanticize the therapist, that there is somebody out there, not yet met whom I don't know. Maybe it's somebody who has written a book that I've read, maybe Jung, so I'll wait until he comes around again! And there's the feeling that without that wonderful unknown person I'm going to hold myself intact. It's really romantic love that we're doing, a kind of idealization, and that's not necessarily the case. There is something to be learned from practically anybody. Now, that doesn't mean not to select carefully, to try and find the best person in your area or your neighborhood, but take a step. We do not love by finding the right love object, it's a state of being. We do not begin to enter therapy by finding the right therapist, it's a state of being and of opening. Do you see what I'm saying?

Audience: Should I go to a Freudian psychologist or a Jungian psychologist or one of the other kinds of psychotherapy like Gestalt? What is the difference?

Richard: Again, it's the *person*, not the school that is most important, but to clarify your confusion I have another suggestion. Go to your local college or university and take a basic course in comparative psychology. It will cost you one semester of your time. It's a survey course in psychology and you can see what Gestalt is all about, what the difference is between Freudian and Jungian theory, what Adler had to say, what some of the more humanistic directions are in psychology. Some of the newer therapies like object-relations, or family therapy, or James Olman's theory of archetypes, and so on. Find out what's right for you. As you're listening and learning, you'll say, "Ah, this strikes a spark in me. This turns me on. I find it exciting." Chances are that which you find exciting will directly relate to what you need. You're not going to do yourself irreparable damage. This is like the relationship between the astrologer and the client. You're not going to destroy yourself by getting into the wrong therapy. If it's wrong for you, you'll begin to realize it and leave, but you will have learned something from it.

Audience: We have read and heard from therapists in other schools of thought that Freud was off base and therapists practicing his theory can be detrimental or restrictive. What do you think?

Richard: I think Freud often gets a bad rap. I think it's not Freud so much as it is Freudians. There is a tendency for certain Freudians to want to wallow around in the muck which has nothing to do with what Freudianism is capable of. And there's a tendency for certain Jungians to levitate and elevate up to the realms of the divine intuitive, to dance around among the gods and goddesses and archetypes, and fail to anchor down at the bottom. So it isn't so much the difference between Jung's theory and Freud's theory as it is that certain types of people tend to be attracted to certain kinds of practice and polarize themselves along certain lines.

It's not too hard to read into Freud his very sexist ideas and here we have a very male, Cronus archetype. Jung seems in many ways more balanced, and brings in the feminine, and honors the anima, and brings in the idea of the Goddess, so he is preferred by women, or those who are searching for the feminine component in their lives, and they will move in the direction of Jung. There's a tendency to be a bit uncomfortable with Freudianism and the split he has within himself in regard to the inner male and female, but not every Freudian practices it that way. It's like I always say, the trouble with Christians is they've forgotten Christ and gotten hooked on Christianity, and the trouble with Freudians is they've forgotten Freud and turned him into dogma. The same thing applies to Jungians. Jung himself said that the thing he dreaded most was that after he died, people would call themselves Jungians.

Remember, you can interview your prospective therapist just like you can interview your astrologer, and just like you can interview your client. And the way you can make an informed choice by doing this interviewing is, for starters, knowing what the different therapies offer. I think that one would choose a therapist very much the way one would choose a good doctor or lawyer—perhaps a recommendation from someone who has had a good experience. Go to the professional organizations to find out who has good standing. Attend a lecture, read somebody's book. Many of you, I suppose, were attracted to this conference because you've heard me lecture, or you've heard a tape that I've done. So, in the same way, you find the therapist that's right for you.

Audience: When I was looking for a therapist it was important to me that he or she should know something about astrology, or at least have an open mind and not put astrology down.

Richard: I hear your point and I think the last thing you said is the determining factor. Obviously, you cannot work with somebody who puts down something that is an essential part of your belief system, but it *is* possible to work with someone who is neutral. I can only speak for myself here, but it would not be necessary for me to work with a therapist who understands astrology or believes in it as deeply as I do, but I would want one who would respect my position and not project his or her negativity. I couldn't work with somebody like that, but I don't have to work with a therapist who I can talk astro-jargon to, or who even says, "This is a wonderful thing, I'd like to know more about it," which puts me in the role of educating the therapist. So, I hear what you're saying and I think that maybe it's even better to find one who is neutral than one who is as pro-astrology as you are. I think neutrality has great healing powers in the therapeutic setting and I think you will find that most good therapists, who are in touch with what they're doing, would not condemn anything meaningful to another person. And insisting that a therapist "speak your language" may be a way of pricing yourself out of the market. Like, "I want a Jungian woman who is 42 years old, who has the Moon in Libra because mine is in Aries (or my mother's was), who is eclectic and transpersonal and nurturing and warm and not intrusive and speaks astrology." It's a very neat way, just like we often do in our relationships, of ending up pricing ourselves out of the market.

Audience: I had a therapist that I trusted and things went well until I asked for his birth data. When I looked at his chart and decided we were astrologically incompatible, I read all kinds of negative things into the situation and ended what had been a productive relationship.

Richard: Yes, I appreciate what you're saying, and we can massacre a personal relationship the same way. Instead of dealing with the *person*, we have this nice little language that enables us to take what we *think* is the person, two dimensionally, off into our ivory tower and natter over it to ourselves and make up our minds who this person is, and what the relationship is supposed to be like. That's one of the reasons (among others), that I do not give out my chart. It's not the desire to be mysterious, or aloof, or elevated. It's because it's too easy to listen to the kinds of things I say, which are often uncomfortable, and say, "Oh, I know why he says that! He's got da-da-da and da-da-da," or "His thing does this to my thing," or "Obviously he's got a debilitated T-square, no wonder he says all these crazy things." It's too easy to use astrology, which is a most brilliant language, as a way of separating ourselves from actual experience.

Audience: I'm curious. Which came first for you, astrology or psychology?

Richard: For me the areas were convoluted. Ever since I was a child, I was interested in psychology and mythology—particularly fairy tales and legends. And from the very first I thought this is more than it appears, this has something to do with me and the human condition, and I was starting to see things archetypally, although I didn't know it. But I had some undergraduate work in psychology before I dropped out of school to get into the theater, which was my greatest experience of practical psychology, and from that I went into astrology and back from astrology into psychology. So it has been a kind of looping thing for me, a spiraling thing, and I keep going back and forth. I would have to say that probably professionally, I went from astrology to psychology rather than the other way around.

Audience: How did you deal with the price you have to pay to be an astrologer? How did you deal with the loneliness of being excluded, or being laughed at, or being thought a fool or a flake?

Richard: When I was a brand new student in astrology, which I consider my first ten years, it was very important for me to proselytize. It's part of that particular time in your life when you believe in something so powerfully, and it has made such an impact on you, yet on the other hand you're a little shaky about it, too. You're not grounded in really knowing in the bottom of your soul that it is so, you have to keep convinced. Therefore I used to get hooked into arguments all the time and, not only that, I provoked them. I'd meet people and say, "I'm an astrologer!" implying "Do you want to debate?" That was important for me at that time because I used these people as kind of teething-rings. By refining what I was thinking through arguing and refuting arguments and dealing with skeptics, I grounded myself more truly in what it is that I believed. Now, if someone comes up to me and says, "I think astrology is nonsense,"

I'll dismiss them because I don't want to get involved with anyone who has a closed mind. It's interesting though, that there are some astrologers who say, "I cannot argue with an open mind." They like the closed mind. It's sort of like the moth that throws itself on the flame. And there are certain people among us (not that there's anything wrong with it) who love to get involved with people who get hysterical about astrology, and there may be a secret shadow issue in that.

To deal with the other part of the question you asked, I myself came from one of those wounded families that so many of us have, and there's the business of how do you take care of yourself? When you are a lightning rod, either because you're well known or because you're standing for something that challenges the least common denominator mentality of the collective around you, it does, in a sense, put you in a lonely place. But the answer to dealing with that is self-nurturing and knowing how to take care of yourself. It's about not getting trapped into the business of "I am the servant of the Universe, I am the channel, I am only existing on the transpersonal level because the personal is simply too much for me." By going into your own work, whatever way it is that takes you into doing that, to nurture your own child, to take care of your life, to make sure that your emotional security needs are met, that *you* are okay with *you*, all this enables you to stand on this rather exposed place in relative safety because the winds that blow do not knock you around as much—you're rooted, you're grounded.

I think the fundamental nexus is the nurturing of the inner person, to ground out and center in. That's why we're constantly going over this business of going down into the labyrinth, because by healing in that area, you create a ground for yourself; that's where the roots are. If the roots are strong, the tree can take a lot of wind; if the roots are shallow, then a strong blow knocks it over. So in growing we must remember that we are *both* root and branch, and we cannot only concern ourselves with reaching up for the sky. We must remember we have roots that are going down toward the underworld, and they have to be developed in balance with the amount of branch we put up to the sky.

Audience: Will you talk about what you see in the future role of astrology? Do you see it gradually becoming more accepted, and what is our part in that in teaching?

Richard: I hate to predict, because I'm usually wrong, since twenty years ago I said, "In twenty years astrology will be taught in all the universities," and I guess I was wrong. But, still and all, I see the process unfolding. I think of the heyday of astrology as just one more of the things that people do, like basket-weaving, meditation, the kinds of things we all did in the late 60s and 70s when there was a broad awakening in astrology. It has changed now. It's narrower, but it's deeper. The people who are interested in it now are much more deeply and sincerely interested and focused on it. The movement that I see happening, and find exciting, is the marriage between astrology and psychology of all kinds. This kind of conference couldn't have been put on fifteen years ago. Why? Because fifteen years ago there wasn't an audience for it, but there is a shift in consciousness, and it encourages me; it excites me. In a sense, we're all missionaries, we're role-models. Each person among us who forges deep insight in terms of herself or himself, who makes the marriage between astrology and other disciplines, models for other people and shows the road to people coming along.

Audience: I think it's important to remind ourselves that there will come a time in our lives when we will not feel the need any longer to look at life through astrology, that it's just one of tools to a way of seeing life. I've known some very old astrologers who at the very end gave it up.

Richard: I'm wondering what *kind* of astrology it is they gave up. There are certain kinds that I would encourage people to give up! For instance, people often say to me, "Don't you carry your chart with you everywhere you go? Don't you carry an ephemeris? Where is your progressed da-da-da?" And when I say I'm not sure of the degree, they're shocked. Well, that's the kind of astrology I'm anxious to give up. I know my own chart, I know exactly what it is, but I don't have to be a walking ephemeris. That kind of astrology I have given up. I would rather have it descend more deeply into my soul. For me it is a passion, and I don't want to give up a passion. The part I have given up is the kind of astrology that binds me in, dependency astrology, umbilical astrology I have given up, and I would encourage you to give it up at the time in your life when you're ready to do that. Many of us still carry our charts around, like our palm, to have someone look at. There's nothing wrong with that. It's a phase, a natural phase that goes on, and we all went through it. The first thing I would do every morning and the last thing I would do every night was check my chart. "Ah, Neptune has moved one more minute of arc, what shall I do tomorrow?" It's a natural phase, and it will pass, but don't throw the baby out with the bath water, it's a wonderful baby.

Audience: What do you think is the basis of the fear around the word astrology, and where does that fear come from?

Richard: The predominant paradigm of our time is the Cartesian,[3] linear, scientific model that everything that means anything can be measured and not only that, but cause and effect can be equated. So for those who believe that, and it is the predominant model of our time (although it's not necessarily the predominant model in every time), astrology seems a-rational, and for that reason, it is extremely frightening. Just as the astrologer is motivated into astrology out of the fear of fate, so is the scientist, and his way of dealing with it is to go for the rationalistic, linear model and that is his basic territory. Anything outside of that is threatening. It's a kind of psychic dying for the rationalistic scientist to open up his mind to what appears to be irrational.

So that's the way it is right now and there's a wound there. I think there's a wound in our world that needs to be healed and I think astrology is one of the bridges. It is a metaphorical bridge that can communicate between these two worlds, so I think there is important work to be done. We see that the scientific world doesn't work either, do we not? I mean, with all of the scientific expertise, we have Chernoble, and new and more deadly weapons that can slide through X-Rays. We see that the scientific model isn't working, and the religious model isn't working, so what is left? Where are we going to go? I think astrology is one of the directions we're using in our search.

Audience: One of the things I find missing in astrology, as it's presented to the outside world, is it very often lacks the image that will

3. Cartesian: of or pertaining to the doctrines and methods of René Descartes, French philosopher and mathematician.

integrate into that rational world because, either by dress or look or behavior, it has an occult, scary, image of soothsayer, pointy hat, and cult. Maybe that's why astrology is turning more toward psychology.

Richard: Yes, and one of our problems is language. We talk *astrologese* to people who don't speak the language, and then we wonder why they're put off or intimidated or resentful. It's so easy if we're *bridge-people* —that's a word Rudhyar liked to use and I love the word. If we are bridge-people, people who reach across, then it is our function to be dual or multiple in our languages. If we're trying to present astrology to a Freudian, as an example, it might not be a bad idea to learn what Libido and Ego and Id means, and in what way we can connect that with astrology. It's not necessary to expect the Freudian to come over into our territory if we're the ones who want to do the convincing.

Audience: I've studied and taken long courses in air-conditioning, but after this week I know my path is in astrology, not air conditioning.

Richard: I know what you mean. I knew I was in trouble when I came to a rehearsal, left my script at home, and had a copy of Alan Leo. I knew right away what direction my destiny was going to take me; the gods were already telling me.

Audience: I think our biggest problem is the horoscope sun-sign columns in newspapers and magazines because people think that's all there is to astrology.

Richard: Yes, I'm really dead set against sun-sign horoscope columns, but Michael Lutin, an astrologer in New York, does his column with humor and such a twist and insightful metaphor that there's a little bit of an "Aha!" in each one of his columns. Astrologers seem to be taken with a deadly seriousness; we forget to see it with a sense of humor, and the lowest-common-denominator-astrology tends to take itself more seriously.

So, now this long week is winding down to its close. I want to thank you all very much for coming and sharing as deeply as you have. It has been an important learning experience for me, and these yearly get-togethers are a renewal. I charge myself with your energy, this feeds me and I feel, going out into the world, that I'm renewed and more open in different places than I was before. Let me just say to you that lots of stuff has happened on a very deep level for you. There is therapy going on here. You didn't know that at the beginning of the week, but I certainly think you know it by now.

Be gentle with yourself, go slowly and digest the material, don't rush around. A lot of stuff on the internal level has been shifted around and dislocated. Sit with the material for a while and let the Magic Thread slowly unwind. Let your dragon coil around the treasure a little bit. Nurse it, nurture it, let it drop down into the proper place. Be very kind to your body and your psyche at this moment. Don't run home and try to put it all together with the charts of all your family. Let the wine stay in the cask a little bit and age. Go slow—be gentle.

INDEX

Other Books by The Wessex Astrologer

The Essentials of Vedic Astrology
Lunar Nodes - Crisis and Redemption
Personal Panchanga and the Five Sources
of Light
Komilla Sutton

Astrolocality Astrology
From Here to There
Martin Davis

The Consultation Chart
Introduction to Medical Astrology
Wanda Sellar

The Betz Placidus Table of Houses
Martha Betz

Astrology and Meditation-
The Fearless Contemplation of Change
Greg Bogart

Patterns of the Past
Karmic Connections
Good Vibrations
The Soulmate Myth: A Dream Come True
or Your Worst Nightmare?
Judy Hall

The Book of World Horoscopes
Nicholas Campion

The Moment of Astrology
Geoffrey Cornelius

Life After Grief - An Astrological Guide to
Dealing with Loss
AstroGraphology - The Hidden link
between your Horoscope and your
Handwriting
Darrelyn Gunzburg

The Houses: Temples of the Sky
Deborah Houlding

The Magic Thread
Richard Idemon

Your Horoscope in Your Hands
Lorna Green

Temperament: Astrology's
Forgotten Key
Dorian Geiseler Greenbaum

Astrology, A Place in Chaos
Star and Planet Combinations
Bernadette Brady

Astrology and the Causes of War
Jamie Macphail

Flirting with the Zodiac
Kim Farnell

The Gods of Change
Howard Sasportas

Astrological Roots:
The Hellenistic Legacy
Joseph Crane

The Art of Forecasting
using Solar Returns
Anthony Louis

Horary Astrology Re-Examined
Barbara Dunn

Living Lilith - Four Dimensions of the
Cosmic Feminine
M. Kelley Hunter

Primary Directions
Martin Gansten

Classical Medical Astrology
Oscar Hofman

The Door Unlocked:
An Astrological Insight into Initiation
*Dolores Ashcroft Nowicki and Stephanie V.
Norris*

Understanding Karmic Complexes:
Evolutionary Astrology and Regression
Therapy
Patricia L. Walsh

www.wessexastrologer.com